PREFACE

The second in the series "Studies in Indian Writing in English," this volume is devoted entirely to the study of Indian fiction in English (IFE) and, with the exception of Raja Rao and some Anglo-Indian women writers of the colonial era, all the novelists studied here belong to the third generation of the Indian writers in English who have broken with the tradition and charted new paths for themselves.

Indian fiction in English is now reckoned to be a literature of world stature. Contrary to what generally happened until the eighties, it has in the past two decades become a favourite with the postcolonial critics. A number of factors have contributed to its new-found status, prestige and global visibility. We shall first focus on these factors and briefly account for the phenomenal success of IFE.

First and foremost, the emergence and enthusiastic reception in the West, of a generation of post-modern novelists—Salman Rushdie, Amitav Ghosh, Vikram Seth, Rohinton Mistry, Shashi Tharoor, Arundhati Roy and Manju Kapoor to cite a few—has elevated Indian fiction in English to new heights. After reading these novelists no critic could continue to have a patronizing attitude to IFE. While the novelists of the previous generations enjoyed much popularity at home but found it initially difficult to reach out to foreign readership, except as some kind of 'sellers' of India, these younger novelists broke every kind of barrier, often with their debut novels themselves, and met a ready acceptance abroad as writers of great merit. Their success has been so phenomenal that Rushdie, who has gone on to become the most controversial living author, declared that Indian literature in English had risen so high in stature that the regional literatures, in spite of their more than a thousand years of history, had been almost dwarfed by it. Whether Rushdie is right or wrong is debatable, but it is a fact that Indian fiction in English of the eighties and the nineties most certainly has the strength, freshness and vivacity which were unknown to the previous decades. Going by the number of international awards it has won, it can be said without much hesitation that the position of IFE is now strong and secure.

Secondly, IFE has been catapulted onto the international stage by the gender consciousness writings of the women novelists. The sustained efforts of great writers such as Anita Desai and Nayantara Sahgal of the earlier generation together with the women's rights struggles nation-wide, opened up ever-new possibilities for the fictional treatment of women's issues. Studies of women writers included in this volume reveal a rare intellectual freedom and artistic integrity on their part. These women writers seem to have consciously or otherwise broken the idol of womanly perfection which Coventry Patmore has described as the "Angel of the House." The consciousness of what men will say of a woman who speaks the truth about her passion was the greatest obstacle that the Indian woman writer had to contend with. Most of these modern Indian women writers have however fought these ghosts and refused to be thwarted by the extreme conventionality of the other sex. It is also significant to note here that while the first generation women writers needed a long period to attain maturity and popularity as novelists, the writers who came on stage during the eighties and nineties were able to attain these twin objectives with a remarkable alacrity. Allowing for individual differences, this is precisely what happened to Shashi Deshpande, Namita Gokhale, Shobha De, Arundhati Roy, Manju Kapoor and Shauna Singh Baldwin, to name a few who readily spring to mind.

Postcolonial literary studies in universities across the world too have had a considerable role in projecting IFE as occupying a position of centrality in debates. Postcolonial criticism prior to the eighties generally tended to privilege writers other than Indian for a variety of reasons, but specially because there was hardly an Indian critic who could measure up to projecting IFE in a favourable light on international forums. The limited recognition the three pioneers of Indian fiction in English, namely Anand, Raja Rao and Narayan, initially gained in the West cannot be attributed exclusively to the critical endeavour but to extra-literary reasons: Anand for his

Marxist leanings and the depiction of various ailments of India from a sociological perspective, Raja Rao for his cultural and philosophical depths and Narayan for his ironic portrayal of Indian reality which helped readers all over the world to 'understand' India. Obvious proof of the critical apathy towards IFE of the pre-eighties period is that a seminal text on postcolonial studies, *The Empire Writes Back* by Ashcroft, Griffiths and Tiffin hardly mentions Indian authors in course of its theoretical discussion, and when it does it is only the Preface to Raja Rao's *Kanthapura* and not a Fictional work! Starting with the eighties however a highly resourceful group of Indian critics has changed the situation for the better culminating in re-evaluation and repositioning of IFE from fresh and genuinely critical perspectives. Homi Bhabha, Gayatri Spivak, Ajaz Ahmad and Harish Trivedi are just four of the famous critics now actively engaged in this critical pursuit.

Having discussed some of the factors that ensured the success of IFE during the past couple of decades, we turn to the most important of all Indian writers in English during the period under reference, namely Salman Rushdie. Rushdie's success as a writer has such varied dimensions that it is almost impossible to fully account for it. The publication of his ground-breaking work *Midnight's Children* heralded a new era in Indian fiction in English and set off a series of chain reactions. IFE could not remain the same after this novel had appeared. *Midnight's Children* has become a point of reference for all the Indian novelists in English ever since. The imaginative re-working of Indian history in a culturally hybrid environment, the innovative use of literary techniques and models fashionable till then only among western writers—especially magic realism—together with a supreme command of the English language and a genius for story telling modelled on the hoary Indian narrative traditions and cultural practices, had established *Midnight's Children* as a trend-setter and classic for all times. Seen in these terms the arrival of Rushdie on the scene with *Midnight's Children* was no less than a literary earthquake. If Anand, Raja Rao and Narayan have been credited with the title of the forefathers of IFE, Rushdie richly deserves to be called the father of its rebirth as modern fiction.

Four remarkable novels—*Shame, The Satanic Verses*, *The*

Moor's Last Sigh and *The Ground Beneath Her Feet*—followed *Midnight's Children*, in which Rushdie avoided introducing too radical thematic and stylistic innovations but stuck to what proved to be a success formula for him. In line with his literary canon, which sees paradoxes as real and meaningful, the *fatwa*, occasioned by his novel *The Satanic Verses*, rather than reducing Rushdie to silence ensured his popularity and made him in the process one of the highly sought after novelists of the world.

Rushdie's novels have generated enormous critical interest for another reason as well: his position of being "neither an Indian, nor a westerner" has added postcolonial studies a new dimension. The debates over colonialism, initiated by Said's *Orientalism,* have developed in such unpredictable directions that now no meaningful postcolonial discourse will be complete without a reference to Rushdie. The paradox of it is that now Rushdie's novels seem to have 'colonised' Indian fiction, de-centering India again. If it is true that Rushdie is the most famous of the Indian novelists today, it is equally true that it is the West rather than India which celebrates his success enthusiastically. Indian critics often make it a point to stress how westernised the Rushdie reader must be in order to fully appreciate his novels; otherwise he will most likely miss the contretemps concerning Indian cultural referents. In this sense perhaps, Rushdie inadvertently runs the risk of setting off a second wave of Orientalism.

There are a few more basic points which may establish Rushdie's 'colonisation'—unintended though it is—of Indian fiction in English. For fear of expansion we will confine ourselves to one single point—that of the diasporic writing. Even though there is no consensus among critics on the precise meaning of this concept, in the pre- and post-Rushdian eras it certainly means two different things. The Indian diasporic writing is a literary entity which needed a cultural shock-wave like *Midnight's Children* to be fully recognised. Writers like Raja Rao, Anita Desai and Kamala Markandaya for instance, are hardly considered part of the Indian diaspora although they too have lived for extended periods outside India. Thanks to Rushdie, the 1980s and 1990s immigrant writers, instead, were readily brought under the description of diaspora, in spite of some of them—Ghosh and Chandra, for instance—insisting that they spend only six months a year abroad. Rushdie is thus wholly responsible for forging and configuring an identity for the diaspora writers. At least two papers in this volume—Shaul Bassi's "The (Un)making of Saladin Chamcha: Rushdie's Subversion of the Bildungsroman" and Christopher Rollason's "Rushdie's Un-Indian Music: *The Ground Beneath Her Feet*"—seek to discuss these and other issues in Rushdie's novels.

Rushdie is not the whole of Indian fiction in English. There has been a rich crop of writers—living in India and abroad–who have continued his legacy in one form of the other. In this long line of writers perhaps Amitav Ghosh comes first. His novels definitely evidence the fusing together of the various fictional genres—travelogue, Bildungsroman, thriller, science fiction, historical chronicle, saga, etc.—eluding classification in the process. We are happy to include in this anthology an article by John Thieme who chooses colonial discourse analysis to study Ghosh's novel *The Calcutta Chromosome.*

Vikram Seth is yet another distinguished member of this new breed of writers. His claim to literary fame rests primarily on *A Suitable Boy* in spite of his equally important other works: *The Golden Gate* and *An Equal Music.* This massive novel surely merits comparison with the huge masterpieces of the 19th century Russian novelists in terms of bulk and multiplicity of characters. Seth's craftsmanship and technical excellence, superb handling of various registers as well as his remarkable ability to blend poetry with fiction, make him one of the most outstanding names in the contemporary fiction. The paper by Pier Paolo Piciucco in this anthology brings out the analogies between *A Suitable Boy* and the Elizabethan drama.

Bharati Mukherjee who made her debut long before Seth and others but gained critical acceptance only during the last couple of decade, is a quintessential Indian diaspora writer—one who gives an authentic fictional treatment to the immigrant experience in such of her novels as *Jasmine.* Sandra Ponzanesi's article on this novel of Mukherjee views it from the feminist and multicultural perspectives.

Although not represented in this anthology, Vikram Chandra,

Shashi Tharoor and Rohinton Mistry are three more noteworthy authors who have won an enviable place for themselves in the world of fiction. Their thematic concerns and styles remarkably vary but they certainly belong to a homogeneous group in that they have all lived in the West and have had their creative sensibility shaped by it, an aspect that seems to heavily characterise their literary identity. Chandra, the last of the three to break on the international literary scene, is a very talented writer whose novels evidence his very personal narrative line in a world of competing literary trends. Tharoor, a UN diplomat, is a lively writer who has made his place with his masterpiece *The Great Indian Novel*, a humorous reworking of the epic *Mahabharata,* and is populated by the avataras of the protagonists of the recent Indian history. Mistry's novels, on the other hand, epitomise life in exile. His nostalgic tone and choice of fictional locales evoke many of Joyce's literary conventions.

The strength—critical and financial—of contemporary Indian fiction in English can be best understood in terms of the incredible success of Arundhati Roy's *The God of Small Things.* If Tharoor has re-written Indian history, Roy has chosen to imaginatively relive her life with the right admixture of bitterness and humour and that by ingeniously making use of the complexity and ductility of the English language as a decolonised Indian writer would. Alessandra Contenti's study of *The God of Small Things* gives an interesting overview of some of the less debated issues centering this novel.

Coming hard on the heels of Roy, several talented Indian women writers have made their appearance on the international literary scene with aplomb. Manju Kapoor and Shauna Singh Baldwin, have for example benefited, as has Roy earlier, from the market-driven publishing strategies and promotional campaigns of the western publishers and have enjoyed smooth launching and sailing. This development has further strengthened the Indian women's literary canon, which has been in the making for some time.

Another woman writer of the new generation who deserves a place of high respect is Shashi Deshpande. Early in her career Deshpande forged her own style and identified her own themes—

family life, focussing specially on women and often probing their mind—which have since become her literary trademark, as Chandra Holm points out in her paper. Holm's analysis of *Small Remedies* in this volume seeks to prove that Deshpande has continued her tradition. In another article her Sahitya Akademi award winning novel *That Long Silence* has been studied by Rajeshwar Mittapalli. Making an extensive use of depth psychology, he proves how its heroine gains a new identity after going through a traumatic experience.

Women's writing has always enjoyed an equal status with the mainstream IFE. It initiated many debates and helped secure a more modern role for Indian women looking for new ideals and models for themselves. The logical extension of these debates was the formulation of a feminist discourse, as the articles by Mary Conde and Joel Kuortti in this volume demonstrate.

Long before all these writers, and alongside them, there have always been the great triumvirate of IFE: Anand, Narayan and Raja Rao most of whose novels, whatever their limitations, are now considered classics of Indian literature in English and are routinely prescribed for study in universities across the world. Gender studies and diasporic writing have slightly eroded their importance in the ongoing debates focussed on Indian literature but it remains a fact that they have always represented the bedrock of IFE. This anthology pays its homage to one of them, Raja Rao, by including Basavaraj Naikar's essay which discusses interpersonal, psychological and philosophical issues in *'The Serpent and the Rope*, a novel that enjoys a strongly divided opinion but continues to be viewed as a cornerstone of the 'twice-born' fiction.

The papers collected in this anthology represent a wide spectrum of critical interests of scholars specialising in Indian fiction in English which has of late indubitably established a powerful and pervasive presence on the world literary scene. A remarkable aspect of this volume is that, apart from Basavaraj Naikar and Rajeshwar Mittapalli, all the contributors to it happen to be either Europeans or Indians settled abroad. The readers will at once recognise that these scholars, by virtue of being uninvolved observers, have brought to the study of the IFE a unique, detached perspective resulting in its objective evaluation. As editors of this volume it has also been our endeavour to encourage the contributors to question prevalent prejudices concerning IFE. We hope that future scholarly studies will keep the debates initiated in this volume alive and possibly find answers to some of them. We also wish to thank each of the contributors for readily responding to our call for papers.

—Editors

CONTENTS

1

Age, Same Rage: Debates over Indian-English Writings

UMA PARAMESWARAN*

In my recent study of Kamala Markandaya,[1] I noted that the earlier generation of Indian writers who lived outside India tended to be called Expatriate writers, whereas the new generation have a new name—Diaspora writers. The Indian diaspora, we must remember, has two distinct phases. The earlier phase, whose writers we tended to subsume under another identity, consists of those who left India between 1875 and 1947 for other parts of the British Empire such as Britain, Fiji, South Africa, the Caribbean. The identity we tended to give them often depended on the language they chose; those who wrote in their Indian mother-tongue were assigned to Indian regional literature, and those who wrote in English tended to be associated either with English Literature or with the country in which they wrote. For example, Punjabi writings of Canadians of Indian descent were read in India as part of Punjabi literature; V.S. Naipaul and Sam Selvon, who wrote in English, were considered part of Caribbean Literature or British Literature. But now, with the emergence of this new identity we call Diaspora Writers, it might be time to revisit such writers, and chart their place in Diaspora Literature, and how their works reflect diasporic sensibility.

My present focus is related to the second phase of the Indian Diaspora, namely, contemporary writers of Indian descent who live

*Professor, Department of English, University of Winnipeg, 515 Portage Avenue Winnipeg, MB R3B 2E9 Canada.

outside India. Within that, I am zeroing in on a specific point in diasporic literature, namely, the differences in the expectations and criteria between writers of the Diaspora and their readers in India. (A line of analysis that I will not go into in this essay is the differences between the perceptions of Indian and non-Indian readers to the same text). I find a growing chasm between these pairs of constituencies.

Ironically, the differences echo the antagonisms articulated in an earlier age between those who chose to write in English and those Indians who wrote, or believed Indians should write, in an Indian vernacular. If the debate is to be summarised in one sentence, one side accuses the other of pandering to the western reader with clichés and stereotypes of pseudo-Indianness, and the other accuses the first of jealousy and fundamentalism.

An Interesting Parallel

Buddhadeva Bose, a Bengali poet and critic, contributed the entry on "Indian Poetry in English," in *The Concise Encyclopaedia of English and American Poets*, edited by Stephen Spender and Donald Hall, which was published in 1963.

Bose says, "The best of Indian-English verse belongs to the nineteenth century, when Indians came nearest to speaking, thinking and dreaming in English," and that those of his own generation who chose to write in English "do not yet realise that Indo-Anglian poetry is a blind alley, lined with curio shops, leading nowhere."[2] He lists in his bibliography six volumes, the most recent of which is Sri Aurobindo's *Collected Poems and Prayers* (1942). Two of the six are anthologies, published in 1918 and 1927 respectively, and the other three are volumes by Toru Dutt, Manmohan Ghose, and Sarojini Naidu, all of which were published before 1905.

This act of editorial arrogance and ignorance is repeated in *The Vintage Book of Indian Writing 1947—1997*, edited by Salman Rushdie and Elizabeth West in 1997 on the occasion of the fiftieth year of India's Independence, though it is directed at another constituency, namely, the vernacular writers.

There was a conflagration of protest at Rushdie's statement that writing created in these fifty years "by Indians working in English is proving to be a stronger and more important body of work than most of what has been produced in the '16 official languages' of India, the so-called 'vernacular languages.'"[3]

There was a similar outbreak of protest against Buddhadeva Bose's editorial stance and statement, spearheaded by P. Lal. However, the difference is that whereas Lal's protest was effective and generated not only discussion but a clear expansion of Indo-English writing, the protest against Rushdie has been ineffective. A conclusion one can draw from these parallels and contrast is that the current neo-imperialism of the west is too powerful to be dislodged. This has its corollaries, as I argue later.

P. Lal

P. Lal is the mentor and leader of the earlier 'new age' of writing. Almost single-handedly (Prof. K.R. Srinivasa Iyengar's critical volume, *Indian Writing in English*, of 1962 aided the process), he helped establish Indo-English literature as an authentic and integral part of Indian Literature. He did this through three major undertakings. He founded Writers Workshop in 1958; it was envisioned as "a group of writers who agree in principle that English has proved its ability, as a language, to play a creative role in All-India literature." It was a discussion group that met on Sunday mornings at Lal's residence in Calcutta.

He also started a bi-monthly journal called *The Miscellany*, which acted as a forum for young writers to express their theory and practice. In the earlier issues of *The Miscellany*, we can find contributions by writers who have become recognised since then —Anita Desai, Kamala Das, Nissim Ezekiel, Prawer Jhabvala....

P. Lal also founded and edited a literary press—*Writers Workshop Books*. Each volume was handbound in exquisite handloom cloth, handset in Alexander typeface and printed on a hand-operated machine by P.K. Aditya. If I mention all this in such detail, it is to pay tribute to the man and his vision of art. I would not be surprised if every Indian writer in English between 1958 and 1980 has had a manuscript, often the first one, published by Writers Workshop in *The Miscellany* or as a separate volume.

Protest against Buddhadeva Bose's Statements

P. Lal spearheaded the rebuttal against Buddhadeva Bose's 1963 dismissal of contemporary Indian-English writing. Writers

Workshop's *Modern Indian Poetry in English: An Anthology and a Credo* was published in 1969. It consists of selections from 132 poets, and the responses of about sixty of them to Lal's questionnaire based on Bose's statements. There are seven questions posed by Lal, but I shall concentrate on two of them which deal with the following two statements by Bose:

> "To the question, 'Why in English?' they give various answers, one being that English is an Indian language—which it is not—another being that English entitles them to a larger audience."

> "The fact is that 'Indo-Anglicans' do not have a real public in India, where literature is defined in terms of the different native languages, and their claim can be justified only by appreciation in England or the United States" (from Bose's encyclopaedia entry which is cited by Lal[4]).

Predictably, almost everyone in this volume took a strong stand in favour of the validity and relevance of English as a medium for their creative output. M.P. Bhaskaran introduced an internecine wrench in the works with his "it is usually the Hindi writers who are most incensed at Indian writing in English.... We do not have this gnashing of teeth in the South at all" (Lal 44). This remark is in the context of the long and bitter debate in the 1950s and early 1960s as to whether English or Hindi should be the national language of administration. The southern regions of India were especially resentful of the imposition of Hindi. On one hand, English was used all over the country and had been one of the factors in fostering national identity, but on the other hand, the choice of English smacked of a perpetuation of colonialism, and it seemed reasonable that a country should have its own distinct national language. However, Hindi was a regional language far removed from the Dravidian languages of the south, which resisted the 'northern' tongue. While feelings ran high for a decade or more, as seen in Bhaskaran's comment, within a decade or two later, the growing spread and influence of cinema did what rhetoric could not do, and popularised Hindi all across the country.

Intriguingly enough, a great many, including such self-confessed unilingual writers as Sasthi Brata, Leela Dharmaraj and Nissim

Ezekiel, and other established writers such as Adil Jussawalla, Keshav Malik and Suniti Namjoshi, agreed with Bose that English is not an Indian language. Several said it is and is not. Tilottama Rajan expressed this dichotomy well: "to call English an Indian language is perhaps unjustified etymologically. It is unfortunate that so many people, with misplaced nationalism, tend to regard it merely as a relic of colonialism" (Lal 421).

Still others, such as Suresh Kohli, K.D. Katrak, N.C. Mahashabde, Arvind Mehrotra, Sujatha Modayil, Kshitij Mohan and Stanley Rajiva, clearly claimed English as an Indian language.

About the issue of the English language opening the door to a wider audience, many chose not to answer the question, and those who answered agreed it did, though they added that this was not the reason they chose to write in English. As Kamala Das has said in her most quoted poem:

Don't write in English, they said,
English is not your mother tongue. Why not leave
    Me alone, critics, friends, visiting cousins,
Every one of you?... The language I speak
Becomes mine....

Gauri Deshpande is one of the few that tackle this question of audience head on, and to say she mainly has an Indian audience in mind. "I do not expect readers not born Indians to derive the total meaning from my poems; however, they are not obscure and are capable of being judged on the same grounds as any other poems are, without any special pleading. But their full appreciation, I am afraid, is reserved for Indians" (Lal 136). I particularly endorse the last sentence because that is my conclusion about Diaspora Literature. I have an average Indian man-in-the-street say to Rushdie in an earlier essay, "You are still writing about.... Indians-in-India, Indians-in-Britain. You can't write about anything else, *mian*, we are your bread and butter, and you with your Angrez-trained mind know which side your bread is buttered. But learn from your own Gibreel that only we will stand by you...*we only are your best readers...*"[5] (italics added for this essay).

Bose had quoted Yeats as saying, "no man can think or write with music and vigour except in his mother tongue." This was one of the main issues in the earlier debate. Editor Ayyub, of *Quest,* stated that, "Fiction and Poetry in English by Indians cannot but be regarded as freakish or at best as highly exceptional" (*Quest* 26 Sept. 1960). This was rebutted by P. Lal in the next issue. In a still later issue of *Quest*, Jyotirmoy Datta continued the debate and argued very cogently, sometimes tongue-in-cheek, that English as used in India was a functional medium of administrative communication but could never be a living language, the way it was in England.

Latika Basu had expressed the same opinion in 1933: "English is not alive in India, and that is why the few writers who were genuinely gifted were hampered in writing English poetry." This sentiment had been expressed by others as well, including David McCutchion. In a long essay on "Indian Writing in English," he says, "I am more and more inclined to agree with those who affirm that English as a medium of expression works as a barrier against real insight into the Indian mind and circumstances" (*The Miscellany,* 29 Oct. 1968: 11). Lal might well have responded "Et tu Brute?" for McCutchion was one of those who published regularly in *The Miscellany*! Again, I would like to point out to Lal's credit that he encouraged dissent and gave equal space to anyone who expressed opinions different from his own.

In the present context, there is no doubt that Indians are fully capable of using the English language, and that they have refuted in no uncertain terms Bose's contention that Indo-English writers can never hope to master the prime poetic requirement, namely, that they change or re-create the English language. Not so incontestable is their cultural sensibility. Raji Narasimhan says, "Somewhere between the Narayan-Raja Rao-Desani age and the emergence of new writers, a blunting of sensibility seems to have taken place."[6] In the present context, more important than the mastery or lack thereof of the language is the overt or covert goal of Diaspora writing. Is it written with an eye towards winning over a western audience, as was the charge that was levelled against Indo-English writers of the earlier age?

David McCutchion, though he has written an appreciative review of Raja Rao's novels, goes on say that Raja Rao can never be genuinely Indian because "you are most yourself when speaking to others like yourself, whereas Raja Rao through his choice of language knows he is writing for non-Indians, which can only make his Indianness self-conscious."[7]

Similarly, Latika Basu's critique of Sarojini Naidu's poetry is relevant to our present debate between Indian and non-Indian readers of Diaspora Literature. Naidu's earlier poetry, like Manmohan Ghose's, had been full of the landscapes of England, and Edmund Gosse advised her to use Indian imagery. She did, in her subsequent poems, and Latika Basu came down pretty hard on her: "She merely continues the picture of India painted by Anglo-Indian and English writers, a land of bazars, with picturesque wandering minstrels and snake charmers."[8] This experience of being buffeted and sandwiched by disparate sets of expectations is replicated in contemporary Diasporic experience.

M.S. Prabhakar, reviewing Raja Rao's great classic, *The Serpent and the Rope*, says, "Anybody with some awareness of contemporary India will recognise *The Serpent and the Rope* for what it is: a cleverly contrived sham, making the best use of myth and Hoary Past....It is all slightly sickening and yet it is these pseudo-Lawrencian metaphysical attitudinisations, based on bogus mysticism, that are apparently admired" (*Encounter* Jan. 1965: 95).

Strong words, but one frequently comes across such vituperative force in Indian reviewers' critiques of contemporary writings.

Since these criticisms have been expressed over four decades, and by many different reviewers, the issue has to be looked at carefully. The parallel between the earlier debate and this one is that control is still held by those outside India. It seems that Indian writers have always needed a white godfather. Most books published by Indian writers in the first century of Indo-English literature had a foreword or preface written by an Englishman. Toru Dutt and Sarojini Naidu had their English godfathers. Even Tagore needed Yeats to give him a hand. McCutchion repeats what others have said before and after him when he says, "Lack of critical standards at home and patronising approval from abroad encourage a certain complacency" (McCutchion in *The Miscellany* above, 22).

But there is also a contrast. Today there is no lack of critical standards at home (in India) but the neo-imperialism of the west is even stronger than the imperialism of old because of globalization of culture. Shashi Deshpande, author of *Small Remedies* and other fine novels, says, "The tyranny of publishers, literary agents, marketing forces and the celebrity-hungry media is trying to snuff out the reader's freedom of choice" (*The Hindu* 2 Jan. 2000).

My question is, are today's writers doing even more purposefully what Latika Basu accused Naidu of doing—pandering to the western reader, spooning them stereotypes of what they want to hear? Shashi Deshpande refers to the controversy over the success of Indian-born novelists of today in the same essay, and says, "Much of the controversy, within the country, as well as the success of English writing outside the country seems to hinge on this fact. It is by addressing readers outside the country, by giving these readers what they want that English [she means Indian writers who write in English] writers have gained their international reputations (as well as royalties that are unthinkable for most Indian writers). This is an often-made charge. Is this a tribute?..."

"Giving these readers what they want." Deshpande tactfully distances herself from this opinion, but the references she makes to other respected readers such as Gauri Deshpande and Harish Trivedi show that there is a strong school of thought that writers are directly or indirectly being influenced into writing what the western world wants to hear about India. In the Diasporic context, I would add "what the western world wants to hear about India, and about Indians everywhere). This has been repeated so often and by such respected individuals that it should not be dismissed. It has often been cursorily dismissed as rooted in jealousy.

One of the writers who does so, and whose essay was the reason why I became interested in this topic, is Vikram Chandra. His essay, "India's cultural commissars' worship 'Indianness' instead of art," appeared in *Boston Review* in February, 2000. Vikram Chandra is the author of *Love and Longing* in Bombay. I am told he is a charming person, and that he lives six months of each year in the United States and six months in India.

In this essay, I find all kinds of antagonisms that perhaps the author did not intend. I find its vindictiveness not just in bad taste but symptomatic of a new power structure that could be as neo-imperialistic as the Coca-Cola-McDonald's empires in that he has access to a market that is way out of the reach of those he is running down. It is a rather hysterical defence of an aggrieved writer whose ego seems to have been assaulted by an Indian critic's words that he has chosen to misconstrue so that he can make a point about this term "Indianness" that is at the core of much of the differences of expectations and criteria between Indian readers and the writers of the Diaspora.

I do not wish to adopt the tone of disdain and condescension that Chandra has adopted in the early part of his essay but I must say in the context of my topic that his tone echoes that of Buddhadeva Bose referred to earlier. Another age, same imperialism.

Indianness

So what is this issue of Indianness that is at the centre of this debate? In the earlier debate, reputed critics such as V.K. Gokak and K.R. Srinivasa Iyengar identified Indianness with the metaphysical quality that we see in the writings of Sri Aurobindo, Raja Rao and R.K. Narayan.

Indianising the English language was another point often mentioned. G.V. Desani, Raja Rao, Mulk Raj Anand and R.K. Narayan used Indianisms and also brought out echoes of the sound and syntax of their mother tongues.

Descriptions of Indian landscape, everyday life, and culinary references were used to give writing an Indian flavour. But whereas these Indianisms were considered strengths by most critics in the earlier debate, they are now considered weaknesses by Indian readers.

Landscape and food are two topics mentioned at length by Vikarm Chandra. Chandra begins with the reading that gave rise to the essay. His fellow-reader, Ardeshir Vakil, was questioned about his reason for spending so much time in his novel describing "bhel-puri." "Was that an emigrant's nostalgia or was it written for the westerners who don't know what "bhel-puri" is?" Chandra goes on to say that the question seemed "preposterous" to him. I cannot quite understand his outrage at this rather clear analysis. Balachandra Rajan in his classic, *The Dark Dancer*, describes how masala dosa is made, and I have always assumed he did so for exactly the same reasons proffered by the questioner. The question that really set off

Chandra seems to be Meenakshi Mukherjee's as to his choice of such chapter titles as 'Dharma' 'Artha' and 'Kama,' which seemed to "signal Indianness to the west."

Chandra takes the comments out of context and goes on to argue his point that in India, books are not assessed "on the basis of the relative merits... but on the perceived Indianness of the authors, and by implication, the degree of their assimilation by the west."

He also mentions the jealousy factor that I referred to above. He reads into the mind of the Indian collective as thinking Diaspora writers cannot be good artists because "the bastards are too comfortable over there and don't have to face Delhi traffic jams and power cuts and queues." He goes a step beyond Buddhadeva Bose's earlier stance and implies jealousy on the part of Indian readers; as I said, neo-imperialism could be even more toxic than old-style imperialism.

New Age of Computers, same rage around the subject of sensibility

I am on several internet discussion groups, and I must say it is a mind-blowing experience to hear so many intelligent and in-depth literary analyses in these on-line groups.

There have been frequent discussions of this topic of what is behind Diaspora writers' focussing on negative Indian stereotypes that western readers want to hear. Some articulate arguments have been made for a writer's freedom to choose his/her material, and that writers' command of language and medium of fiction should be the yardstick, and not his/her delineation of India. However, a fair number of discussants, some living in India and some in North America, have taken a stand similar to Basu and Prabhakar.

Here are two extracts on two novels that have been well received by many.

Man from Matunga (pen name of an on-line writer who posts his reviews on his web site) says of Raj Kamal Jha's *The Blue Bedspread:*

> Over the past few months I have been reading many Indian English authors and I am getting more and more convinced that more often than not I am wasting my time.

> .....
>
> And the hang-loose parts. Incest between the brother, and sister is introduced, but never really further explored. Pederasty between the father and the brother is talked about and then forgotten. Or maybe all these are just ways in which to pack in as many "hot topics" as possible to make the book interesting and saleable.

Siddhartha Singh, writing from Delhi, says of Pankaj Mishra's *The Romantics:*

> Newspapers tell me that this book is being lapped up in the West. I simply cannot understand why. Why do intelligent, educated people insist on reading about an India that is poor, filthy and totally mired in depravity, superstition and poverty? Agreed that is one part of the country. But definitely not the only or even the most predominant part. This inaccurate depiction of India only distorts the true picture. Why does the West prefer to read *The Blue Bedspread* and *The Romantics*, and no other books like *Shadowlines,* or *The Madwoman of Jogare*? (The latter two do not in any way gloss over Indian poverty or problems, but they do not sensationalize them).

A simple answer would be that the latter books are not readily available in the west. But a more complex analysis would look at why they are not available. Is it because it is not what "readers want?"

When I wrote to Siddhartha Singh for permission to quote him, he gave another instance of an interesting exchange that took place at a discussion of Sunny Singh's *Nani's Book of Suicides.* He writes:

> A critic said that this novel lacked an 'Indian Flavour.' She said that when you read Rushdie or Vikram Seth or some others, you could immediately find an 'Indianness' in the narrative. This novel, she said, did not have a liberal sprinkling of Indian words, or other such characteristics.
>
> To this, the author replied that she had been taught to speak Hindi and English properly, i.e. no mixing. She also said that she could not cook, hence the absence of any "tadka" passages!

("Tadka" is a culinary phrase referring to the final garnishing of the dish, and that the author refers to a culinary image shows that Vikram Chandra's article has reached a wide audience.)

As a Diaspora writer myself, I am conscious of the various pressures faced by a Diaspora artist. In a paper on Deepa Mehta's films, presented at the Israel Association of Canadian Studies in June 2000, I said, a Diaspora writer has to perform in a three ring circus, simultaneously in all three rings. "In one, the trapezes and hoops are held by the new homeland; in the second, the tight rope bridges the two sides of their self-identity with their ethno-cultural community on one side and their demanding Muse on the other; in the third ring, the tamers are their peers in their original homeland."

Not an easy task. Which is not to say that the rage *against* diaspora Indian-English writers is not as justified as the rage *of* the Indian-English writers of the earlier age. Before dismissing these comments against the Diaspora as an overdose of nationalistic fervour, one needs to look between the lines of Diaspora writings to analyse the presence of various factors such as western readers' neo-imperialism, western publishers' marketability requirements, the liminality of the Diasporic world, authors' psychological hang-ups about their original homelands (Naipaul's *Area of Darkness* is a prime example from an earlier age), and "the Anglomania which seized some upper-class Indians in the early years of British rule." The Anglomania referred to by Bose has two aspects—the linguistic, which time has shown to be irrelevant in that today English is one of India's languages, and the cultural, about which critics such as Raji Narasimhan, quoted above, speak, and which has to be a relevant factor in any theoretical constructs being set up for the new area of study we call Diaspora Literature.

NOTES AND REFERENCES

1. Uma Parameswaran, *Kamala Markandaya* (Jaipur: Rawat, 2000).
2. Buddhadeva Bose, as quoted in P. Lal, ed. *Modern Indian Poetry in English: An Anthology and a Credo* (Calcutta: Writers Workshop, 1969) 5.
3. Salman Rushdie and Elizabeth West, eds. *Vintage Book of Indian Writing 1947 -1997* (London: Penguin, 1997) x.
4. Bose in Lal above 4.

5. Uma Parameswaran, *SACLIT: An Introduction to South Asian Canadian Literature* (Chennai: East West Books, 1986) 221.
6. Raji Narasimhan, *Sensibility under Stress: Aspects of Indo-English Fiction* (New Delhi: Vikas, 1976) 18.
7. David McCutchion, "Indian Writing in English," *The Miscellany* 29 (October 1969): 11.
8. Latika Basu, quoted by McCutchion 44.

2

Grounded in Fiction: Women Inscribing the Indian Landscape

MARY CONDÉ*

I have chosen to look at landscape "the single most telling signature of western identity," as it has been called (Comer 11), through the female gaze of Englishwomen writing about India before Partition, with a rather briefer look at Indian women writers after Partition.

The first thing to be said is that the Englishwomen were not necessarily interested in presenting their female gaze as female: Charlotte Despard wrote anonymously; Bithia Mary Croker started writing as "B.M. Croker," Alice Perrin as "A. Perrin," Fanny Emily Penny as "F.E. Penny," and Olivia Douglas as "O. Douglas"; J.E. Muddock, Sydney Carlyon Grier, Maxwell Gray, John Travers, I.A.R. Wylie, C.M.K. Phipps, J.M. Graham, M.J. Colquhoun, H.M. Cadell, and E.W. Savi were all women. E.W. Savi's novels even included deliberately misleading reviews with remarks like "Mr. Savi knows his India well" (Standard) and "Mr. Savi knows his India very well" (*Aberdeen Journal*).

However, their gaze is presented as English, with titles like *The Englishwoman*, *The Anglo-Indians*, *An English Girl in the East*, *England Hath Need of Thee*, especially when romantic love was their main focus, which it usually was. One of the major discoveries of Mills & Boon, after it was founded in 1908, was I.A.R. Wylie,

*School of English & Drama, Queen Mary, University of London, Mile End Road, London E1 4NS, England.

author of *The Rajah's People* (1910) and *The Daughter of Brahma* (1912). Joseph McAleer completes his recent study of Mills & Boon by quoting John Boon's comparison of his phenomenally successful former company "to a new British Empire of sorts," and his rider (with a broad smile) that "'I hope it won't have the same fate!'" (McAleer 290) The connection between these two empires is underlined by a letter written to Alan Boon as late as 1966 by Gladys Fulbrook, agreeing that Cyprus was a "risky" setting for her novel *One-Man Girl* because

> In view of the steady crumbling of the old British Empire, no one would bat an eyelash if we walked out of Cyprus to-morrow—and no woman would want to identify herself with that background (McAleer 261).

Although McAleer is not explicit about this, it appears from his account that not a single Mills & Boon was set in India after 1947; the consciousness of India as an imperial possession was crucial to the presentation of landscapes by romantic novelists as managed by strong and attractive men. Typical in this way is K.M. Edge's *The Shuttles of the Loom* (1909), which opens by following the sweeping glance across a southern Indian forest of John Grange, a Deputy-Conservator of Forests in the Vengaimalais, and then explaining what informs this glance (a comprehensive and accurate knowledge of every tree) and what this knowledge entails (a heavy responsibility). Grange must make himself active in this landscape, and inscribe himself on it, by building bridges and demarcating boundaries, but he is an impassive presence within it:

> Though he stood in the midst of forests he loved, no muscle of his face moved, and his expression was hard (Edge 4).

Grange's face effectively becomes a landscape of its own for the reader to decode as he decodes the forest, but man and forest remain quite separate. Face as landscape also appears in Ethel M. Dell's massively best-selling *The Way of an Eagle* (1912), in which Nick Ratcliffe's face is desperately searched by the soldier who must confide his daughter to him

> as a man who views through field-glasses a region distant and unexplored (Dell 1912: 11).

The difference between these two novels is that although Nick Ratcliffe and John Grange are both primarily interesting to their creators as potential lovers of their heroines, Nick Ratcliffe ends happily married to Muriel in the "peace unspeakable" of the Indian mountains, "that those silver crests lifted into the splendour of Infinity" (Dell 1912: 543), while John Grange finds his peace by dying of cholera almost immediately after he marries and being buried in the landscape he has helped to shape:

> His body was fitly given to the land for which he had spent his manhood, and in which his influence must remain long after he himself was forgotten (Edge 339).

Landscape here is not just a predictor of a man's attitude to a woman (masterful and loving), but represents another kind of romantic embrace.

The harshness of Englishmen's lives in India, often insisted upon, is usually insisted upon through an introduction via the landscapes they are attempting to control. It is a path in the Hindu Kush which opens the story of Alan Laurence, the Engineer subaltern of Maud Diver's *Candles in the Wind* (1909):

> The path was no more than a six-foot mule track and an unpleasant one at that; a knife-scratch across the harsh face of desolation, whose dominant features of rock and stone and sharply jutting spurs were unredeemed by the least suggestion of tenderness in outline or tint (Diver 11).

Like a very similar description of a track which "was the most unroadlike possible" (in a chapter called "The Back of Beyond") in a novel by Sydney C. Grier (Grier 31), this implies contrary expectations on the part of the reader (tenderness, a roadlike road), and it is an important component of the *English* gaze that an English landscape (which, indeed, often opens the novels) is always predicated as the norm by which an Indian landscape is measured. In times of crisis especially, English landscapes will flash upon the inward eye of the hero, "green and peaceful," or covered with "cold mists on the hill tops," as they do in two Mutiny novels" (Gray 67; Steel 1897 32) but their memory can, at the best of times, dull the pleasure taken in India. Ethel Duff-Fyfe in *The Relentless Gods*

(1910) explains why the approach to Calcutta up the River Hoogly "is by no means beautiful or impressing"; it is because

> With the remembrance of the soft green of the English landscape still fresh in mind, everything looks … as if enveloped in a haze of dust. The turgid river is a thick yellow colour, sandy, or rather muddy shores, grass, trees, animals, houses and boats have all the same tint—a dull, uniform brownie grey (Duff-Fyfe 1910: 30).

Duff-Fyfe suffers the same indignant disappointment when she turns to the city, observing that

> There is this resemblance between the Strand in London and the Strand in Calcutta—that they are both narrow, both important and overcrowded thoroughfares, but here the likeness ceases. The dear old London Strand with the theatres close by, the ever ready and attentive policemen at the corners, and the perfectly regulated traffic, is as the Garden of Eden compared with the dusty, vilely smelling road so called in Calcutta (Duff-Fyfe 1910: 33).

Alice Perrin is similarly discouraging in *The Charm* of the same year:

> A small station in the plains.
>
> To those who know Upper India the words will perhaps recall the vision of an isolated little spot marked on the vast level of the country by a group of whitewashed bungalows standing within mudwalled enclosures; a few scattered trees and dusty hedges of aloe and cactus; a tangled patch of native town linked to the English quarter by a broad, metalled road; and, all around, stretches of barren land and tracts of tall, dry grass relieved by the mango groves and temple tops of occasional villages and their radiating acres of close cultivation (Perrin 1910: 17).

Perrin's main purpose here is to explain why such a posting would not be attractive to an ambitious young Englishman, but her description is notable for (and typical in) its emphasis on the tiny size of the settlement in comparison with "the vast level of the country," its implied commendation of the English presence (the bungalows here *standing* and *white-washed* in contrast to the *tangled patch* of native town), and its appeal to the élite group of readers "who know upper India." Knowledge of an Indian landscape is an aspect of the imperial possession of it, in some sense guaranteeing the moral validity of the imperial possession of it; the next best thing is a knowledge of an imperial centre like the "dear old London Strand" to function as an opposite.

The writers themselves did not neccssarily have the first kind of knowledge; I.A.R. Wylie left Mills & Boon when the firm deprecated her dropping of Indian settings as she tartly recorded in her memoirs.

> They liked my adolescent fairy stories about Sahibs, Mem-Sahibs, ayahs and Boottrees. On no account was I to write about anything about which I knew anything (Quoted in McAleer 44).

Nor had Ethel M. Dell ever been to India: she got it out of books. At her death *The Times* ranked her as one of the four or five most popular novelists in the English-speaking world, and generations of readers formed their ideas of India from her work, despite what have been called her "highly romanticised notions" (Miller 89-90). Highly romanticised notions, however, whether conveyed by novelists with firsthand information or not, were presented by the publishers as authoritative ("Mr. Savi knows his India very well"), and various guarantees of authenticity were often placed at the beginning of the narrative, ranging from the dedication to a maharajah "in memory of a very happy visit" (Alice Eustace's *Flame of the Forest*, another Mills & Boon) to the assurance that the author had "represented the *Lady's Pictorial* and several other periodicals at the Imperial Durbar" (Charlotte Cameron's *A Durbar Bride*). There is a strong impulse within the novels themselves to present their landscapes not only as authentic, but with an authenticity under threat, either "from the foot of the globe-trotter" (Croker 1886 I: 1-2), or because (paradoxically) they are safe from would-be lady novelists, like the wilder scenery round Shimla in *A Pinchbeck Goddess* (1897) by Alice M. Kipling, Rudyard Kipling's sister (Kipling 1897: 200). In B.M. Croker's *Her Own People* (1903), Captain Malcolm Haig tells a lady at dinner that a novel called *Thrills from the Hills, or the Curse of the Khitmatgar* seems to have its facts taken from fiction and its local colour from Earl's Court (which is tactless, as the lady is the (lady) author's sister). He, who has been in India for seven years, significantly declares that

> "... the truth is that India—real India—is to the European a closed book!" (Croker 1903: 25)

in the face of his dining companion's confidence that although she has never been there, she has read about it, "'which amounts to almost the same thing'" (Croker 1903: 25-26). Croker is of course trading on exactly this confidence in her reader, that the closed book may be opened by the novelist.

But, again paradoxically, readers were constantly reminded of the "unreality" of the "real India." Flora Annie Steel opens *Miss Stuart's Legacy* (1893) as if with a stage direction:

> An Indian railway station in the first freshness of an autumn dawn, with a clear decision of light and shade, unknown to northern latitudes, lending a fictitious picturesqueness to the low arched buildings festooned with purple creepers (Steel 1893 I: 1).

Here Steel follows the tradition of describing Indian landscapes in terms of their difference from English landscapes, their properties "unknown to northern latitudes," but when she speaks of a "fictitious picturesqueness," she means it not in the sense of a deceptive or false picturesqueness, but a picturesqueness suitable for fiction. A critic has remarked of the huge readership of the more than hundred and fifty adventure stories for girls by Bessie Marchant in the first quarter of the twentieth century that

> It is not difficult to see why. In beautiful distant lands, wonderful girls undergo thrilling adventures ... (Bratton 201-202).

What is striking about the use of India as a suitably beautiful distant land, however, is many fictional characters" awareness of it as an artificial setting. May Crommelin's heroine Roma in *Pink Lotus* (1914) finds the landscapes of the Jhelum valley "unreal" and like a "fairy forest" (Crommelin 80), and English heroines routinely speak of *enchantment*. "'It's like an enchanted land,'" says Peggy to Noel (who is actually more interested in shooting buck and crocodiles) in *By Request* (1927) (Dell 1927: 197). Julia in Gertrude Atherton's *Julia France and Her Times* (1912) says to Nigel,

> "One secret of enjoying the East is to forget the West. And for at least a year I was intoxicated—drunk is more expressive—with its enchantment..." (Atherton 269).

But most *enchantment* depends precisely on remembering the West. As Hermione exclaims in *An English Girl in the East* (1913),

> "I love India already ... it's so different from everything else. There's a glamour about everything" (Kirby 151).

The "everything else" (England), often with specific connotations of "rain and mud and fog," is set favourably against what is called in *Olivia in India* "this afternoon land" of India (Douglas 70). Some writers attribute the "magical" aspect of India almost solely to the interplay of climate and landscape. In *Dilys: An Indian Romance* we are told of the palm groves and giant grasses that

> In a cold grey atmosphere the scene would have been dreary and depressing; but under the tropical light of a South Indian sun, the landscape was full of colour (Penny 1905: 3-4).

However, the passage significantly continues with the sinister detail that

> The newcomer gazed across the yellow sands at the gleaming water and azure sky until he was well-nigh blinded (Penny 1905: 4).

Having established India as glamorous and romantic, novelists are often concerned (in the same novel) to establish it as a place of loneliness, labour, and deprivation: a curious contradiction which is echoed in the double insistence on India's brilliant colours and "dull, uniform brownie grey." Indian landscapes are read in terms of famine and the aftermath of famine in several novels: for example, Mrs C.E. Phillimore's *Two Women and a Maharajah* (1906) (Phillimore 42), Olivia A. Baldwin's *Sita* (1911) (O. Baldwin 77), Alice Perrin's *The Stronger Claim* (1925) (Perrin 1925: 5). The implications here (again contradictory) are that the country and its climate are implacably hostile to human beings (so that, for example, even the sun is described as sinking "with angry reluctance" in a novel called *East of Suez* (1901) (Perrin 1901: 1)), and that the

Indian population is not responding with a proper energy to this recurring crisis. Even the insects, reptiles and birds which inhabit the grey rocks and bushy scrub near Bangalore in F.E. Penny's *The Unlucky Mark*, are said to be accepting "fate without question" (Penny 1909: 20), whereas you would hardly expect them to do anything else.

English deaths in India, on the other hand, are often regarded as especially tragic because consciously resisted by those who die. As a doctor who has been in Lucknow for many years observes in a novel of 1842, "'every Briton, wherever he spends his life, likes to close his eyes in his own land'" (Monkland I 27). Young Bertie Seton, mauled by a leopard in *Late in Life* (1896), whispers as he lies dying, "'Oh! awful to be buried in India—no one to come and look at your grave —'" (Perrin 1896 I: 43). His sense of being absorbed into an anonymous, alien landscape is confirmed by the chapter's closing words,

> That same evening, he was laid in the dreary, dusty little cemetery, and the hot winds howled over the bare grave until the rains came, and then the coarse rank weeds sprang up and covered it (Perrin 1896 I: 43-44).

Here the landscape itself effectively becomes a desecration of the grave in obliterating it, although Perrin was also emphatic that, as another writer puts it, meditating on "the men of England,"

> it is because of those lonely, scattered graves ... that our hold on India is as strong, as unshakable, as it is (Peterson 1913: 280).

In this novel, *The Lure of the Little Drum* (1913), Esther, who deserts her man of England, her decent, patriotic husband, for a native prince, recovers some of her own decency and patriotism in death, being buried in an unmarked grave beside another, faithful, wife, so that

> When the sun drops down behind the Bholpur forest, the white cross on the other grave flings a shadow across Esther's resting place (Peterson 1913: 349).

In a similar way, the "living hell" of an unfaithful Englishwoman, now living in an English seaside town,

> sinking gradually from one depth to the one beneath it, a prey to drink and other evils too dreadful to mention (Duff-Fyfe 1913: 306),

is contrasted with the heavenly peace of a nun, Mother Mary, buried near a tiny Mission Church in "the land of sunshine" (Duff-Fyfe 1913: 307). Even England, as a landscape, is outranked here by the triple claims of death, sexual abstinence and good weather in India.

The evidence of death was of course a major tourist attraction in India—as long as the death had happened long enough ago. The narrator of *The Land of the Lotus* (1914) is oppressed by the "world of sinister horror" lurking in the gardens around the Towers of Silence in Bombay (Graham 120), whereas in *The Flying Months* the long description of the tombs at Bijapur concludes:

> There is nothing harsh, or repellent, or suggestive of decay. Soft sun-warmed beauty reigns, and an extraordinary quiet (Peard 1909: 259).

Ruins, more generally, had a pleasantly melancholy impact, and two historical novels, Margaret Horton Potter's *The Flame-Gatherers* (1904), set in 1205, and Ena Fitzgerald's *Patcola* (1908), set in 1602, draw attention to this contemporary effect (Potter 3-4; Fitzgerald vii-viii).

Indian landscapes were useful to the novelist (especially the novelist who only knew India from novels) in conveying vague suggestions of some excitement which never had to be very clearly articulated: the yellow cornfields and jungle clad mountains of *The Daughter of Brahma* seem to hold "some secret, some mystery," remarks Wylie (Wylie 1912: 33). The actual locations themselves are often very vague, even though very few authors owned up, as Alice and Claude Askew did in 1912, to having chosen

> a purely imaginary Province for the scenes of their story which are laid in India (Askew n.p.).

Flora Annie Steel, although she spent twenty years in India, also created an "imaginary province" in writing about the Moghul emperors in *King-Errant, A Prince of Dreamers, A Mistress of Men and The Builder*, novels which, because they were set in the past, enabled her to tap into the same vague mysterious melancholy of an Indian landscape, like this one lying beyond the Taj Mahal:

> ... The faint streak of the river showed like a curving snake through the blue haze which was India, and beyond India the world. A world that was hastening through space—whither wards? (Steel 1928: 177)

Indian landscapes, because of their inscriptions by transient empires, were particularly liable to make writers wonder where the planet was hurtling, unless they included mountains, which, in their sublime, uninscribed grandeur, were particularly liable to make writers wonder about their characters' relation to the planet. They reduce Fay in *The Anglo-Indians* to "this little girl, this atom of life" (Perrin 1912: 4), and make May in *The Heart of a Maid* accept a man she does not love because

> The great grey hills were very vast and solemn in the dim light; looking at them she felt dwarfed, and of no importance: they had stood and would stand for centuries. What did her insignificant little life matter, after all, how spent, or with whom? It was all so small and contemptible (Kipling 1890: 6).

This, of course, has to be taken with a pinch of salt because after all *The Heart of a Maid* is predicated on the notion that the heart of a maid is important; often, indeed, it is a large landscape which lends a lone individual an importance. A Maud Diver novel of 1931 opens:

> Honor Meredith folded her arms upon the window ledge of the carriage and looked out into the night: a night of strange, unearthly beauty.
>
> The full moon hung low in the west like a lamp. A chequered mantle of light and shadow lay over the mountain barrier of India's northwestern frontier, and over the desolate levels through which the train, with its solitary English passenger, sauntered at the rate of seven miles an hour, halting to take breath—for ten or fifteen minutes—at embryo stations set down in a land of death and silence (Diver 1931: 377).

Honor (whose name does indeed denote *honour*), solitary because clearly the Indian passengers might as well be absent, and therefore the figure who redeems India from "death and silence," not only has the perception which renders the scene beautiful but is the civilised measure by which the speed of the train and the size of the stations become absurd.

A similarly solitary figure crosses a landscape at the opening of Alice Clifton's *An Unwilling Wife: A Tale of the Indian Mutiny* (1890):

> In the early morning of one of the last days of May, in the year 1857, a single English horseman, attired in the white linen clothing and solar topee usually worn by officers of the army instead of uniforms during the hottest months of the year, was riding over a wide, sandy plain in one of the northwest Provinces of India (Clifton 1).

Despite the opening date, the Mutiny is actually very perfunctorily treated in the novel, but that opening date does give this noble knight pricking o'er the plain a special poignancy, in his double whiteness, in his isolation, despite his companions, and in his tininess in relation to the wide plain which he traverses.

John Church, just appointed Lieutenant Governor of Bengal at the opening of Sara Jeannette Duncan's *His Honor and a Lady* (1908), is observed by two Indians who are going "about the business of the Queen Empress" in Hassimabad (Duncan 1) as he goes to tell his wife the news. Duncan describes the landscape in terms of its varied life, and noise, and then comments that

> Nevertheless there was a boundless stillness—a stillness that might have been commanded. The prodigal sun intensified it, the trees stood in it, a red and dusty road wound through it, and the figure of a man, walking quickly down the road, seemed to be a concentration of it (Duncan 2).

The (otherwise extraordinary) equation of a *walking* man with a concentration of *stillness* expresses Duncan's confidence in Church's capacity to bring a stability to Bengal and at the same time her recognition of India's lack of capacity to change, very similar to that of Nina Stevens in *The Perils of Sympathy* four years earlier. Stevens, also reading a landscape in Bengal, comes to the conclusion that the active, policing presence within it, beside the village well, of "strongly formed, fair skinned, golden hued" Englishmen "denoted modern rule," because to her their picturesque, racially demarcated bodies means that rural India, "unchanged from far distant ages," is accepting a new order; she immediately qualifies this by characterising this as

> The new order that ever rises in the East, not changing the old, but springing up by its side, gradually to overshadow it (Stevens 27).

The same reservations are expressed in *Cecilia Kirkham's Son* (1909) through the observation, within a "commonplace enough" Indian landscape of brown grass, dusty trees and sunbaked road, not of a group of Englishmen but a crowd of Indians, who are standing listening to the Bengal Cavalry at the Dharwad garrison playing "God Save the King," and are described as

> some huge, dark, unknown, yet concrete creature, anchored to the spot by sound (Combe 12).

The crowd, that is, is recognized as anchored very precariously in this imperial space.

The ability at least to respond to a landscape, if not read it, is an important moral register for characters, which is why landscape is rarely treated brusquely by authors, although M.J. Colquhoun in *Every Inch a Soldier* does impatiently conclude one description, "But to return to our story" (Colquhoun 1888 I: 34). When an admirable character is indifferent to a landscape, his creator is liable to leap in to defend him. Beynon, another manager of landscape—the chapter heading identifies him as "Beynon, of the Irrigation Department"—is looking out over the River Ganges, but

> looked at it all, and saw nothing, principally because he was thinking of his work—he very seldom thought of anything else—and also because he was so accustomed to the scene … (Perrin 1901: 2).

explains Alice Perrin, and only the most empty-headed of flirts, like Ursula à Beckett's Sybella, remain completely indifferent to Indian scenery (Beckett 277); more common is the experience of Frances M. Peard's Patty when she sees the broad treeless plain and mountains near Peshawar:

> A new dumb awe struck Patty which she could not have explained, but which kept her silent (Peard 1904: 31).

The narrator of May Edwood's *The Autobiography* of a Spin (i.e. *flirt*) is explicit in congratulating herself on her delighted response to the landscapes around the hill station of Murree:

> ... It must be a very hard nature indeed that is not affected in some way by all these wonders and beauties.
>
> You are astonished that I have any such feelings, but I am endeavouring to show you the worst and the best of me (Edwood 161).

A sensitive response to landscape is not only an important register of moral fibre, but of race. Of course, in some of these novels this is exactly the same thing, and Indira Ghose in *Women Travellers in Colonial India: The Power of the Female Gaze* quotes Mrs Colin Mackenzie, author of *Six Years in India* (1857) who had expatiated with a sublime lack of self-awareness on the inferiority of "the subject race":

> The Hindustanis are very apathetic to scenery. I have never known one to stop to admire anything. My husband cross-questioned a chaprassy (from Delhi I think) to find if he had any appreciation for the beauties which surrounded him. Not in the least. He said the pain in his legs in running up and down hill with messages was not to be expressed, and that if it were not for the wants of his stomach he would not stay here a day (Mackenzie 173, quoted in Ghose 49).

In a novel of 1908, the mixed-race Bulbul, named after the Indian nightingale which features in so many descriptions of Indian landscapes, redeems himself morally and becomes "an unconscious poet" as he describes the beautiful landscapes of his home in Mhudapur (Duff-Fyfe 1908: 255), but in this very curious narrative (Ethel Duff-Fyfe's *The Nine Points*) he is cheated out of his English inheritance, with the author's complete approval, precisely because India is his home. The fact that he gives way to the English impostor Fred Carvill, surely in a subterranean commentary on English imperial claims, shows what a "true gentleman" he is!

In a novel of 1904 the mixed-race Averine, born in India,

reveals her moral inferiority, and her sexual rapacity, at a party on the Thames, for while her companions are thinking sedately only of the sedges and the river, "she sat dreaming of the passionate beat of the monsoon driven surf upon the west coast of India" (Penny 1904: 15).

Conversely, in *A Bottle in the Smoke* (1912), Mrs. Fellowes demonstrates her essential decency by enjoying the beauty of an Indian beach because it suggests to her "'one of the vanished haunts of my girlhood'"—in England (Rae 220). *A Bottle in the Smoke* is a convoluted narrative in which the good mixed-race character is discovered to be English, and the bad English character is discovered to be mixed-race, a doubly convenient outcome which we could have anticipated if we had tracked their respective attitudes to landscape—although even the evil Alfred, when gazing out over a beautiful starlit garden, does experience "one of those moments of self-revelation which visit even the basest and shallowest of human hearts" (Rae 199).

Gardens, and particularly their management, are especially important as moral touchstones; gardens in India, however, do not "challenge the grand sweep of the masculinist gaze" (Rose 112) as at least one feminist critic has suggested they usually do. The huge and beautifully designed gardens of the Moghul Emperors (star features in Flora Annie Steel) are proof of the high level of their civilisation, whereas in the India of 1911 the political and sexual waywardness of a rajah is demonstrated by the "wild profusion" of the flowers in his palace garden, "without the restraining influence of the pruning knife" (Penny 1911: 45). English gardens in India, with their mixture of exotic blooms and suburban order, are, as a metaphor for harmonious imperial rule, often meticulously described, the individual flowers carefully enumerated, as they are in E.W. Savi's *Baba and the Black Sheep* (1914) (Savi 1914: 1), but here the idyllic scene on the west bank of the Ganges is shattered by the irruption of the English girl who lives in the bungalow; to the horror of the Englishman who looks on, she shoots a mad dog. There is a very similar sequence in F.E. Penny's *Love in the Hills* (1913), in which a visiting Englishman is soothed by the mixture of English and Indian flowers in the heroine's garden in the Nilgiri Hills, where

> The homely sweet William grew cheek by jowl with the gardenia, and the humble snapdragon lifted its spikes of yellow and orange flowers under the shelter of a flaming poinsettia (Penny 1913: 9).

This idyllic scene is shattered by the appearance of "Teddy," a bear who is one of the heroine's many pets, which attempts to maul him. Although elsewhere in F.E. Penny the garden is more conventionally a personification of the heroine, for example in *A Mixed Marriage* (1903), where the new blossoms opening their petals after a night's destructive rain and the "unsullied" butterflies hovering over the flowers represent Lorina, rescued from a harem (Penny 1903: 266 to 267), here the bear, like the mad dog, appears to be a trope of erotic power, the more powerful for appearing unexpectedly amid the flowers. Honor Meredith (she of the railway journey) also impresses the hero by shooting a mad dog in the compound (Diver 1931: 401). Perhaps there is—quite simply—for female readers the imaginative pleasure of shooting down a prey, far from the "ever ready and attentive policemen at the corners."

The Englishman the bear attempts to maul, a captain in the Royal Engineers, stationed near Ootacamund, has just been wandering in the jungle, where he has been taking pains to monitor and collate its different sounds:

> More than once he seated himself on a wayside boulder to watch and listen; and each time he discovered in the chorus a new voice that had escaped him before (Penny 1913: 2).

The birds, frogs, lizards, bees, water and foliage that people this beloved landscape are regarded here and in many other novels with just as much, if not more, affection as human figures, who are often no more than local colour. Brenda Lisle in *A Blind Alley* (1911), delighted by "the quaint Eastern aspect of all she saw" (Savi 1911: 155), notes that

> Children swam and dived like brown water babies, and young girls balanced earthen vessels full of water on their heads ... (Savi 1911: 157).

The narrator of *Primus in Indi's* (1885) is similarly very taken by the fact that from his "solitary tent ... in a thick shady grove near a temple" he can watch "tall, elegant girls draped in simple muslin" drawing water from the river in large red earthen vases (Colquhoun 1885 II: 107-108). The particular attraction of such a feature of the landscape is put most cogently by F.E. Penny in *Dark Corners* (1908), writing about her heroine in South India:

> The morning was perfect, and the figures seemed to Olwen to harmonize with the beauty and peacefulness of the scene. In that remote valley how many generations of women had trodden the path to the river, clothed in garments of a similar fashion, and bearing brazen water vessels of the same shape? (Penny 1908: 300)

Actually Penny's title refers both to supernatural goings-on and India itself, the two being closely connected, and Olwen immediately witnesses a murder (Penny 1908: 302), but she is momentarily soothed by this picturesque historical pastoral, without any reference to the actual lives of the women. In Eliza F. Pollard's *The White Dove of Amritzir* (1897), we are told of Colonel Melville and the girls Ruby and Kate, as they ride from Calcutta to Delhi, that

> what amused them most was when they passed through the villages with their mud huts, squalid and untidy in the extreme, for then the whole story of Eastern life unrolled itself to their eye and minds … (Pollard 78).

Indians can be seen as positively sullying an Indian landscape with their presence. Margaret Peterson declares in the rather appropriately titled *Dust of Desire,*

> as everyone knows, it is an almost herculean task to make an Indian community live in cleanliness according to the sanitary laws of any other civilisation (Peterson 1922: 35).

Earlier Florence Marryat had been "particularly charmed" by the sight of the plentiful mulberry bushes around Bangalore, but distressed by the idea that Indians should touch them, because

> There is something in the idea of gentlemen who never wear any clothes picking the fruit you eat which is not at all appetising (Marryat 6).

Closely connected with the threat of dirt and nudity is what Pollard described as the *untidiness* of Indian landscapes, whether it is "a confused dream of feudalism and Gothic Middle Ages" in the case of a rajah's castle near Lucknow among "dark masses of unfamiliar foliage" (that is, unfamiliar to an English eye), (Gray 73) or (Lucknow again) "a vast chaotic mass" (Phipps 89). It is out of this vast chaotic mass that the novelist must construct her story. J.E. Muddock in *The Great White Hand* ("the great white hand" meaning British imperial rule) offers this recipe for the construction of Cawnpore:

> ... you must take a big plain with lots of cocoa palms about, and a broad river running through it. Then get many hundreds of bamboo and mud huts; a few marble palaces, some temples with gilded minarets, a few big public buildings, a hospital or two, a goal, and a quantity of miscellaneous structures, such as an arsenal, barracks, etc., shake them all up together, and toss them out on the plain, and there you have your Cawnpore (Muddock 136).

Muddock is here not only referring to the incoherence (as she sees it) of the landscape, but writing about the creative imagination in which diverse elements are "shaken all up together" to produce a fictional territory, a fiction located within a fiction, "the idea, the scheme, and the intention," as Duncan called the British Empire in India (Duncan 216).

How might contemporary *Indian* women's fiction differ from some of the texts I have mentioned? (I have looked briefly at some fiction *in English*, written by that tiny minority of Indians at ease in English—which is, however, a tiny minority of more than 30 million). Much of this fiction is written outside India and has the same predisposition as the Englishwomen's fiction to filter one landscape through another, India usually set against Britain, Canada, or the United States. Anita Rau Badami's *Tamarind Mem* (1996), for example, opens in a cold and snowy Canada, narrated by the daughter of the "tamarind mem" (bitter woman) of the title, the "other" against which she remembers the India of her childhood, an India literally inscribed by her father, a railway engineer, but also imaginatively inscribed by the labourers with whom he works, who have to offer coconut milk and pink rose petals to Ganga to coax the river out of her sulks (Badami 43). The second half of the novel is narrated by Kamini's mother, in a way which makes us understand her bitterness, but ends triumphantly with her using the railway maps which her husband had given to her daughter so that she could track his journeys, to plot her own as she crisscrosses India on a kind of secular pilgrimage for her own amusement, rejecting her daughters" appeals for her continued emotional support:

> No way, honeybun! I do not belong to anyone now. I have cut loose and love only from a distance (Badami 266).

"Pilgrimage" is the title of a short story by Padma Perera (1985), in which the protagonist's restless travelling across India and gorging on her landscapes is likened by a chance acquaintance

> to a *Bharat darshan*: the age-old ideal of a pilgrimage across the length and breadth of the country to be vouchsafed the sight, and thereby the blessing, of your whole holy motherland. Holiness was too doubtful a dimension for the likes of him, but he had seen the countryside all right. From the southernmost tip of Cape Comorin, where three seas meet, all the way north to Kashmir for an object and abject lesson on poverty in paradise; then slowly east to the low-lying, thatch roofed, mudwalled villages of rural Bengal, its ponds choked with incomparable blue of water hyacinths, its air with the stench of jute rising in the ditches; then southwest again to the hamlets strung along the canals of Kerala, whose beguiling, amphibious children slipped smooth as otters from doorstep to water and back again … (Perera 93-94).

Here "poverty in paradise" is seen with a pang, but by a spectator absorbed in his own feelings, and the children of Kerala are figures in the familiar picturesque pastoral. Moreover, this is a gaze conditioned by a particular predicament: the protagonist travels only to sublimate his illicit love for his stepmother, not his love for his holy motherland. Here landscape offers only a tepidly romantic embrace, of an unsatisfactory rather than a tragic kind.

In another story of illicit love, Sunetra Gupta's *A Sin of Colour* (1999), the interplay of character and physical environment is theatrically exaggerated, as Debendranath Roy reflects of his elder brother's wife,

> She hated too to tread barefoot upon any surface, and he had seen her squirm in agony as her toes were splashed with mud on a monsoon day as she picked her way through the puddles upon the cracked pavements. He had seen her recoil in horror from the oily skin of a weed choked pond as it stretched to fill her sandals while she pleaded with her sons to wade back out. And each time he had feasted on these anxieties, to him they wcrc profoundly sensual ... (Gupta 35).

Although not usually in a positive way, characters seem less separated from the landscape in Indian women's fiction. Rather than appearing as isolated figures within it, they are often compared with it. In Anita Desai's *Fasting, Feasting* (1999) the face of Mira-Masi, another restless pilgrim, begins "to look muddy and was streaked with deep lines like a riverbed that has run dry" (Desai 53). In Shauna Singh Baldwin's *What the Body Remembers* (1999) Sardarji owns not only apricot orchards but his new young wife Roop, whose skin is described four times over as "smooth as a new apricot beckoning from the limb of a tall tree" (S. Baldwin 15, 31, 66, 159). Another repeated image is of apricot buds sprouting from between Roop's legs, to be plucked by Sardarji and given to his first wife Satya, who is to take charge of Roop's babies (S. Baldwin 25, 471). After the cataclysm of Partition: "Women and children are being sorted between the two countries like apricots brought in from the orchard" (S. Baldwin 466).

Priya, who narrates Namita Gokhale's *Paro: Dreams of Passion* (1991), imposes her own sexual disgust on the backdrop of her encounter with her predatory boss B.R.:

> And I think of the sea at Marine Drive, the first time that he kissed me—vast, ugly and compulsive. I yielded almost immediately to the pressure of his plastic lips; but a part of me held back, observant and detachedly clinical. I stared instead at the coy moon hiding behind the white clouds, and watched the restless ocean regurgitate its teeming refuse back on to the black sullen rocks (Gokhale 8).

There is a similar sequence in Dina Mehta's *And Some Take A Lover* (1992), set just before Independence, in which the female protagonist is also sexually disgusted and yet successfully seduced.

Her married suitor stops his car in order to court her, and is absorbed into the static, urban scenery:

> The curving sweep of Marine Drive, wearing a circlet of lights, was tranquil. He sat motionless, like a statue that had been lowered into place behind the steering wheel, his marble hands resting on it. A diamond on his little finger glowed coldly (Mehta 18).

Roshni, by contrast, is absorbed into the sea, feeling "a tide in her blood" and sensing herself "on the edge of a new territory" (Mehta 20). Their conversation is also of a new territory: the England in which Rustom now, for materialistic motives, longs to live permanently, arguing that as Parsis they are both aliens in India,

> "'And our days are numbered after the British leave'" (Mehta 18).

Roshni finally finds happiness with the Hindu Sudhir who is working for Indian independence; they declare their love for each other in a landscape which is heavily inscribed with India's history, on the lawn of the Prince of Wales Museum, beside a statue of George V, the dome of the museum towering in the background, "all glare in the sunlight, lending a mediaeval atmosphere to the garden" (Mehta 175), this last detail confirming the transience of the imperial control represented by the statue, while Roshni's recollection of happy childhood picnics in the garden signals an assent to colonial memories.

Bombay's Marine Drive enjoys a bad press as a moral signifier, appearing in two more novels of the "nineties as a contaminated location, each time expressing an anxiety about how a landscape, or vista, may be purchased. Anxieties about the possession of land are interestingly pervasive. The heiress Devina in Sujata Sabnis's *Silent Whispers* (1996) looks out of the window of her flat and:

> Out there, in front of her, spread the whole expanse of the Arabian Sea, magical in its changing colours, in the chimera like movements of its waves. She loved to stand there for hours, just watching the sea, and its chameleon moods. Turbulent, calm, mischievous or mature, playful, angry, constantly changing yet always the same. This heartbreakingly

> beautiful vista had been the clinching factor in her decision to buy the flat. The reason why she had happily paid the exorbitant price the seller had asked for though her lawyer had told her that she was paying too much (Sabnis 23).

There is the same emphasis on money in Nirmala Moorthy's *Maya* (1997), in which the protagonist's father has had corruptly "to pull strings" for a flat from which Maya has

> a spectacular oceanfront view of Marine Drive, the palm-fringed promenade that was a scenic spot in Bombay. The curving halfmoon of its twinkling streetlights had earned it the name of the "queen's necklace" (Moorthy 26).

In each case the view has been bought too dearly. Devina, who has had a split personality since she was a child ("constantly changing yet always the same"), has forgotten that she acquired her wealth through murdering her parents. Maya, like her siblings, has no space or privacy because Marine Drive, as its picture postcard description suggests, is attractive to a horde of visitors which routinely displaces the family.

Even in a very different kind of novel, *Nurjahan* (1994), Jyoti Jafa's latter-day version of Flora Annie Steel's Moghul sagas, a beautiful prospect is shown as coming with a price. The seventeenth-century empress is first seen by her emperor husband Jehangir as she sits dreaming

> by the edge of a small round lily pool. Tiny striped squirrels, birds in gilt cages and drifting butterflies made this garden on the banks of the Ravi, outside the walled city of Lahore, a place of enchantment (Jafa 26).

Later, her daughter by her first husband sits talking to a prince

> beneath the spreading branches of a mango tree.
>
> Bright plumaged birds twittered through the garden, peacocks strutted across the lawns, trailing pure white feathers along the green grass. Little slave girls ran about, shooing them away from flower beds (Jafa 135).

Her daughter is actually using this conversation to find out the truth about her murdered father, and these miniature landscapes encode the oppressive aspects of the civilization to which their beauty bears witness in their images of imprisonment and enslavement.

The emotional development of Prema, the protagonist of Usha Ananda Krishna's *A Turbulent Passage* (1996), is demonstrated through her ability to acknowledge the reality of her own landscapes. When her husband and children move to Bhimsarai and she stays behind in Calcutta, she fantasises that she is in Manhattan or Paris (Krishna 52). When she is driven to the outskirts of Calcutta by her husband's friend Arjun, who is trying to seduce her, she looks with pleasure at an idealized version of landscape,

> The famed lushness of Bengal, ... clusters of picturesque huts, thatched or tile roofed, any poverty romantically screened off by banana plants, hibiscus shrubs and mango trees (Krishna 83).

As the sun sets she becomes acutely aware not only of what she sees as her sordid situation, but of "the raddled sky and litter-pocked mudflat" (Krishna 228). Finally, when Prema abandons her unconsummated and unsatisfactory relationship and travels out to Bhimsarai to be with her husband, Krishna opens a chapter with a long and consciously informative passage which explicates in blunt and unromantic terms the scene which Prema is seeing for the first time:

> Bhimsarai is a small town in one of India's northeastern provinces, at the point where the Ganges, wandering a little from its course, makes a small loop. The first settlers built their huts here in this fertile patch and gradually, because of the increasing importance of river transport the village gained prominence and grew to a town and thereafter the district headquarters.
>
> Seventy years ago there were indigo plantations on the banks of the Ganges, but with the invention of chemical dyes this industry became an anachronism … (Krishna 63). (and so on)

Prema, now that she is anchored back in reality, is able to absorb the evidence of all his intelligently, and even to interrogate, with amusement, the "reality" of a landscape refracted through history and art, noting that she is being driven along "the famous "Red hills of Bhimsarai" featured in books of the Raj," and commenting on the plumes of sugarcane waving mistily from behind the huts, and the river shining whitely in the morning light, that it is like a set from *Gandhi* (Krishna 64).

Chchanda, who guiltily becomes the mistress of her beloved aunt's husband in Indrani Aikath-Gyaltsen's *Daughters of the House* (1993), even though her entire life is structured by what she calls her family's "sentimental geography" (Aikath-Gyaltsen 1993a: 16), reflects very consciously on the "appropriate" symbolism of the landscape of her family home:

> The old acres, sold like so many others to tenant farmers, had shrunk until there remained only the grounds arranged in a little crescent at the river's edge: scarcely two acres in all, of which perhaps a quarter served as a kitchen garden, while the rest, all thickets and Thom brakes, was occasionally cut back to preserve a few tall deodars that plunged into the sky, swaying in the March winds like so many demented witches against a background of confused clouds, soiled a little from the smoke of the chimney. And nothing else, besides a gulmohur tree that had been struck by lightning, a rubber tree that oozed gum, and a garland of madhumalati overgrowing a little lawn where the crabgrass strangled the last crocus and the last rose tree reverted to a briar. The wilderness triumphed here, over all that man had done. It was even more so in the animal kingdom: a furtive cat, a few fowls that laid their eggs under the bushes, and everywhere else fugitives, nomads, overhead and underground—the insects, the birds, even a squirrel making off with a precious vegetable, a mongoose crawling among the eggs and another mongoose among the hens (Aikat-Gyalten 1993a: 11).

Like the "wild, overgrown garden" in Kerala (A. Roy 1) which opens Arundhati Roy's *The God of Small Things* (1997), this garden expresses deterioration and decay, but also shameful theft. Aikath-Gyaltsen's second novel, *Cranes' Morning* (1993) is named for the landscape perceived with delight by the old woman Vidya as belonging to the cranes, as they fly above the terraced hills of Chhotanagpur before a rainstorm (Aikath-Gyaltsen 1993b: 3) for here the landscape spells a human imprisonment, just as it does for the protagonist of Deepa Shah's *The Solitude of Surabhi* (1997), who commits suicide in her despair. As she opens her story, she describes her surroundings:

> Hemmed in by hills on three sides the town in the valley feels closed in, claustrophobic, in the silence of the early dawn (Shah 1).

Another, less tragic, protagonist feels similarly oppressed by her surroundings in Anurada Marwah Roy's *The Higher Education of Geetika Mehendiratta* (1993), but reflects more ironically upon them, commenting on the inappropriate name of Desertvadi in Rajasthan that

> It is not quite a desert, and a vadi (valley) only because it is surrounded by hills.
>
> This inappropriateness would dawn on the bureaucrats whenever a dignitary visited the place, or whenever there was a proposal to attract more tourist trade to the town. Once, the Municipal Council had all the roof tops neighbouring the railway station painted a dirty salmon pink. But Desertvadi could never be called "pink city" because that name had been usurped by Jaipur which was far more exotic and attracted far more foreign currency than Desertvadi could ever hope to. Another time they built fountains in the centre of the marketplace, so that the fountains combined with the few lakes that the town had, could heighten the valley aspect of the name. That very year severe water shortage hit Desertvadi. Not only did all the taps run dry, but the lakes also evaporated. Nevertheless, the dry lakes continued to fascinate the few impecunious tourists (foreigners), but that is another matter, they had other reasons.
>
> In that town of indeterminate character there was nothing to do except cry, make a phone call or masturbate, that morning (A.M. Roy 1).

Far from being glamorous or enchanting, some at least of contemporary fictional Indian landscapes seem to lack a significant inscription for their inhabitants (as opposed to the tourists, the new colonisers, for whose benefit a romantic inscription is attempted).

It is perhaps more difficult to conjure up emotion now because of contemporary technology. A Pakistani writer, Kamila Shamsie, observes:

> To set foot once more on the soil of one's homeland. Modern airports deny us this symbolic gesture. No soil, not even tarmac. Instead we step into an elevated corridor which carries us through to passport control, luggage claim and customs clearance (Shamsie 85).

There is the same antipathy for dirty peasants (for example in Manjula Padmanabhan's "Hot Death, Cold Soup") but usually a *lack* of antipathy for the material legacies of the British Raj, which are often merely noted as adding a picturesque element to the landscape (just as Moghul tombs had done for the earlier writers). There is no sense of landscape being managed for a noble purpose, or of surrounding landscapes endowing small human figures with importance, although these surroundings may console the restless travellers within them; rather, these small human figures tend to be metaphorically absorbed into the landscape.

Lacking the titillating consciousness of writing fiction driven fiction about an imperial possession, Indian women writers inscribe Indian landscape with moral criticism, sadness, entrapment—or simply dreariness.

NOTE

1. Although I.A.R. Wylie is in some sense Australian, and Sara Jeannette Duncan Canadian.

WORKS CITED

Aikath-Gyaltsen, Indrani. a *Cranes' Morning*. New Delhi: Penguin Books India, 1993.

——. b *Daughters of the House*. London: Phoenix House, 1993.

Askew, Alice and Claude. *The Englishwoman*. London, New York, Toronto and Melbourne: Cassell, 1912.

Atherton, Gertrude, with Roberta Eel. *Julia France and Her Times*: A Novel. London: John Murray, 1912.

Badami, Anita Rau. *Tamarind Mem*. Harmondsworth: Penguin, 1996.

Baldwin, Olivia A. *Sita: A Story of Child-Marriage Fetters*. London, Edinburgh, New York, Chicago, Toronto: Fleming H. Revell, 1911.

Baldwin, Shauna Singh. *What the Body Remembers*. London, New York and Toronto: Doubleday, 1999.

Beckett, Urusula à. *In Extenuation of Sybella.* London: Stanley Paul,

Bratton, J.S. "British imperialism and the reproduction of femininity in girls' fiction, 1900-1930." Ed. Jeffrey Richards. *Imperialism and Juvenile Literature.* Manchester and New York: Manchester UP, 1989. 195-215.

Cadell, H.M. *Ida Craven.* 2 vols. London: Henry S. King, 1876.

Cameron, Charlotte. *A Durbar Bride*. London: Stanley Paul, 1912.

Clifton, Alice. *An Unwilling Wife: A Tale of the Indian Mutiny.* London: Remington, 1890.

Colquhoun, M.J. *Primus in Indis: A Romance.* 2 vols. London: Chapman and Hall, 1885.

——. *Every Inch a Soldier.* 3 vols. London: Chatto & Windus, 1888.

Combe, Mrs Kenneth. *Cecilia Kirkham's Son.* Edinburgh and London: William Blackwood and Sons, 1909.

Comer, Krista. *Landscapes of the New West: Gender and Geography in Contemporary Women's Writing.* Chapel Hill and London: U of N Carolina P, 1999.

Croker, Bithia Mary. *A Bird of Passage.* 3 vols. London: Sampson Low, Marston, Searle, & Rivington, 1886.

——. *Her Own People.* London: Hurst and Blackett, 1903.

Crommelin, May. *Pink Lotus: A Comedy in Kashmir.* London: Hurst and Blackett, 1914.

Dell, Ethel M. *The Way of an Eagle.* London: Ernest Benn, 1912.

——. *By Request.* London: Fisher & Unwin, 1927.

Desai, Anita. *Fasting, Feasting.* London: Chatto & Windus, 1999.

Diver, Maud. *Candles in the Wind.* Edinburgh and London: William Blackwood and Sons, 1909.

——. *Captain Desmond, V.C.* London: George Newnes, 1931.

Douglas, Olivia. *Olivia in India: The Adventures of a Chota Miss Sahib.* London, New York, and Toronto: Hodder and Stoughton, 1913.

Duff-Fyfe, Ethel. *The Nine Points.* London: John Long, 1908.

——. *The Relentless Gods.* London: John Long, 1910.

——. *Written On Our Foreheads.* London: Chapman & Hall, 1913.

Duncan, Sara Jeannette. *His Honor and a Lady.* London, Edinburgh, New York: Thomas Nelson and Sons, 1908.

Edge, K.M. (Mrs C.T. Caulfeild). *The Shuttles of the Loom.* London: John Murray, 1909.

Edwood, May. *The Autobiography of a Spin.* A Story of Anglo-Indian Life. Calcutta, Bombay, and London: Thacker and Spink, 1893.

Embree, Ainslie T. "Imagining India: English language fiction set in post-independence India." Eds. Robin W. Winks and James R. Rush. *Asia in Western fiction.* Manchester: Manchester UP, 1990. 71-84.

Eustace, Alice. *Flame of the Forest.* London: Mills & Boon, 1927.

Fitzgerald, Ena. *Patcola: A Tale of a Dead City.* London: Greening, 1908.

Ghose, Indira. *Women Travellers in Colonial India: The Power of the Female Gaze.* New Delhi: OUP, 1998.

Gokhale, Namita. *Paro: Dreams of Passion.* Calcutta, Allahabad, Bombay, Delhi: Rupa, 1991.

Graham, J.M. *The Land of the Lotus.* Bristol: J.W. Arrowsmith, and London: Simpkin, Marshall, Hamilton, and Kent, 1914.

Gray, Maxwell (Mary Gleed Tuttiett). *In the Heart of the Storm: A Tale of Modern Chivalry.* London: George Newnes, 1903.

Grier, Sydney C. *England Hath Need of Thee.* Edinburgh and London: William Blackwood and Sons, 1916.

Gupta, Sunetra. *A Sin of Colour.* London: Phoenix House, 1999.

Jafa, Jyoti. *Nurjahan.* New Delhi: Lotus, 1994.

Kipling, Alice M. (Writing as Beatrice Grange). *The Heart of a Maid.* Allahabad: A.H. Wheeler, 1890.

——. (Writing as Mrs J.M. Fleming). *A Pinchbeck Goddess.* London: William Heinemann, 1897.

Kirby, Margaret. *An English Girl in the East: A Tale of Japan and India.* London: Andrew Melrose, 1913.

Krishna, Usha Ananda. *A Turbulent Passage.* New Delhi: UBSPD, 1996.

Marryat, Florence (Mrs Ross Church). *"Gup." Sketches of Anglo-Indian Life and Character.* London: Richard Bentley, 1868.

McAleer, Joseph. Passion's *Fortune: The Story of Mills & Boon.* Oxford: OUP, 1999.

Mehta, Dina. *And Some Take a Lover.* Calcutta, Allahabad, Bombay, Delhi: Rupa, 1992.

Miller, Luree. "The Himalayas in Fact and Fiction." Eds. Robin W. Winks and James R. Rush. *Asia in Western fiction.* Manchester: U of Manchester P, 1990. 85-99.

Monkland, Mrs. (Published anonymously.) *The Nabob at Home; or, The Return to England.* 3 vols. London: Henry Colburn, 1842.

Moorthy, Nirmala. *Maya.* New Delhi: Penguin Books India, 1997.

Muddock, J.E. *The Great White Hand or The Tiger of Cawnpore: A Story of the Indian Mutiny.* London: Hutchinson, 1896.

Padmanabhan, Manjula. "Hot Death, Cold Soup." *Hot Death, Cold Soup: Twelve Short Stories.* New Delhi: Kali for Women, 1996. 1-67.

Peard, Frances M. *The Ring from Jaipur.* London: Smith, Elder, 1904.

——. *The Flying Months.* London: Smith, Elder, 1909.

Penny, F.E. (Mrs Frank Penny). *A Mixed Marriage.* London: Methuen, 1903.

——. *The Sanyasi.* London: Chatto & Windus, 1904.

——. *Dilys: An Indian Romance.* London: Chatto & Windus, 1905.

——. *Dark Corners.* London: Chatto & Windus, 1908.

——. *The Unlucky Mark.* London: Chatto & Windus, 1909.

——. *The Rajah.* London: Chatto & Windus, 1911.

——. *Love in the Hills.* London: Chatto & Windus, 1913.

Perera, Padma. "Pilgrimage." *Birthday Death day and Other Stories.* London: Women's P, 1985. 73-94.

Perrin, Alice. *Late in Life.* 2 vols. London: Hurst and Blackett, 1896.

——. *East of Suez.* London: Anthony Treherne, 1901.

——. *The Charm.* London: Methuen, 1910.

——. *The Anglo-Indians.* London: Methuen, 1912.

——. *The Stronger Claim.* London, Calcutta, Sydney: George C. Harrap, 1925.

Peterson, Margaret. *The Lure of the Little Drum.* London: Andrew Melrose, 1913.

——. *Dust of Desire.* London and New York: Andrew Melrose, 1922.

Phipps, C.M.K. *Douglas Archdale.* A Tale of Lucknow. London: London Literary Society.

Phillimore, Mrs C.E. *Two Women and a Maharajah.* London: John Long, 1906.

Pollard, Eliza F. *The White Dove of Amritzir.* A Romance of Anglo-Indian Life. London: S.W. Partridge, 1897.

Potter, Margaret Horton. *The Flame-Gatherers.* London and New York: Macmillan, 1904.

Rae, Mrs Milne. *A Bottle in the Smoke: A Tale of Anglo-Indian Life.* London, New York, Toronto: Hodder and Stoughton, 1912.

Rose, Gillian. *Feminism and Geography: The Limits of Geographical Knowledge.* Oxford: Polity, 1993.

Roy, Anuradha Marwah. *The Higher Education of Geetika Mehendiratta.* New Delhi: Orient Longman, 1993.

Roy, Arundhati. *The God of Small Things.* London: Flamingo, 1997.

Sabnis, Sujata. *Silent Whispers.* New Delhi: Har Anand, 1996

Savi, E.W. *A Blind Alley.* London: Digby, Long, 1911.

——. *Baba and the Black Sheep.* London: Hurst and Blackett, 1914.

Shah, Deepa. *The Solitude of Surabhi.* New Delhi: Penguin Books India, 1997.

Shamsie, Kamila. *Salt and Saffron.* London; Bloomsbury, 2000.

Steel, Flora Annie. *Miss Stuart's Legacy.* 3 vols. London and New York: Macmillan. 1893.

——. *On the Face of the Waters.* London: William Heinemann, 1897.

——. *A Prince of Dreamers.* London: William Heinemann, 1908.

——. *King-Errant.* London: John Lane, Bodley Head. 1912.

——. *Mistress of Men.* London: William Heinemann, 1917.

——. *The Builder.* London: John Lane, Bodley Head, 1928.

Stevens, Nina (Mrs F. Griffiths). *The Perils of Sympathy* London: T. Fisher Unwin, 1904.

Wylie, I.A.R. *The Rajah's People.* London: Mills & Boon, 1910.

——. *The Daughter of Brahma.* London: Mills & Boon, 1912.

3

Coming Together: The Central Problem in *The Serpent and the Rope*

BASAVARAJ NAIKAR*

One of the most difficult problems of human life is living together and in the most intimate and complete of these, marriage, the coming together of man and woman, the challenges are even greater. This involves a continuous, dynamic adjustment, an acclimatization, occurring on many planes—physical, psychological, moral, emotional and even philosophical. *The Serpent and the Rope,* like all other meaningful novels, concerns itself with this central problem of life i.e., the problem of coming together of two individuals, Rama and Madeleine, from two different worlds. The problem which essentially is of marriage—has more than its normal share of challenges in this case in as much as the man is an Indian with a decidedly metaphysical turn of mind concerned with the invisible eternal realities of life and the woman, a Westerner from France, with a diametrically opposite temperament intensifying the normal feminine concern with the tangible realities of the living earth. They happen to meet in Paris University and fall in love. Their love starts of course with the basic sexual attraction for each other. This attraction naturally is the more intense because of their different colour and nationalities. The novelty and the strangeness that surround them hold a special fascination that irresistibly draws them towards each other. Madeleine, for example, likes, nay, loves Rama's golden hair and the live tradition of India of which he is to her an embodiment: "Look at this pale skin beside your golden one.

*Professor of English, Karnatak University, Dharwad, India.

Oh, to be born in a country where tradition is so alive that even the skin of her men is like some royal satin, softened and given a new shine through the rubbing of ages" (19). Much the same way, Rama also is attracted by Madeleine's beauty: "For an Indian this golden hair seemed always something unearthly, magical and of moonbeam and of raven silver" (20). Rama's culture, quite different from hers, enthralls her soul as much as a mystery does a romantic imagination. Her thrill of being loved by him is seen in her desire to be physically touched by Rama: "...She wanted to be touched by me, to be held by me, to know the knowing that has made knowing a single presence" (61). Even Madeleine's relatives like Tante Zoubie are so pleased with him that they think: "Oh, you Brahmin boy, who came to make this Charantaise happy" (91). Madeleine's overwhelming fondness for Rama, and her eagerness to die in India, the strange land, signify her romantic love for him: "I am happy I shall die in India. You will burn me; won't you Rama?" (68). Her willingness to merge her identity into her husband's and achieve the necessary cultural synthesis expresses itself in her desire to give her child an Indian name: "you know Rama, women must have names from their mother's side" (92) implying thereby that her son should be named after a Rajput King. Madeleine grows so much attracted to him that she feels lost in the absence of her husband; "Yesterday I felt lost without you" (136). All this adoration for Rama's virtues does not blind her to the other, not so charming, aspects of his person. She knows, for example, that Rama suffers from asthma, and she does not, therefore, allow him to carry the heavy suitcase; "There is no he-man in the world of God.... But the she-woman of France is just made to carry the burden for a Brahmin" (139). Thus between a young woman and a young man set out to achieve the consummation of a successful marriage, there is no lack of passion, nor lack of willingness nor effort, nor ardour to achieve the understanding necessary for it.

But in spite of these hard efforts, the couple fail to achieve the union of minds; to break the invisible walls that divide soul from soul; to achieve conjugal harmony. Though they live together physically, they do not come together psychologically and spiritually. They may love each other but they do not always understand each other completely. The reasons for this soul-to-soul distance are many. Madeleine somehow feels that Rama cannot understand her feelings, probably because he is a man. A certain masculine indifference on his part makes him neglect her feelings and desires. And the dominant self-centeredness in his nature has an additional detail to intensify it; and he hails from a different cultural background, of which he is especially proud; and then there is his temperament, different from hers. And so to find a kindred soul who can understand her feelings and problems, Madeleine turns to Katherine Mansfield's novels: "No man can understand a woman, Rama, no, never." "Only can a woman speak of a woman. We are no angels. But we are no beasts" (164). Behind all their surface gaiety, there is an undercurrent of dissatisfaction. Many times Rama feels as though he married her just the previous day: "Then she would kneel by me—just my bride. Yesterday I felt married to her as never before" (84). Until now he has not achieved that spiritual affinity with her, which he should have by this time. Though living together, they have not come together in the real sense of the term. Rama feels this matrimonial dissatisfaction quite often: "Last night she rose as she always has, with a simple gesture and on my sick bed in the chapel of Montpalais, when the night was clear as one's knowledge of oneself, she became my wife again and I called her many sweet names" (84). The phrase "She became my wife again," connotes that she was not his wife until then in the real, spiritual sense. They can only attain the matrimonial union superficially in a momentary emotion or a physical gesture, but never the abiding sympathy or the marriage of minds.

Like Madeleine, Rama also is overwhelmed by a kind of darkness. Deep in his heart there is a certain restlessness, turmoil and a sense of the meaninglessness of it all. This feeling is lurking in his soul right from the beginning: "Once again it happened last night—that same emptiness, the mango-seed like kernel that lay within me, and I remembered what Grandmother had said of the mango-seed ... but she was not happy either" (149). Another time, Madeleine tells Rama, "Be happy, my love, be happy." "But I was not happy" (162), says Rama. When in despair Madeleine turns to Buddhism Rama grows even more restless. He experiences a sort of spiritual crisis of identity, which becomes unbearable to him. Metaphysical problems stir his soul to the utmost: "Yes, I say to myself, 'I must leave this world, I must leave, leave this world.' But Lord, shall I go, where? How can one go anywhere? How can one go from oneself?" (399). After much rigorous, ceaseless cogitation, Rama realizes his desideratum in life. He comes to know that what he needs most is a Guru to show him the spiritual path, the ultimate reality of life, the rope which Rama had mistaken for the serpent, the illusion or *maya*. Madeleine is sensitive enough to understand that Rama will not be happy with an ascetic for a wife. Each of them becomes a stranger to the other. The gap between them widens until she voluntarily suggests divorce to him. Ultimately, compelled by these circumstances, Rama seeks separation from her and returns to India in order to lead his life at the lotus feet of a Guru.

There is more than one reason for their failure to come together. Many of their cultural idiosyncrasies act as barriers in their coming together. Though an agnostic in the beginning, Madeleine believes in superstitions. She believes more in Rama's power of healing than in the doctors. Though a heathen, after the death of their son, Pierre, she starts attending the morning masses. Her soul is groping in confusion and is struggling for some faith. She begins fasting on Fridays and lights candles to the Virgin. The death of Pierre makes her religious but not philosophical. She is not able to attain to the detachment Rama has mastered. But Rama's approach is altogether different: it is of a man, and what is more, of an Indian whose soul has its roots in the immemorial philosophic past. For him, "Pierre was never dead: I could feel him in my loins" (41). Rama, deep in his heart, is not worried because death for him is not the end of life but the continuation of it. So it is not as agonising to him as it is to Madeleine, the Westerner. This philosophical attitude towards life makes Rama take the death of his son easy and lightly which to the mother is a shock. This is the evidence of a basic gap between two different cultures. As a result, Rama, despite his subtle and mystical explanations, fails to console her.

The cultural difference, in fact, is seen in their diametrically opposed attitudes and responses to Pierre both alive and dead; Rama's is the Eastern mystic soul, metaphysical; Madeleine's the practical and emotional. For Rama, Pierre was not happy but happiness itself. Madeleine says, Rama is more interested in Pierrot's sonship than in his being Rama's son. She accuses him: "Your impersonal approach was strange to me, you yourself so impersonal" (36). "You people are sentimental about the invisible, we about the visible. And to me you were the invisible made concrete, so visible, incarnate, beside me—and my husband" (37). This contrast in approaches proves that their cultural edges are not blunted yet. She further accuses him: "You make the simple too big, and everything human seems ridiculous before you" (37). Here Rama's Indian tendency to exalt everything to divinity at the cost of humanity, and Madeleine's tendency to see life geocentrically are in contrast. Madeleine is irritated to see that her countrymen's humanness is looked upon by Rama as insignificant. This difference can be seen throughout the novel.

Rama is so impersonal and abstract in his approach to life that one wonders if he has a concrete physiological existence at all: "I wondered," says Madeleine, "whether I could really love a thing so abstract as you" (40). Rama with his perpetual philosophical preoccupation gives such an impression to Madeleine that she doubts: "I wonder if Indians can love" (40).

The cultural polarity is also seen in their attitude to time and punctuality. A Westerner is always very particular about time, whereas an Indian is notorious for unpunctuality. This is evidenced in Rama's late return to Paris. Rama knows: "She would be unhappy first, then angry, knowing that Indians are so undependable" (58). "But this Indian haphazardness, like the towels in the bathroom that lay everywhere about, was exasperating to Madeleine" (58). This makes it clear that they are unable to drop their cultural peculiarities, or, what is more significant, achieve a workable assortment of them that would not land them in an emotional disarray.

Even in their religious bents of mind differences exist. George can understand an Indian better than Madeleine can. A Westerner, Madeleine expects intellectually and logically convincing answers to the problems of life. A typical woman, she wants some faith or the other to cling to—a faith based on an emotion which is the woman's bridge to life, whereas Rama, an Indian, is easily satisfied with the mystic-cum-metaphysical answers about life. A Catholic, George is also like Rama, a fanatic. Madeleine listens to the stodgy, metaphysical discussions about Truth, History and Christianity carefully and curiously, but she is more puzzled than convinced by them. This is because, as Madeleine says, "Fanatic as he [George] is, his Catholicism makes him understand India more than I do pagan that I am" (63).

The national-cum-cultural opposition is perceivable in their knowledge about their own countries. Madeleine, for example, knows that the Europeans have been civilized only recently, thereby accepting the cultural superiority of India. She writes: "After all, we Europeans have only been civilized for a thousand years. And what you may pardon in me, Savithri may not" (116). Rama assures Madeleine that Indians were a very tolerant people, and the 'barbarities' of Madeleine might amuse Savithri more than hurt her" (116). In the same way Rama also knows how faith plays an important role in Indian life. Rama says, "Yes, we Brahmins do make engineers, doctors and even military men today, but it is like one of those pillars in the inner courts of our old houses—though eaten by wood lice it continues. Not that it supports its roots, and the rest is held by air, by faith.... We've the fitness to know, not the sinews to act, we the real impotent of the earth" (145). In these opinions we have an indication of Madeleine's meekness contrasted with Rama's chauvinism and a smack of egoism.

The cultural extremities can be seen in their diverse concepts of wife-husband relationship. She designates him as an impersonal husband who can glorify and worship her without ever showing the familiarity a husband ought to. She says, "All evening I had talked of you to Tante Zoubie and to Catherine I spoke especially of the respect you show to me, for you a woman is still the other, the strange, the miracle. You worship women even if you torture them. But I like to be tortured and be your slave" (95).

Another point of divergence can be observed in the Indian's over serious and the European's relatively light-hearted approach to life. Madeleine is so much fed up with her husband's philosophical grimness that she would like to go and seek the warmth of living, tangible, humanly cheerful company of ordinary human beings. "Sometimes," says Madeleine, "I want to run away from you just to listen to stupid innocent laughter, like Tante Zoubie's or go to a circus and see the clown make everyone laugh—this high seriousness reminds me of poor Werther. I am not serious, you know, Rama, and one day perhaps, I shall run away" (136).

Rama's *vedantic* philosophy enables him to maintain a certain balance of mind of which Madeleine is incapable. He is neither elated by pleasure nor depressed by pain. This is evidenced in his response to the news of his wife's operation. Instead of getting apprehensive or worried, he bursts into guffaws of laughter: "In the bathroom, later when I stepped on the wash-slab I felt above both, like a child looking at the kite in the sky. I thought of George and laughed at Leibnitz and the monad and all that. I saw the yellow and white of the kite and the snake-like tail that the wind swept curling whirling on itself and leaping up back against the sun. The winds blew cool and fresh. I laughed as a child laugh, playing with the subtleties of the breeze. I was happy. The world is a happy place for anyone to live in: look at the ants in the Lal Bagh.... I laughed hilariously the whole afternoon, playing country chess, first with Little Mother and then with Saroja when she woke from her siesta. In the evening I took them all to the cinema" (215).

Another of the most important factors responsible for their failure to adjust to each other, is their philosophic-religious beliefs. Rama believes in the superiority of the Indian way of life. Though he knows that "to wed a woman you must wed her God" (15), he never makes any attempt in this direction because he remains a fanatic of his own God, sometimes fascinatingly, and sometimes irritatingly. Rama's defence of Indian people and their character is dogmatic and exasperating: "We forget evil easily. Naturally we love the good" (62) as if a non-Indian cannot do so. On the contrary, Madeleine, far from defending her countrymen, is ready, though light-heartedly, to admit their weakness: "For the European, Truth can only be attractive when it is perverse" (301). Rama holds the conviction that India stands for Truth and therefore she has no history, whereas other nations have history because they do not stand for Truth: "France is a battle for humanity." "India has no history, for Truth cannot have history" (101, 102). As to what man must aim at in life, Rama says that "man must seek not purity of mind and body but to be purity itself. Man must not wish to taste the sweetness of sugar, but one must become, as the Vedantins say, sweetness itself" (111). Rama is always preoccupied with the most fundamental philosophical problems of life: "The Brahmin is never contemporary—he goes backward and forwards in time, and so has a sage to begin with the genealogical tree and a *Guru* to end the cycle of birth and death. Where, I ask you, where was I to build a house, a home? By what river or tank or temple corridor?" (125). Rama points out how only Indians have questioned the ultimate aim of life. "We are ... deadly serious, about everything, that we are perhaps the only nation that throughout history has questioned the existence of the world, of the object" (332). Once seeing the love-game between George and Catherine, Madeleine asks Rama to explain why these things happen in life, Rama answers that Catherine likes George because she wants a mate. George loves Catherine not for Catherine's sake but for the sake of self in her. Madeleine is fascinated by these mystico-metaphysical answers, but she never shows any sign of satisfaction with them. Sometimes Madeleine dares to taunt him about certain topics which occupy her mind. For example, she points out the inferiority of woman to man and untouchability in India: "So that the pariah may have his separate well, and the woman slave for men" (62). To this Rama makes no answer. We have here an encounter between an intuitive, mystic, Indian husband and an intellectual, logically minded French wife.[1] Consequent upon the dissatisfaction with her husband's puzzles, she turns to Buddhism to find her own answers. She starts reading Buddhist texts and ultimately ends up as a Buddhist ascetic. She sleeps on a bed made of boards and thin mattress; renounces all luxury; speaks only three hundred words a day; acquires some power for oracles. She starts talking in Buddhist philosophical terms. She calls herself a vestment of eighteen aggregates. At the same time, Rama also grows more and more acutely a Brahmin. Hence the rift between them grows wider and renders mutual adjustment impossible.

The person mainly responsible for her transformation or voluntary religious conversion is, of course, Rama. As she herself says: "I was an atheist, with a horror of the Church. You it was Rama, with your Brahminism that gave me the eyes to see" (317). Rama acts as a catalytic agent who transforms Madeleine, while remaining himself unaffected, and incapable of doing to himself what he could do to another being. So he has to seek a divorce from her only to come back to India, to seek the aid of a *Guru.*

The failure of Rama and Madeleine to come together is generally ascribable to their different personal idiosyncrasies, national and cultural backgrounds, convictions, temperaments and attitudes to life. Though an agnostic and a pagan at the outset, she has a latent desire for some faith to cling to. And this desire of hers gets materialized in her voluntary conversion to Buddhism through Rama's influence. A typical Westerner with her intellectual and scientific bent of mind, she could not comprehend her husband's Indian, mystic and metaphysical interpretation of life and his equally mystic and metaphysical self at least as he projects it to her. She, therefore, is drawn towards Buddhism which is less mystical, less puzzling and confusing than Hinduism. In it, she finds relatively simple, clear and unparadoxical answers to the questions nagging at her soul—answers such as 'life is full of suffering,' Peace is repudiation of desire' and so on. In this way there is a growth in Madeleine from agnosticism to some sort of faith; from being a pagan to being a Buddhist. But Rama never grows. One might say he goes round in circle and return to the starting point. From the beginning to the end, he remains a Brahmin and that too fanatically so. Not only that, he indirectly tries to win her heart towards Brahminism but finding her leaning towards Buddhism, gives up the attempt. He remains utterly indifferent to her feelings. His failure to attune himself to Madeleine's life is solely attributable to his philosophy—a philosophy that tells him that all experience, indeed all life is, a mere illusion. His Madeleine, Pierre, Tante Zoubie, Uncle Charles, his ex-beloved Savithri, Paris and its life—all these visible phenomena are only appearances, the serpent for him. Hence all this spiritual restlessness and disillusionment. His cardinal aim is to attain reality, i.e. the rope. Only the invisible Supreme Brahman is the reality for him. That is why he decides to go back to India to attain this Reality with the help of a Guru. Apart from their individual, national, cultural and religious differences, Rama's philosophy mistakenly or otherwise breeds a metaphysical egoism in him, fails him in achieving the connubial concord. This exalted concern with 'Self' hardly lets him appreciate European culture, whose concerns are of the immediate and the present, at least for his wife's sake. He remains a God-hungry Brahmin and never becomes a true husband for Madeleine. In fact, *The Serpent and the Rope* can be designated as the tragedy of philosophy of an Indian Hamlet. Rama, who is a scholar, a romantic and a sensitive person, should, with all these qualities, have had no difficulty in achieving matrimonial harmony with his wife. But his philosophy makes him indifferent to the reality of the world of which Madeleine is an essential part. He looks at life through the *Vedantic* lenses, whose vision might light up the path to the heart of God but not to that of a woman of flesh and blood, passion and love. It is this philosophy that makes him impersonal. Sitting in his ivory tower of metaphysics, he looks down upon the earthly Madeleine and her surroundings. In the perception of wifehood he does not see his wife. In the pursuit of sonship of Pierre, he forgets Pierre. With his preoccupation with the self, for which both he and Madeleine are mere instruments, he neglects Madeleine the woman. Obsessed with the ultimate aim of life, he ignores life itself. His godly preoccupations render him unhuman not only to Madeleine but to others as well. The couple fail to come together not merely because of temperamental incompatibility but also because of the incompatibility of their philosophies.

NOTE

1. Had she been a German girl, who is generally romantic and idealistic and could have loved and easily responded to the Indian husband's philosophy, this problem would not have arisen at all.

4

The Trauma of a House-wife: Shashi Deshpande's *That Long Silence*

RAJESHWAR MITTAPALLI*

With a gift for sharp psychological insight into the subtleties of human mind and society and aided by a richly evocative, unassuming and unpretentious style, Shashi Deshpande is perhaps ideally suited to tread the labyrinthine tracts of human psyche and creditably represent it in fiction. Her novels—particularly *The Dark Holds No Terrors* and *That Long Silence*—are an education in the psyche of people who lose their capacity for rational thought on being subjected to traumatic experiences.

Jaya of *That Long Silence* when required to face a traumatic situation temporarily seeks shelter in neurosis which evades her responsibility as an adult individual for her without her being aware of it. Her suffering has a beneficial effect on her. It initiates the process of self-discovery in her which leads in the last analysis to her fresh perception of life. She emerges at the end of the ordeal as a woman with a certain willingness to compromise with life's problems while earlier she showed a surprising lack of accommodation and expansiveness.

Jaya Kulkarni is an apparently satisfied house-wife. Having married a responsible man, Mohan, and blessed with two children, Rahul and Rati, and a home and material comforts, she seems to have almost nothing to ask for in life. To achieve this stage of fulfilment as a woman Jaya has systematically suppressed every

*Associate Professor, Department of English, Kakatiya University, Vidyaranyapuri, Warangal, India.

aspect of her personality that refused to fit into her image as wife and mother. Two such most important aspects are: her writing career and her friendship with Kamat which need clear understanding at the very outset.

Jaya has been a short-story writer of moderate success. Although Mohan takes pride in the fact of being the husband of a writer, he strongly objects to her themes which he suspects to have strong autobiographical overtones. On a particular occasion he says:

> 'They will all know now, all those people who read this and know us, they will know that these two persons are us, they will think I am this kind of man, they will think I *am* this man. How can I look anyone in the face again? And you, how could you write these things....'

She however feels that she has related her experience only after transmuting it into something entirely different. But she has been "scared of hurting Mohan, scared of jeopardising the only career I had, my marriage" (144). So in spite of her best judgement she gives up writing fiction and settles down to writing middles to newspapers which pose no problem to anyone.

Kamat exists in the novel as a shadowy figure. He is an advertiser and lives alone above the apartment of the Kulkarnies at Dadar, Bombay. Unlike the other men he has no reservations against doing "unmanly" things like cooking. He is sympathetic and objective and conducts himself with ease and grace in the company of women. Jaya's attachment to him cannot be termed platonic although it falls short of a full-fledge affair. Of all the qualities that endeared him to her she particularly notes his treatment of her as an equal. While every man she meets puts on a different face and a false smile, making his condescension all too palpable, with Kamat she comes into herself:

> it had been a revelation to me that two people, a man and a woman, could talk this way. With this man, I had not been a woman. I had been just myself—Jaya (153).

In spite of the "so asexual" nature of their relationship, it is significant that she has never known how to address him. Nevertheless it is in his presence that she becomes uninhibited and sheds the crippling silence she imposed on herself as part of erasing every public sign of her identity. She gets from Kamat the best of her father's concern for her—reassurance and comfort—and the best of attention that she would like to have from Mohan. He can chide her like her father when she is in the wrong:

> I'm warning you—beware of this "women are the victims" theory of yours. It'll drag you down into a soft, squishy bog of self-pity. Take yourself seriously, woman. Don't skulk behind a false name (148).

He can encourage her like an elder brother: "spew out your anger in your writing, woman, spew it out" (147). And he can pay beautiful compliments like a lover: "your name is like your face" (152). Consequently she confides in him things she would never dare mention to Mohan. It is to Kamat that she turns for solace when one of her stories (which she wrote pseudonymously) is rejected by many editors. When she feels particularly sad about her father Appa's death, she involuntarily finds herself in the comforting embrace of Kamat. For a split second she is unable to distinguish between him and Appa. Her body responds to his gentle look, voice and touch and momentarily her ego and id clash with the ferocity of two combatants. She recounts the experience:

> There had been nothing but an overwhelming urge to respond to him with my body, the equally overwhelming certainty of my mind that I could not do so. Later, there had been confusion (157).

But she instantaneously rejects the instinctual urge—it is not in the interest of safeguarding her marital bliss. At home that night, however, she deliberately arouses desire in Mohan and makes fierce love to him in an apparent displacement. In her case and in the case of many others, she reasons, the man-woman relation, especially within the boundaries of marriage, is dictated by treachery, deceit and betrayal. Yet the pretence has to be maintained. Perhaps it is the same realisation which makes her behave callously on the death of Kamat.

> That night, while having dinner, I had thought, someone I know is dead, I saw him dead. And I had been detached from

that woman who had seen him, remote from that experience (157).

Her writing and Kamat are not all that she has given up for the safety of her marital citadel. She has systematically insulated and alienated herself from everything and everybody that posed the remotest threat to the peace of her home. Deshpande concretises Jaya's plight in the well-known childhood bed-time story of the wise sparrow who built a house of wax and the foolish crow who built hers of dung. On a rainy night the crow's house collapses forcing her to seek shelter at the sparrows. The sparrow is so possessive of and attached to her home that she keeps the crow waiting, out in the rain, for a considerable time. She allows the crow in only when she is thoroughly drenched and then guides her to the hot pan to warm herself. The foolish crow hops onto it and gets burnt to death.

Jaya's married life has been lived almost on the same lines as the sparrows. She has built an edifice of security around her husband and children believing it to be a burrow into which she can crawl, reptile like, and feel safe (148). Attending to the needs of the husband and tending and caring for the children become her full-time occupation. She states in unequivocal terms that Mohan is her profession, career and means of livelihood (75) and as Kamat points out she derives a strange satisfaction in making him dependent on her. Unconsciously following her aunt's advice to treat her husband as a "sheltering tree" (32) she, like Gandhari of the *Mahabharata* symbolically bandages her eyes and grows blind to his weaknesses. Like Sita who followed her husband into exile, she follows Mohan into the concrete jungle that is Bombay (11). (Significantly the column she maintains is entitled "Sita"). Once there, like a faithful wife she takes to wearing huge dark glasses, gets her eyebrows shaped and hair cut short to look exactly like the wife of an executive. In the process she becomes dwarfed and annihilated as an individual but it all goes unnoticed even by herself. Her protest, largely unconscious, remains wrapped in an uneasy wordlessness finding its occasional expression in such acts as her adamant patronage of Kusum, whose feeblemindedness she seems to borrow for a while.

Her absorption into the family fold is so total that from a fiercely independent girl she gradually deteriorates into the "stereotype of a woman: nervous, incompetent, needing male help and support" (76). The thoughts of the collapse of marriage, particularly those relating to the possibility of Mohan's death, keep constantly haunting her:

> I had lived in constant panic that he would die. I had clung to him at night, feeling with relief the warmth of his body, stroking his chest, letting my palms move with his even deep breaths. The thought of living without him had twisted my insides. His death had seemed to me the final catastrophe. The very idea of his dying had made me feel so bereft that tears had flowed effortlessly down my cheeks. If he had been a little late coming home, I had been sure he was dead. By the time he returned, I had, in my imagination, shaped my life to a desolate widow-hood (96-97).

In fact, apprehension of disaster has always been active in the depths of her unconscious. She quite often wonders why it is that "wars always took place in other countries, tidal waves and earthquakes occurred in far-off, unknown places, that murder, adultery and heroism had their places in other people's lives, never in ours?" (4). And the disaster does take place in her life in the shape of a serious threat to her much prized and carefully built marriage and its temple, home.

Mohan gets involved in a shady deal and consequently faces enquiry into charges of corruption. If the enquiry is carried on he will stand every possibility of losing his well-paid job which will mean terrible insecurity. Jaya is at once reminded of the army wives, Mohan has told her about, who were reduced to destitution on their husbands' being thrown out of jobs and arrested later. In the Indian context it is instructive to understand why Mohan has resorted to corrupt means of making money. Sudhir Kakar views that super-ego, the moral agency, is weakly differentiated and insufficiently idealised in Indians. Whereas in the West an individual's behaviour is constantly regulated by the proscriptions of the super-ego, in a Hindu it is regulated by what he calls "communal conscience." He explains that communal conscience which comprises family and *jati* norms "is a social rather than an individual formation: it is not 'inside' the psyche. In other words, instead of having one internal sentinel an Indian relies on many external 'watchmen' to patrol his activities and especially his relationships in all the social hierarchies."[2] This creates a situation in which clandestine infringement of moral and social norms is a thing not to be much worried about. In this light "dishonesty, nepotism and corruption as they are understood in the West are merely abstract concepts"[3] for an Indian. It is the primacy of relationships that pervades through the life of an average Indian rather than primacy of healthy social values.

Mohan is by no means an exception. He has been a dutiful son, in spite of the inhuman treatment meted out to him by his father and by extension he is a dutiful husband. He regularly sends money to his family and makes it a point to attend the death anniversary of his father every year and even bears the entire expenditure of it. While working at Lohanagar as a small time engineer he makes himself a scapegoat in the corrupt deals of the CE for securing spacious living quarters for his family. And after moving to Bombay, encouraged by his colleague Agarwal, he accepts illegal gratification again so that his family might live in comfort and his children might attend good schools. He says:

> 'It was for you and the children that I did this. I wanted you to have a good life, I wanted the children to have all those things I never had' (9).

They move from their posh Churchgate house to the small flat in Dadar to evade the enquiry. Mohan takes the misfortune in his stride. At the most, in an apparent case of "projection" he accuses Jaya of being indifferent (116) and storms out of the house.

To Jaya the experience turns out to be traumatic. The insecurity caused by the possibility of Mohan's losing his job, his subsequent disappearance coupled with the running away of her son who has been vacationing with their family friends, Rupa and Ashok, comes as a terrifying prospect to her. The carefully built sparrow-house appears to be cracked and the insides cruelly exposed.

> It was like a house collapse during the monsoon. There was something desolating about the ease with which that had seemed

> so substantial fell away, almost contemptuously leaving behind an embarrassing nakedness (174).

This realisation hits her with the force of a bolt striking a tender tree. As has been pointed out earlier she has been expecting something terrible to befall her and consciously welcomes it now:

> there had been for me that other waiting.... Waiting fearfully for disaster, for a catastrophe. I always had this feeling—that if I have escaped it today, it's still there round the corner waiting for me; the locked door, the empty house, the messenger of doom bringing news of death. With Mohan's confession, I was actually relieved. Here it was at last—my disaster. No more waiting, no more apprehension, no more fears (30).

Yet the conscious bravado does not sustain at the unconscious level. She therefore cringes, and unable like Savitri of the myth [with whom she fondly compares herself (11)] to dog her husband's tormentors, neurotically breaks into a dialogue with herself subjecting everything that matters to her in life to minute analysis perhaps in the spirit of Yajnavalkya's scholarly wife Maitreyee (with whom too she compares herself at several places).

She considers, like a rational individual, several options for dealing with the crisis such as suicide (11) and plain confession of the crime (31) and dismisses them all as impracticable and ultimately lets her psyche take its own measures to manage the crises. She lives several days in a traumatic state. Her thoughts go back and forth in time triggered by the slightest provocation but constantly return to the traumatic event. Traumatic neurosis is usually a result of an emotional shock wherein the subject feels his life threatened. Sometimes it acts as a precipitating factor and reveals an already existing neurotic structure. But mostly it manifests itself, in cases where the trauma is a decisive factor in itself, in the form of symptoms that incessantly strive to "bind" and abreact the traumatic experience. On account of the low level of tolerance that Jaya is bestowed with, an earlier traumatic experience, that of her father Appa's sudden death, is precipitated by the present exceptionally intense stimulus. Both have shattered her equilibrium. Appa meant a great deal for her, and his death was premature and sudden and it occurred at a crucial time in her life—when she was writing her school final examinations. His death rendered Jaya's family homeless and left her bereft of an emotional support. But at that time, although she took seriously ill, the comforting hand of her elder brother saved her from further psychic crisis. The present loss of her second home which she has so carefully nurtured, apart from being of traumatic proportions, comes as a repetition of it. But now there is none whom she can turn to, not even Kamat. She is required to grapple with the trauma all by herself even if it means an upset of her equilibrium and emotional poise and it must be said to her credit that she emerges triumphant, crowned with a new understanding of herself and the world, at the end.

The partial relaxation of the ego's control over the working of her psyche, during this period, give her a changed perspective of the nature of things and human relationships. The most important of them is a free play given to the super-ego which can be equally disastrous as the id when not properly managed by the ego. After experiencing the trauma Jaya seems to become at once excessively concerned about the moral side of what she has done so far and what she should have done but did not. Freud observes in this regard:

> ill-luck—that is, external frustration—so greatly enhances the power of the conscience in the *super-ego*. As long as things go well with a man, his conscience is lenient and lets the ego do all sorts of things; but when misfortune befalls him, he searches his soul, acknowledges his sinfulness, heightens the demands of his conscience, imposes abstinences on himself and punishes himself with penances.[4]

Indeed Jaya pours out, during her neurotic spell, her innermost thoughts and makes an unqualified confession of her "sinful" acts which she never confided in Mohan again for fear of jeopardising marital security. She feels freshly guilty about her clandestine fictional endeavours:

> I had written even after that confrontation with him (145).

> It hadn't been Mohan's fault at all. And it had been just a coincidence, though it had helped, that just then Mohan had propelled me into that other kind of writing [middles] (148).

Her soul-searching, occasioned by the enforced leisure and coupled with a neurotic spell, also makes her dig into the long forgotten past and feel sorry for such things as the third child which she has not let live. With the help of her brother she happened to secretly terminate her third pregnancy. She now comes to think about it as her "great act of treachery against Mohan" (130). As she probes deep into this significant event of her life the guilt feelings assume greater sharpness and poignancy.

> But now, as if it had been waiting for its cue all these years, a shadowy figure in the wings, guilt sprang out at me. I thought of the unborn child with dread and a piercing sorrow. I invested her—yes, it would have been a girl—with all the qualities I missed in Rahul and Rati (131).

Jaya is almost convinced at a point that the misfortune that had suddenly engulfed her family is entirely of her making—of her failure as a wife and mother (185).

Apart from the unusual activation of the punitive elements of the super-ego Jaya's psyche sets a wide variety of painful reactions in motion—something which is very much characteristic of traumatic neurosis—to naturalise and bind the flood of mobile instinctual energy. Rumination on the traumatic event, insomnia and recurrent nightmares and dreams, feelings of detachment and disorientation, adverse somatic reaction and relative lack of control over one's actions are the readily available tools of the psychic apparatus which are pressed into service in Jaya's case. Everyone of the defence strategies that Jaya resorts to, emanates from, is structured around and finally returns to the single traumatic event of the sudden disintegration of her conjugal life.

Shashi Deshpande's use of dreams as a literary device, comparable to that of Graham Greene in their subtlety and pointedness, allows her to describe in symbolic and artistic terms the reality about the life of her heroines. The partial relaxation of the ego's control during sleep enables the dream-work to symbolically present the unconscious motivations of the dreamer. Consciously Jaya tries to explain to herself her and Mohan's fugitive status in terms of the slightly bizarre image of village women hiding only their heads when found easing in the open. But in her nightmares and dreams her desolate helplessness come more poignantly alive. Jaya's first nightmare, coming as it does at a crucial turning point in her neurotic reaction, reveals many conflicting tendencies within her. In the dream she sees Mohan and herself walking together. Soon she is left behind, and for some reason, has to pass through a house. She is helped into the house by a girl. Once she is in, she realises with shock that she is alone, fears that she will not be able to find Mohan anymore. She is then led into a room where a number of girls are present. Although she feels that they sympathise with her none of them comes forward to help her. She feels ill and utterly helpless and lies down like a corpse. The girls around her discuss her predicament in low tones. Not much later however, Mohan appears on the scene and asks her to hasten to a waiting taxi. But as she runs after him, she realises

> *that it is too late anyway, we will never be able to make it, we will never be able to get away, it is all my fault, all my fault...* (86).

The dream presents, in a classic case of condensation and displacement, her entire marital experience, her present predicament and her unconscious wishes. The house she passes through is the marital edifice. She is led into it by society (symbolised here by the more acceptable and seemingly agreeable girl and later by a group of girls). Once, she is inside the house, no help comes forth. She has to make a home herself. She does not even understand Mohan fully. And then comes the catastrophe of the enquiry into the charges of corruption. Society, which she has thought to be on her side suddenly turns hostile. Her degradation is discussed by everyone. (In fact she literally shivers at the mention of the enquiry by her younger brother Ravi [111] and her neighbour Mukta's oblique reference to her unusually long stay at the Dadar flat). She fervently wishes to get away from her present predicament. Tradition has it that a wife should seek her husband's help. And so Mohan appears there with a taxi. But her belief in Mohan's ability of deliverance is not strong enough to blissfully give herself into his care. She therefore thinks again that it is very late, the escape route is closed. She finds fault with herself because she is unable to do anything to help Mohan in his hour of need except neurotically rave and grieve.

While Jaya's first dream is a sort of wish-fulfilment, her second dream, occurring much later, is expressive of her utter frustration. By now Mohan has deserted her and she has already borne the resultant additional psychic conflict. She experiences a stab of anguish whenever her servant-maid, Nayana, makes a direct reference to her unenviable plight. It is at that specific point that Jaya recounts her "crazy recurrent dream."

> I was looking for a toilet, I was desperate, I had to find one, I'd disgrace myself if I didn't find one at once. And yes, there it was—the immense relief, and then the over-powering shame as I realised I was in a public place surrounded by people staring at me steadily and silently (161).

Jaya and Mohan have hoped to escape publicity by moving to the Dadar flat. That such a thing is not possible is evidenced by Jaya's dream. She unconsciously perceives what is at the back of the mind of most of their acquaintances and it comes alive in the dream.

Feelings of detachment from the self, experience of split personality and a sense of disorientation too are expressive of neurotic conflict. The seeds of a split personality have always been present throughout her seventeen-year old married life. Her name was changed to Suhasini by her in-laws soon after marriage. Ever since, "Suhasini" has been her marital identity. Now that this identity is in crisis she feels disoriented. On a secret visit to her posh Church gate house, to which her marital identity has been almost fixed, she sees her divided self clearly.

> And now nothing seemed to connect me to this place, nothing bridged the chasm between this prowling woman and the woman who had lived here. I was conscious of a faint chagrin at her disappearance. Wasn't I who had painfully, laboriously created her? Perhaps, for that very reason, she could not evade me entirely, and she appeared to me, only a faint wraith of herself, standing near this table, hand poised over a vase of flowers (168).

As her conflict reaches climacteric proportions she makes an even more frank admission of "a feeling of total disorientation" (177) and experiences detachment "from everything," even from her "own body" (177).

A relative lack of self-control over one's actions is again quite in keeping with the logic of neurotic suffering. Jaya's involuntary actions, "mad actions" in common parlance, are almost always precipitated by a specific incident in the present. But at the same time they can be easily traced back to the one great affliction, that of the shocking disintegration of her home the security of which she has uncritically taken for granted. The beginning of it is precipitated by Mohan's own disappearance. She experiences a fine quivering in her abdomen which has always been for her prelude to a panic. She does not have Kamat now to assure her of her significance and sanity nor the distant relative, mad Kusum, against whom to test her sanity. Inevitably therefore her "sense of confusion" and turmoil meet her "with brutal force" (125).

> I could feel myself gasping, drowning in the darkness, the wild, flailing, panic-stricken movements that I was making taking me lower and lower into the vortex....
>
> *Take your pain between your teeth, bite on it, don't let it escape....*
>
> I came floundering out of the depths, thinking—am I going crazy like Kusum? (125).

In spite of her categorical assertion of her sanity on the next page she indeed sacrifices some of it to relieve herself of the excruciating mental pain forced on her by circumstances. Apart from such apparently "crazy" actions as mumbling and speaking plain nonsense she experiences a brief spell of utter mental confusion as things move to a finale. This time it is triggered off by her witnessing a cruel scene at the bus-stop. After the secret visit to the Church gate house she waits for some time at the bus-stop. It is raining heavily. She looks around and finds a very beautiful young girl smoking a reefer and two men roughly kneading her small breasts. Her imploration to stop the indecency evokes only a hearty laughter from the men. She feels so humiliated and helpless that she flees the scene as if pursued, in the pouring rain. In her unconscious she identifies the girl at the bus-stop with her daughter Rati and the prospect of a similar future for Rati (a part of her secure home) drives her crazy. Somehow, she returns home and deliriously goes on ringing the bell of her apartment and then bangs on the door. It is ultimately Mukta who takes the key from her bag and opens the door. All along Jaya keeps raving incoherently. She continues to be in delirium even the next day.

The impact of this specific incident coupled with the cumulative effect of the events of the past few days has been so deep on her that her psyche transfers some of its tension to her body which reacts adversely under the pressure. She plunges head-long into high temperature. In fact she has always reacted in a similar manner whenever under great stress. She happened to fall dangerously ill following Appa's death too.

While on the one hand Jaya's psyche reaches almost the point of total disintegration under the intense pressure and force of adverse circumstances, deep within her, involuntarily again, a defence process is also set in motion. Dreams, neurosis and all the other aspects we have discussed so far, themselves are basically defensive in nature. Another defence device that comes handy to Jaya, partially aided by her experience as a writer, is her reliving, at every point, in her imagination of the significant moments of her not short life. The exercise helps her above anything else, to come to grips with the reality as it presents itself. It is in this context that the stream of consciousness technique adopted in the novel, is artistically most gratifying. A smooth linear development of the narrative would not have facilitated the to and fro movement in time of Jaya's consciousness. Jaya's unfolding of her story in bits and pieces, moving back and forth with remarkable felicity, borders on the incoherent, necessitating the stream of consciousness technique. Shashi Deshpande's use of the technique reminds us of Dorothy Richardson of *Pilgrimage* in that there is a significant assertion of authorial voice and autobiographical under-currents, of Virginia Woolf of *The Waves* in that both are concerned with private visions of life and private symbols in presenting character which never succeeds in becoming typical, and also of James Joyce of *Ulysses* in that the disparity between man's aspirations and actual achievements gave a comic vision to Joyce, whereas for Deshpande a tragic resignation and a conscious, not spontaneous, reconciliation with the world.

The technique has been very effectively used by the author to reveal the psychic being of Jaya, of what she is rather than what she does. In this process of dramatising her consciousness (quite often Jaya also engages her two selves in an imaginary dispute) her essential nature gets verbalised and lends itself for examination. "The problem of character depiction," says Robert Humphrey, "is central to stream-of-consciousness fiction. The great advantage, consequently the best justification of this type of novel, rests on its potentialities for presenting character more accurately and more realistically."[5] Indeed the character of Jaya as it emerges at the end of this interesting exercise is a person divested of all self-deceptions, falsities and artificialities that she has all along been living with. She considerably sobers herself on making certain key discoveries about herself. While earlier she contemplated suicide, she now dismisses it as being silly (183). Mohan's telegram from Delhi informing her that everything is fine and a changed Rahul's return do help her in this process. But now such things seem to be of marginal importance. The picture of the emotionally, physically and socially secure world of which these people have been seemingly permanent members has vanished from her imagination forever. The Mohan's wife image is no more relevant for her as she tells us:

> I'm not afraid anymore. The panic has gone, I'm Mohan's wife, I had thought, and cut off the bits of me that had refused to be Mohan's wife. Now I know that kind of a fragmentation is not possible (191).

Her new perception of life, implied here, is that the members of her family, herself included, are independent individuals with distinct identities—a view which imposes no responsibilities and their loss or separation entails no insecurity and emotional trauma. She knows that in material terms things will continue to be as they always have been. She will continue to be the wife of Mohan and mother of Rahul and Rati, and when required, will "bite on" her "pain," but now self-consciously so, of her own accord. She has seen for herself that outside the family fold a woman is subjected to the unbearable harshness and cruelty of society. She has therefore to compromise with the realities of life. Citing the authority of the *Gita* she resolves to be the master of her choice which she hopes will enable her to be on equal terms with Mohan and to "erase the silence" (192) between them. She has indubitably gained the moral courage and necessary resourcefulness required for the purpose.

Yet she has to make life possible in the present and therefore put up with the realities of life with an awareness of the advantages of accepting the established values. That alone, it seems to her, promises a modicum of spiritual and emotional fulfilment in this world.

In conclusion, it may be observed that the exigencies of life presented themselves in the form of traumatic events to Jaya. Her psyche has not been well-equipped to meet them. As a result the flood-gates of anxiety have been suddenly opened and at this psychological moment irrationality qualified her response to the situation. However, soon she has mustered up enough inner strength to stage a return to normalcy. The experience has provided her with an ideal occasion for growing introspective and thus make important discoveries about herself and redefine her relationship with the world.

NOTES AND REFERENCES

1. Shashi Deshpande, *That Long Silence* (New Delhi: Penguin Books, 1989) 143-44. Parenthetical page references in the text are to this edition.
2. Sudhir Kakar. *The Inner World: A Psychological Study of Childhood and Society in India* (New Delhi: OUP, 1981) 135.
3. Kakar 125.
4. Sigmund Freud, *Civilization and its Discontents* (Harmondsworth: Penguin, 1985) 318.
5. Robert Humphrey, "The Functions of Stream of Consciousness," *Perspectives on Fiction,* ed. James L. Calderwood and Harold E. Toliver (New York: OUP, 1968) 258.

5

Potent Remedies: Themes and Techniques in Shashi Deshpande's *Small Remedies*

CHANDRA HOLM*

In *Small Remedies*[1] using the stories of two women—Leela, the trade union activist and Savitribai Indorekar, the ageing diva of the Gwalior Gharana—as the background, Shashi Deshpande explores her favourite theme of a woman set on a journey of self-discovery, a journey which will bring past and present within a single pair of brackets, which will heal the wounds even if it does not provide all the answers. Madhu who introduces these two women into our lives is not a mere passive story-teller like the chronicler in Pushkin's "Boris Gudenow." She is very much of a mitgestalter, a creator with great potential. Though her intention is to write the biography of Savitribai Indorekar, Madhu, in coming to Bhavanipur, is attempting to unravel the puzzle that is past, present, and future, understand the vagaries of time's hands and find remedies to the blows life so nonchalantly hands over.

During the course of this journey, we witness various stages of Madhu's life: as the motherless daughter of a successful doctor in Neemgaon, her friendship at that time with Munni, Savitribai's daughter, her big-eyed worship of Savitribai and Ghulam Ahmed, her moving to Bombay to Leela and Joe's place when her father dies, the beginnings of her love for English literature due to Joe's influence, Tony's becoming her brother "with a determination that

*University of Applied Sciences, Olten, Switzerland.

was much at variance with his usual lackadaisical attitude" (203), her job as the assistant editor of *City News*, her friendship with Tony's friends Chandru and Som, her marriage to Som (the birth of their only son Adit fills her life with such radiance that she feels like a devotee telling her god, "What can you give me, my Lord, I, who have everything?" [89]), and finally the rift between the couple and the death of Adit.

Madhu is not alone on this journey. She has companions: Lata, a young and lively woman, Hari, her quiet husband (both strangers till now but they have offered Madhu their home during her stay in Bhavanipur), Tony, Tony's Rekha (both visit her in Bhavanipur under one pretext or the other because they are concerned about her), Hasina, who is Savitribai's companion and student, whose music takes Madhu a great way along the healing path, and Som, whose very absence underlines his place in her life, who leaves her in peace, allowing her time to come to terms with life, in her own way. And finally there are memories that keep her company. Innumerable memories. Memories of all those incidences, words, gestures that have shaped her life. Memories which show her vulnerability, her capability. And memories she wants to get away from.

Small Remedies is a complex novel. It is a novel about myriad feelings—love, courage, honesty, truth, trust, death, the pain associated with death, about music, about the power exerted by time and by words. It is a novel in which past and present are intermingled, in which the word chronology has no meaning. Madhu—reflecting Deshpande's own thoughts—feels that writing Savitribai's history would be easy if Time is the only connecting factor. But, she says,

> I can't do this. No one can. We don't live our lives this way, we don't see our lives this way. We see our lives through memory and memories are fractured, fragmented, almost always cutting across time (165).

Thus the novel is not a story told along a straight line, but it cuts across the timeline; Madhu's own memories as well as those evoked by the association of the people around her acting like the only points to hold on to. These memories are so fresh that the border between past and present is easily obliterated.

The novel opens with the sentence, “This is Som’s story” (1). It turns out soon that it is rather Madhu’s story. Madhu, who, enclosed in a fog of bereavement caused by the death of her only son, seventeen year old Adit, while mulling over past incidents, remembers her quoting once T. S. Eliot’s words, “In the life of one man, never the same time returns” (3). The occasion was a small gathering after Joe’s—Leela’s husband’s—death. Som was telling them about the party Joe’s students had thrown at the retirement of their beloved teacher. And how after a marathon party, Joe had remarked, “that was wonderful, absolutely wonderful. Shall we do this again tomorrow?” (3) It was then, out of the blue, that Madhu had quoted Eliot’s famous sentence from *The Murder in the Cathedral*. Words which had silenced everyone assembled there, words which had shown them how ominously empty life can be. It was Tony who with a light remark had saved the situation, pulling them back from the abyss.

Thinking of this incident now, Madhu feels that you can neither undo nor repeat what has happened, that the past is irrevocable, that “Time moves on relentlessly and you have to go along with it” (5). There is no other alternative. Absolutely none. There is no cure to life’s ills, no prevention.

> That the Ganeshas in niches, the decorated thresholds, the mango leaf torans, the Oms, the Swastikas, the charms and amulets—[are all designed] to keep disaster at bay, to stave off the nemesis of a jealous god (81).

Nothing like that will help. No mantra can ward off the evil eyes. Even thinking philosophically that “to get happiness, you’ve got to accept the sorrow and the pain as well” (81) is futile; such thoughts do not make it any easier to bear the past, do not lessen the pain.

Having abandoned all such charms and mantras, Madhu has come to Bhavanipur to write the story of Savitribai’s life. Is this an occupational therapy, a much needed medicine for a mother devastated by the death of her son killed in a bomb blast? Would this writing of the life of the ageing Savitribai help her answer the one question that has preoccupied her since Adit’s death: “how does one live with the knowledge of a child's death?" (155) Because in writing about Bai, she would be dealing with the relationship between Savitribai and her daughter Munni, her childhood friend. Munni was the daughter "whose existence Bai has obliterated" (168) for the sake of her career. The girl rejected her famous mother and took the name Shailaja Joshi, "who died, by a strange coincidence," like Adit, "on the same day, victims both of them of the same madness" (154) that gripped the country in the aftermath of the Babri Masjid incident in Ayodhya.

When Madhu accepted Chandru's offer to write this biography, she certainly did not bargain for the silence Savitribai exercises with respect to Munni. It was as if Munni did not exist. Never existed. It was as if those years when Munni and Madhu were neighbours in Neemgaon where Madhu's father was a doctor did not happen. All those years ago in Neemgaon, Madhu could not comprehend why Munni so disliked her father, the tablaji, Ghulam Ahmed with whom Savitribai was living. Now in Bhavanipur she is taken aback at the business like reception she gets from Savitribai at their first encounter, at the manner in which she has wiped out her years in Neemgaon. Then it is too late to say, "I'm Munni's friend Madhu. Remember me?" (29)

Madhu realises that Savitribai has mapped out the story that she wants her to write. But Madhu knows that there are three books here.

> Firstly, there's Bai's book, the book Bai wants to be written, in which she is the heroine, the spotlight shining on her and her alone. No dark corners anywhere in this book, all the shadows kept out of sight, backstage. Then there's Mays and Yogi's book. As publishers they are interested in a book that is controversial. Trendy. Politically correct, with a feminist slant. A book that will sell (125).

And then there is her own book, for which she is searching for the real Bai in the jungle of words she has collected. Which is the real Bai?

> The pampered child? The young girl who discovered what her life was going to be? The young woman who gave up her secure and respectable married life, abandoned her child and

> eloped with her lover? The woman who is in search of her genius, of her destiny? The great musician, the successful Savitribai Indorekar? (283)

To find the answer to this important question, Madhu has to travel a long way.

Meanwhile, Leela re-enters her life. Through Hari she discovers that Leela, her mother's eldest sister, was also the eldest sister of Hari's grandmother. When Madhu's father died, it was Leela and Joe who had provided her a home. It was they who had pulled her out of the emptiness that life had become. Till Hari mentions Leela's social activities, Madhu had not thought much about those aspects of her beloved aunt. Leela the trade unionist, the activist, the rebel was too remote a person for Madhu who could only think of the love she got from Leela, of the true love that shone in the lives of Leela and Joe.

Now trying to establish the identities of the real Leela and Savitribai amidst all the facts she has collected, Madhu sees parallels between the lives of these two women. She thinks,

> I've begun thinking that in writing about Bai, I'm writing about Leela as well. And my mother and all those women who reached beyond their grasp. Bai moving out of her class in search of her destiny as a singer, Leela breaking out of the conventions of widowhood, looking for justice for the weak, my mother running in her bare feet, using her body as an instrument for speed—yes, they're in it together. But they paid the price for their attempts to break out (284)

She realises "that both were courageous women, that both were women who worked for and got the measure of freedom they needed, that both were ready to accept wholly the consequences of their actions," (284) and that, more importantly, whatever happened, they still went on with their lives. Madhu has now accepted the simple truth that it is not necessary to know all the answers to the questions that life throws up. "That what we call truth has nothing to do with the truth that emerges through words" (255).

With this understanding, the realisation dawns upon Madhu that life has simply to be lived, no matter what happens, even when things look so very abysmal. That truth comes home to Madhu not abruptly but slowly as she witnesses the lives around her. One such instance is an upanayanam ceremony she witnesses in the Bhavani temple, a ceremony that is marked with muted pain and grief. The death of the father had not meant that the upanayanam could not take place. Life had to go on. Watching the mother of the boy whose upanayanam it was, Madhu thinks,

> so many of us [are] walking this earth with our pain, our sorrow concealed within ourselves, so many of us hiding our suffering, going about as if all is well, so many of us surviving our loss, our grief. It's a miracle (315).

In this moment, Madhu is like Kisa Gotami whose search for someone who can bring life back to her dead child had taken her to the great teacher Gautama Buddha himself. On seeing the distraught mother fiercely holding the lifeless body of her child in her arms, Buddha had told her that he would be able to bring her child back to life if she would bring a fistful of mustard seeds from one such home where there has been no death. Gautama Buddha's Kisa Gotami had then gone—with a heart brimming with hope—in search of the mustard seeds that would revive her son. The people in all the homes on whose doors she had knocked upon were ready to give her a handful of mustard seeds but from none could she accept the life giving seeds as there was no house which was not visited by death. Kisa Gotami, who goes from door to door, realises, finally, that in a man's life death is as certain as birth, goes back to Buddha with a calm mind, joins his sangha, and finds peace. The search for tiny mustard seeds had acted like a soothing remedy to what had come across like an eternal pain.

Madhu's troubled heart is stilled when she listens to Hasina singing a Vachana by Akka Mahadevi, a saint poet of Karnataka. It is a night performance held in the Bhavani temple on Guruji's (Savitribai's guru, Kashinath Buwa's) death anniversary. During what is her first major performance Hasina sings, "I saw a dream, I saw a dream" (319) as a repeated affirmation of the vision of not only the poet but of all kinds of people through the ages. Madhu feels,

She's speaking of my dreams too, so many of them, all woven

> about Adit. And Som's dreams for his son. It's all over now, there are no more dreams left for me, for either of us (319).

She knows that even if there are no dreams left for her because of Adit's death, life has to be lived. That nothing works against our mortality.

> Mustard seeds to protect us from evil, blessings to confer long life—nothing works. Simple remedies? No, they're desperate remedies and we go on with them because, in truth, there is nothing else (315).

Does this mean that there are no remedies in life? Of course, there are remedies. But the remedies that are available are small remedies—an affectionate hug like the one Tony gives Madhu, a moment coloured with true understanding like the one she shares on the beach with Joe a short while after her father dies, the words of a song like the ones sung with feeling by Hasina, even the aroma of hot oil and of curry leaves roasting in it, the splutter of mustard seeds when one is hungry. This revelation is what makes Madhu ask herself at the very end of the novel,

> 'How could I have ever longed for amnesia? As long as there is memory, there's always the possibility of retrieval, as long as there is memory, loss is never total' (324).

This was the same Madhu who had thought, at the beginning of the story, "of the totality of loss" (5), its irrevocability.

Small Remedies clearly bears the stamp of Shashi Deshpande's writing. In the manner typical to her writing the story is revealed through the inner consciousness of one central character; life around is focussed through the eyes of this character and understood through the mind of this one character. Not just in this aspect but also in her special way of looking at details, love for imagery, in her deliberately slow manner of unveiling the plot that is full of sudden twists and turns, in her ability to look into the depths of human heart and give expression to the feelings buried in there, and in the very honesty with which her central character confronts her own life, in the importance given to dreams to unravel events, this is a Deshpande book.

Like in her other novels, the house in *Small Remedies* reflects its inmates. "In spite of being a slapdash kind of household, there's no chaos in it; only the disorder that comes from constant flux, the movement of life" (21). It is Lata, the effervescent Lata, who is the mistress of this house, who is constantly on the move, and who by moving seems to imbibe new bouts of energy. The description of the very first night and morning which Madhu spends in this new house in Bhavanipur is so rich with details that it comes across like a miniature painting. One feels more like a spectator than like a reader. It is a book where no image, no description is superfluous. Like the path Madhu chooses out of three available ways to approach Savitribai's house. "There is the main approach," Madhu says,

> along the road and through the non-existent front gate, ... there's another, the shortest route, which involves entering from the back of the house and going past a disused well and the dilapidated remains of a row of rooms, which were once the servants' quarters. There's a third way, the one I now regularly take, stepping over the sagging barbed wire and going through the mango grove to the right of the house. Here, the undergrowth has been cleaned. The grass is growing back, but even as it grows, it carries the impress of my feet, and I can see the faint outline of the path I followed the previous day (72).

It is like memories, like a slate from which the writing can never be wholly erased, where "the impressions remain, faint scorings that can be deciphered by those who know what was there earlier" (154). Another such graphically emotional, yet tautly restrained episode in the book is the one which describes Adit's death. The pages depicting the uncertainty of where her son is, Madhu's waiting for him through the violence ridden days, her search for him on the crowded streets of the city even when Som tries to convince her that Adit is dead, and her final acceptance of the inevitable truth are some of the most poignant ones in contemporary Indian literature.

Small Remedies is also a novel that clearly marks the development of the personal philosophy of the writer. No farther than the epigraphs of the books need to be looked at, to understand the core of Deshpande's philosophical thoughts, and to trace their development. If the epigraph "You are your own refuge; there is no other refuge.

This refuge is hard to achieve" (from *The Dhammapada*) of her first novel, *The Dark Hold No Terrors* (Vikas Publishing House, 1980 / Penguin, 1990) indicated that the only support Saru can find is within herself, the epigraph "Father of the earth, protect us; Father of the sky, protect us; Father of the great and shining water, protect us,—To which God shall we offer our worship?" (from *Rig Veda*) of *Small Remedies* points at the futility of searching for a God to whom we can offer our homage. It tells us that there is no such homage that can protect us, that there is really no protection from life's disasters. All that we can hope for are remedies, and for these we do not have to look beyond the little acts of kindness that people around us extend to us.

In what has become her hallmark Deshpande offers in this novel an India that is unsimplified. It calls for the undivided attention of the reader. For a serious reader, the reading—and rereading—of *Small Remedies* promises to be an enriching, a satisfying experience. True to Deshpande's other works, *Small Remedies* is also a treasure of ideas and sentences every reader would want to usurp and make his own. It is a book in which Shashi Deshpande surpasses herself as a writer and underscores her place in the scene of international literature in English as a writer to be read, to be respected.

NOTE

1. Shashi Deshpande, *Small Remedies* (Delhi: Vikingc/Penguin Books India, 2000). Parenthetical page references are to this edition.

6

Bharati Mukherjee's *Jasmine*: The Exuberance of Immigration, Feminist Strategies and Multicultural Negotiations

SANDRA PONZANESI*

1. Postcolonial Anxiety

Bharati Mukherjee is not only the most commercially successful among women writers of the Indian diaspora, but also the most controversial narrator of Indian cultural identity in a multicultural context.

It is not a coincidence that her literary model was originally V.S. Naipaul. She shares with the Caribbean author not only the common Indian Brahmanical background but also the tackling between native values and Western ideology in a way that has been considered provocative by many postcolonial critics. However, their most important common trait concerns the investigation of the migrant identity.

As noted above, Naipaul belongs to the old form of Indian diaspora, that of indentured labour, and his Caribbean origin is as important as his Indian ancestry. Mukherjee is a free diasporic; she belongs to that group of intellectual migrants who expatriated for a better education and who were backed up by solid financial resources. This is surely true for Mukherjee whose wealthy family in Calcutta controlled an important pharmaceutical company. Educated in the best school in Calcutta, the Loreto Convent school for girls, she picked up that distinguished English accent that survives even her

*Belle van Zuylen Institute, University of Amsterdam, The Netherlands.

long North-American residence. She studied English and Ancient Indian Culture at Calcutta and Baroda University where she obtained a first class degree. When confronted with a choice between accepting the arranged marriage planned by her father or accepting the grant to enter the Writers' Workshop at the University of Iowa, she chose the latter.

Mukherjee openly declared her affiliation to V.S. Naipaul in her introduction to *Darkness: Days and Nights in Calcutta* (1977), a collection of short stories based on her experiences in Canada, co-authored with her husband Clark Blaise:

> Like V.S. Naipaul, in whom I imagined a model, I tried to explore state-of-the-art expatriation. Like Naipaul, I used a mordant and self-protective irony in describing my characters' pain. Irony promised both detachment from, and superiority over, those well-bred post colonials much like myself, adrift in the new world, wondering if they would ever belong (2).

The irony mentioned by Mukherjee is inherited by the two authors through the British tradition of satire. The ironic tone in Mukherjee's first works, *The Tiger's Daughter* (1972) and *Wife* (1975), will be replaced in her later phase by a more personal style.

Despite her declaration, that her poetics is similar to that of Naipaul, she later began to disagree with him about his negative vision on the Third World. She dissents from his view of the colonized people as helpless and doomed to failure because of their peripheral location. Mukherjee attempts a narrative and ideological response to V.S. Naipaul's view of the postcolonial world by writing a short-story entitled *Jasmine*, published in her collection *The Middleman and Other Stories* (1988) which sets her female character in the Caribbean:

> I very deliberately set the story in V.S. Naipaul's birthplace because it was my "in" joke, challenging, if you like, Naipaul's thesis of tragedy being geographical. Naipaul's fiction seems to suggest that if you are born far from the center of the universe you are doomed to an incomplete and worthless little life. You are bound to be, if you are born like a Jasmine, an Indian in the Caribbean, a comic character, you come to nothing. So I wanted to say, "Hey, look at Jasmine. She is smart, and

> desirous, and ambitious enough to make something of her life."[1]

Mukherjee's inspiration is taken from a friend's housekeeper, a Caribbean woman of Indian origin whose energy was dictated by her desire to re-make herself and by the need to improvise morality. Thus Mukherjee creates her model of the fighters, women who have to adapt and struggle for their own survival. In this way the writer highlights that the Third World's subject in its imbrication with gender, ethnicity and migration cannot indulge in Naipaul's assumed paralysis, but on the contrary goes through an intense phase of transformation, not preservation.

However, as the author likes to underline, assimilation is not a one sided process.

> I say we haven't come to accommodate or to mimic, we have changed ourselves, but we have also come to change you.[2]

In Mukherjee's stories—of the making and imagining of the immigrant identities in America—female subjectivity forms the primary site of dislocation. The writer assumes the standpoint from where there is always a celebration of assimilation and little nostalgia for roots and authentic belonging. On this aspect she profoundly differentiates herself from Naipaul.

Whether Mukherjee convincingly articulates the exuberance of immigration in her novel *Jasmine* (1989) is the scope of my analysis. Unlike her short story, of the same title, the novel is not based on a Caribbean female character, but on a migrant Indian one.

Flowers and Other Influences

In order to understand Jasmine's contribution to the postcolonial debate it is here relevant to briefly discuss V.S. Naipaul's famous essay "Jasmine," a milestone for postcolonial consciousness. "Jasmine" appeared in the *Times Literary Supplement*, 4 June 1964, and was republished in Naipaul's essay collection, *The Overcrowded Barracoon* (1972). In this essay the jasmine flower is used as a leading metaphor for the disconnection between the colonial natural world and the possibility of its representation through the English language imposed by the colonizers. Naipaul recalls that when he was young in Trinidad he was familiar with the scent of the flower without knowing its name. Later in his life while visiting an old lady in British Guyana he smells the scent of a flower:

> I knew the flower from my childhood; yet I never found out its name. I asked now. "We call it jasmine." Jasmine! So I had known all those years! To me it had been a word in a book, a word to play with, something removed from the dull vegetation I knew. The old lady cut a sprig for me. I stuck it in the top buttonhole of my open shirt. I smelled it as I walked back to the hotel. Jasmine, Jasmine. But the word and the flower had been separating in my mind for too long. They did not come together.[3]

Naipaul attempts a critique of the imposed colonial language which for postcolonial writers means the disconnection between the signifier and the signified, the wording of a world and the reality of it, as culturally and geographically separated. This creates anxiety and fear in adopting the language used in such influential literatures as English since, for example, English cannot express the Caribbean atmosphere but conveys, instead, an alien mythology:

> There was, for instance, Wordsworth's notorious poem about the daffodil. A pretty little flower, no doubt; but we had never seen it. Could the poem have any meaning for us? .... To us, without a mythology, all literatures were foreign. Trinidad was small, remote and unimportant, and we knew we could not hope to read in books of the life we saw about us. Books came from afar; they could offer only fantasy.[4]

Naipaul's often quoted statement is not only based on the postcolonial dissymmetry between language and representation, but also on the strong assumption that a writer's vision could never be individual, nor could he be separated from his own society. From this assumption Mukherjee will move completely outwards. In adapting Naipaul's botanical figure Mukherjee contests the paradigm of origins in the Third World as a hindrance for success in favour of the word jasmine as flowering possibility. First she disengages the development of Jasmine's identity from any idea of collectivism and traces for her a clear path of rampant American individualisation. Secondly she disengages herself from any other postcolonial model.

She never thinks of herself as being part of a larger school, even though she has claimed affiliation with Naipaul:

> I'm uncomfortable being bracketed with other expatriate Indian writers, like Salman Rushdie and Anita Desai. I'm simply writing about characters whom I know and who interest me. At the same time I think I am a new kind of American writer for whom novels have a big social, historical moral component.[5]

Mukherjee distances herself from her Indian origin since she wants to be defined as an American writer who expands the border of the American canon. This shift of positionality within the literary world was made by Mukherjee when she decided to move from Canada, where she was racially assaulted for being "dark-skinned." to the United States. Here she came to terms with her uprootedness and underwent the transition from the "aloofness of expatriation" to the "exuberance of migration" (Mukherjee, *Darkness*: 1977, 3).

In a famous article which appeared in *The New York Times Book Review*, "Immigrant Writing: Give us Our Maximalists!" (28 Aug. 1988) Mukherjee accuses the American writers of not including in their narration the faces and voices of the immigrants, who colour and dominate all American cities, from buses to universities. "I don't think we are on Ellis Island anymore," she states, presenting a view of American society which can no longer afford to exclude new narrative models. If minimalist writings predominate, and this is supposed to be "American fiction" then we need to revise the literary canon, she argues, because there is a blind spot in American writing. She lists the reasons for the success of minimalism: "clever, mannered, brittle ... Minimalist techniques seem a healthy response to too much communication, too much manipulation, and too much of everything in a society that promotes its sports, its causes and its candidates in slick sound-bites." Mukherjee reacts, therefore, to the minimalist shorthand agenda since she sees in it a dangerous white strategy to eschew the exotic, exuberant embrace of the 60's culture, and with it the multicultural panorama of the eighties. She invokes the Maximalists, the Expansionists, under which immigrants, expatriates, exiled people can enumerate themselves as part of the new American canon, and a more real one. It is an attempt to oppose the imposed mainstream as an illusory "majority" and turn the gaze to the "minority voices, the immigrant voices, the second generation Jews and Italians and Irish and French-Canadians. We may look a little different, and carry different-sounding names, but "we mustn't be seduced by what others term exotic. Don't choose to be an exile out of fear, or out of distaste."

With these concluding lines Mukherjee professes her new philosophy on migration. Fight against the "static ghetto of little India," don't choose the rear position, don't play the victim, you are part of America and America is made out of you. With this revisionary slogan, which the Indian critic Malashri Lal has defined as "the Maximalist Credo,"[6] Mukherjee not only intends to expand America but to change it, adding the minority point of view, not clear-cut assimilation, but transformation. The transformation affects both sides and it is in this binary, but fluid interaction between origin and modernity, traditional values and emancipation, collectivism or individualism, that Mukherjee's female characters are constructed and developed.

It is this letting go of her Indianness and her "roots" that positions the author as controversial. She claims, in fact, to have overcome her "Indianness":

> I have joined imaginative forces with an anonymous, driven underclass of semi-assimilated Indians with sentimental attachments to a distant homeland but no real desire for permanent return. I see my "immigrant" story replicated in a dozen American cities, and instead of seeing my Indianness as a fragile identity to be preserved against obliteration (or worse, a "visible" disfigurement to be hidden), I see it now as a set of fluid identities to be celebrated...Indianness is now a metaphor, a particular way of partially comprehending the world.[7]

Whereas Naipaul anxiously searched for his ancestral roots in India, Mukherjee departs from it with great casualness. She makes of her mother country an India of the mind, as in Salman Rushdie's tradition, and it is exactly this aspect that bothers Indian writers and critics who see their cultural heritage used by Mukherjee as a magician's hut from which icons and myths can be picked up and blended in a literary style apt for the Western audience.

Mukherjee is often accused by her Indian critics of creating fables, tall-tales and not realistic depictions, and of using Orientalising icons to market her books in the West. However, some critics who have developed a psychoanalytic reading of Mukherjee's texts, especially female Indian academics,[8] have rightly observed that these recurring images can be read as the unconscious level of Mukherjee's narrative, which shows that her Indianness has not been overcome but returns constantly as a perturbation. I will postpone my judgement until the end of my analysis of *Jasmine*, the novel that launched Mukherjee as an American writer and which contains the embryo of Mukherjee's recurrent themes about gender, migration and identity. These issues are better controlled and developed in her more recent novels *The Holder of the World* (1994) and *Leave it To Me* (1997) which, however, lack the freshness of Jasmine's naiveté, both as far as content and literary achievement are concerned. *The Holder of the World* is a historical novel with a science fiction tinge which stretches the making of America and its ancestors back to the glorious Mogul times. *Leave it To Me* is another fable of female identity dealing with Indian roots and the adoptive identity of her heroine's Italo-American family imbued with urban slang and pastiche. Mukherjee seems to have exhausted her model of uprooted heroines, and even though she glues them to new environments and coins a new jargon for them they lack the verve of Jasmine's recklessness.

2. American Dream

Jasmine is a Bildungsroman rewritten around the postcolonial, postmodern and feminist agenda. The novel focuses on Jasmine, an underage village girl from Punjab, who ventures as an undocumented woman and as a widow to the Unites States, where her fate will be "rewritten."

The *fabula* level of the novel, which is represented by the series of events narrated, does not coincide with the *story*, which is how the events are organised and conveyed. Therefore, the novel unfolds with a non-chronological order of events creating a rather cinematic effect which makes it hard to follow the shifts in location, focalisation and time. The narration is in the first person and the time and setting is Baden, Elsa County, Iowa, when Jasmine is aged twenty-four. The fabula, instead, begins in Hasnapur, a village in Punjab when Jasmine is aged seven. The bold events which have allowed her transformation from the ill-fated village girl, Jyoti, to the self-assured emancipated American woman, Jane, are told in a narrative reversion.

> I'm twenty-four now, I live in Baden, Elsa County, Iowa, but every time I lift a glass of water to my lips, fleetingly I smell it. I know what I don't want to become (5).

The dialectic interplay between the diegesis (past) and the narration (present), separated in time but ideologically intersecting with each other, makes the evaluation of this novel a more complicated affair than it would at first seem. The distance between past and present time also represents the distance between two cultures. But the translation of the past life privileges the language of the present life and therefore becomes an example of what Spivak calls "translation-as-violation."[9]

The past is therefore constructed through constant flashbacks from the Baden location of narration, which function also as flashforwards if we consider the time-setting of Hasnapur in Punjab where the fabula begins. Jasmine is not Jasmine yet, she is called Jyoti (which means light) and is a seven year old girl, the fifth of a long line of daughters:

> God's cruel, my mother complained, to waste brains on a girl. And God's still more cruel, she said, to make a fifth daughter beautiful instead of the first. By the time my turn to marry came around, there would be no dowry money left to gift me the groom I deserved (40).

Jyoti is presented as an unlucky child, born female, too late to profit from her beauty, and intelligent. She was a whiz in Punjabi and Urdu, good at counting and at reading and the first likely candidate for English instruction. Furthermore bad fate seemed to be forecast for her. First Masterji, the English teacher who supports her education, dies in a Sikh terrorist attack. Then, as described in the opening page of the novel (with a scene under a banyan tree) the astrologer foretells Jyoti a life of widowhood and exile. Jyoti protests against the old man's craziness which cannot hold her future. "Fate is Fate" (4), he tells her. Jyoti reacts to the astrologer's attempt to reduce her to nothingness by falling down and making a starshaped mark on her forehead which she interprets as "my third eye." The third eye becomes the figuration for Bhabha's in-betweenness, for that location of hybridization and ambivalence which allows the subjugated subjects, in this case a female subaltern, to operate in the vacuum of hegemonic authority and create their own empowerment. Jyoti starts the war "between my fate and my will" (12), by creating her own interspace for individual growth.

If bad luck seems to persecute Jyoti according to Hindu wisdom (she loses her father before he can marry her off) a strange logic seems to be at work for her. She will be free, in fact, to marry at the age of fourteen her brother's friend, Prakash, a twenty-four year old electronic student whose voice she falls in love with. Jyoti states at this point "I was a sister without dowry, but I didn't have to be a sister without prospects" (70). Prakash plays the modern enlightened man; the wedding is, in fact, not a religious one: no dowry is exchanged. He refuses to live with his extended family and moves with Jyoti to Amritsar, the biggest city in Punjab. He renames her Jasmine to remove from her any trace of traditional dutifulness since as he says to her "only in feudal societies is the woman still a vassal" (77). She is not Jyoti, the village girl, anymore but Jasmine, a modern city woman. Prakash wants to be called by his first name, whereas in traditional India women address their husbands formally. He also prohibits her from having children for the time being, and he encourages her to read his manuals to improve herself and cherish a better future for them both, probably in America, the land of possibility, in order to break away for good from the Indian atavism and immutability.

> *Pygmalion* wasn't a play I'd seen or read then, but I realize now how much of Professor Higgins there was in my husband. He wanted to break down the Jyoti I'd been in Hasnapur and made me a new kind of city woman (77).

The voice narrating the events is that of Jasmine in Iowa at the age of twenty-four. However, the comments and political insights offered come from backstage and betray the narrator's ideological point of view. For example when we read:

> He was basically an old fashioned Indian patriot, with a lot of Gandhi and a lot of Nehru in him (88).

We are aware that this cannot be Jasmine's standpoint since her role the novel is of the naive, but resourceful migrant woman, who tries to survive in America and make ends meet. She is portrayed in the "doer" role, as the woman making herself with no time for reflection or nostalgia. These cultural and political afterthoughts therefore come from an external omniscient voice which sets the whole novel into an ideological and culturally located frame.

There is, in fact, a distance between Jasmine and the authorial centre. Jasmine has a limited awareness. The author has the bigger picture. The bigger picture of the author contextualises *Jasmine* historically and geographically. She was born eighteen years after partition. Her family was from Lahore and had aristocratic connections. However, with the division of Punjab and their forced migration from Lahore to Hasnapur they become simple peasants. Jasmine has already inherited a tradition of exile and migration from her family. At the age of sixteen, she is planning to move with her husband, who dreams of his own Vijh & Wife shop, to the United States. It is the period of the Sikh separatist movement, when Sikh terrorists kill Hindu men and women because they are seen as rapists and whores. Sikhs claim a separate Punjab state from India and under the protection of Pakistan, whereas India fears a total disintegration of the nation state that had been based on secular principles. With Mukherjee we have to keep counting to establish the dates and historical situations of events. For a careless reader these are superfluous data, the added layer to the unfolding life story of Jasmine.

We are now at the beginning of the eighties, a period when several separatist movements take hold in India. Communalism condemned by Gandhi and Nehru had retaken possession of the nation after Indira Gandhi's declaration of the state of Emergency in 1977 which abolished many rights of speech and of freedom in order to protect the supreme unity of the Indian nation. However, Indira Gandhi's paranoia led to imprisonments and dismissal from public functions and created an atmosphere of political unrest and a growing distrust in the Indian democracy. This climaxed in Operation Blue Star in 1984 when Indira Gandhi sent Indian troops into the Golden Temple in Amritsar. The result was a bloodbath and the murder of the Sikh leader. A chain of repercussions took place all over the country, the most serious of which was the murder of Indira Gandhi herself four months later at the hands of her own Sikh bodyguard.[10]

The novel is historically set in the years of tension (the early 80s) preceding the events, Sikh terrorists going round Punjab on scooters, planting bombs. Prakash becomes a target because he had told his Sikh friend Sukhwinder that "There's no Hindu state! There's no Sikh State! India is for everyone" (66). And is therefore murdered for his secularist vision. Jasmine is seventeen and widowed as the astrologer had foretold. In her confusion she can only find direction in her old Indian dutifulness. She decides to go to America to commit *sati*, burning herself along with her husband's suit at the site where he would have gone to university.

However, fate has a few surprises for Jasmine. She travels by plane to Amsterdam and starts acknowledging her uprooted identity and her minority status in the big airports' lounges. Transmigration begins:

> We are the outcasts and deportees, strange pilgrims visiting outlandish shrines, landing at the end of tarmacs, ferried in old army trucks where we are roughly handled and taken to roped-off corners of waiting rooms where surly, barely wakened customs guards await their bribe. We are dressed in shreds of national costumes, out of season, the wilted plumage of intercontinental vagabondage. We ask only one thing: to be allowed to land; to pass through; to continue (101).

In order to illustrate how Jasmine manages to escape her Indian fate, and the dead ends that many immigrants have to face in the States, Mukherjee highlights a series of strategies that makes possible successful Americanisation. Her model is based on the adaptation to American otherness through a concatenation of permutations while keeping Indian diversity only for strategic purposes. A rather "opportunistic" credo which works magic in America, the country of "opportunities." I will now illustrate the many transformations undergone by Jasmine in order to become Mukherjee's heroine of immigration.

Lost Highways

Jasmine's passage to America is characterised by a traumatic experience, the first and the worst, in a long series of adaption, which requires her to improvise morality in order to survive. The transformation of identity from dutiful submissive widow into assertive, criminal and individualistic American woman is in full swing.

On arrival in Florida Half-Face proposes accompanying Jasmine to a motel in order to protect her because she is young, beautiful and Asian and could tempt bad guys. However, Jasmine ends up being the prey of her own assumed saviour. Half-Face drives her in the darkness in an unknown direction to a filthy motel along the highway, the perfect place for an American crime. Here Half-Face becomes the villain and rapes her. For Jasmine it works as a terrifying rite of passage, since "for the first time in my life I understood what evil was about" (116). Her claim to be a mourning widow on a mission does not protect her from the assaults of Half-Face, who on the contrary asserts his hegemony as male and as a white rapist by saying:

> Look, just don't fuck with me. I been to Asia and it's the armpit of the universe (112).

The transformation of identity starts from this moment. Jasmine contemplates her suicide, but the shower seems to waken Jasmine up from her suicidal drift. She has a mission to fulfil, and because of the mission she cannot die yet. Therefore, she needs to use her imagination to sort herself out, and once again her Indianness suggests a course of action.

We have many intertextual references to this location in a motel along the highways. From the classic Hitchcock's Vertigo to the plays of David Mamet and to David Lynch's postmodern Lost Highways, the motel is the perfect site to express American mobility and transitoriness. Judie Newman has not casually entitled her article on Jasmine "the Madwoman in the Motel,"[11] taking the motel as key metaphor for the illustration of chaos theory as applied to Jasmine. This intertextual approach foregrounds a very different way of envisaging what appears anarchic and chaotic as constituting instead a form of fruitful order in which the woman and her relation to dislocation are the key figures.

Kali and other Goddesses

Another strategy used by Mukherjee is to recur to Indian mythology in order to validate passages that would be considered "unrealistic" according to Western standards, but perfectly legitimate within a fictional account. Mythic concepts are attempts to mediate the gap between continuity and change, and this poetic principle is applied by Mukherjee to reinforce her transformative model.

While following the fabula level of the novel we see, in fact, that the rite of passage takes an unexpected turn. Jasmine slices her own tongue with a blade, and with her mouth full of blood she moves towards her villain. Just one stroke of the blade on his throat and the scene of the murder is perfect:

> I wanted that moment when he saw me above him as he had last seen me, naked, but now with my mouth open, pouring blood, my red tongue out (118).

Jasmine's full transformation, from the victim into a vengeful goddess, seems to be reinforced by imagining herself as the reincarnation of Kali:

> The room looked like a slaughterhouse. Blood had congealed on my hands, my chin, my breasts. [...] For the second time in three months, I was in a room with a slain man, my body bloodied. I was walking death. Death incarnate (119).

In order to express the agency of an Indian woman, her empowerment and capability of action, Mukherjee recurs to the old trick of invoking mythology to solve a difficult impasse. Possessed and transformed by the rage of the Goddess Kali Jasmine undergoes a quick shift of identity. From dutiful lost widow she is now a free murderess in search of multiple reincarnations.

This aspect has been criticised especially by Indian critics since Mukherjee seems to recur to easy icons of the Hindu mythology to market them to the West and to illustrate very unlikely passages in her novel. For example, the reason why Jasmine will never be prosecuted or wanted by the police for her crime is a technicality that does not interest Mukherjee. The writer's plan is to develop a female ethnic identity into an American assimilated at any costs. Mukherjee's creation of fables rather than realistic descriptions does not hinder her from the investigation of diasporic imagination. Juggling a bit with Hindu mythology, a bit with the American dream, Mukherjee creates the illusion of a continuum between the Indian female oppressive identity and the new invigorating, multiplying American subjecthood. Jasmine survives innumerable beginnings and ends, she has "hurtled through time tunnels" (240) and cries "through all the lives [she has] given birth to, [cries] for all [her] dead" (241). She steps from the old world ethics of submission, helplessness and doom to the exciting new ethnics of adventure, risk and transformation. Only when recurring to reincarnation does Mukherjee succeed in creating histories that are twisted, tangled and intertwined.

> With the first streaks of dawn, my first full American day, I walked out the front drive of the motel to the highway and began my journey, traveling light (121).

The question of travelling light is crucial for the American celebration of mobility, conquering of space and recycling of identity. However the shedding of an Indian personality, with its precise code of clothing, must be replaced by that stereotypical American motto that you must walk in "running shoes." Therefore one imagery substitutes for another, a superficial change of skin is enacted.

Multiple Politics: Dress, Addressing and Exoticism

Lillian Gordon, the first among Jasmine's many rescuers, introduces Jasmine to the first concept of American life: no backward glance, which entails the loosening of concepts of origin, language and belonging and a survival which means go America! Jasmine begins from this stage to be indirectly demarcated as "different," "special," "lucky" in comparison to other immigrant women. To play on her peculiarity will be Jasmine's winning card to integration, but she needs to "walk American," Lillian exhorts her:

> Now remember, if you walk American and talk American, they'll think you were born here. Most Americans can't imagine anything else (134-35).

She is not Jasmine the city girl anymore, she is Jazzy, the American illegal immigrant, full of promises and possibilities. She moves to Manhattan to work as a paid nanny. Taylor and Wylie Hayes are a glamorous and emancipated couple with an adopted daughter, Duff. Jasmine will be renamed Jase by Taylor and will start her transformation into a sophisticated American woman.

Taylor becomes Jase's American instructor; he teaches her about all the advantages of democracy. When Wylie moves out of the family home to move in with the wealthy Stuart Eschelman, Jasmine registers the change as a drama:

> In America, nothing lasts. I can say that now and it doesn't shock me, but I think it was the hardest lesson of all for me to learn. We arrive so eager to learn, to adjust, to participate, only to find the monuments are plastic, agreements are annulled. Nothing is forever, nothing is so terrible, or so wonderful, that it won't disintegrate (181).

Jasmine profits, however, very quickly from the new situation; she adapts. Taylor becomes Jase's metropolitan lover who turns Jasmine's colonial subalternity into American subjecthood through renaming and educating her. I consider the dividing line between patriarchal embodiment and female assertion as very ambiguous in the novel as these passages indicate. When Jase is obsessed with unwanted goods arriving by mail, Taylor instructs her how to return them. He writes in thick marking pen RETURN TO SENDER and explains to her: "That's all you need to do, he explained. If something gets too frightening, just pull down an imaginary shade that says RETURN on it and you can make it go away" (186). Taylor is giving her a demonstration on how to use America to make it the home you like. You can push away the *Unheimlich*, scary feelings of not belonging and threat and preserve the *Heimlich*, the serenity of a luxury apartment in New York. You just need to know how to transform unsettledness and helplessness into belonging and empowerment. When Jase gets a glimpse of her *Unheimlich* in Central Park, recognising in the hot-dog car vendor, Sukhwinder, the Sikh terrorist who had killed her husband (and who she thinks is coming after her to kill her too), she is stricken by terror. She leaves everything behind and flees to Iowa, incapable of applying Taylor's technique of "Return to Sender." Sukhhwinder can also be interpreted as a figure for Jasmine's own otherness and alterity, her open ambivalence with which she has not yet come to terms. My perception of Sukhwinder is a sign of her multiplicity, of the different women within herself, which are not completely compatible, are not fluid and transformed in the same self.

In Iowa Jasmine's resettlement is once again provided by a man, Bud Ripplemeyer, a fifty year old banker. He represents the American Uncle Scrooge, the emblem of capitalism. Iowa is the territory of transition between old and new America, it is the middle location for hybridisation. Bud, who is the prototype of the strong white rich American, ends up in a wheelchair, with an Indian wife and an adopted son, Du, a Vietnamese refugee. Despite her pregnancy and her reconstructed home, Jasmine, renamed Jane by Bud, decides to abandon Bud and their adoptive son, and moves West with Taylor "greedy with wants and reckless with hope" (241), which is the novel's closing line. Once again the suggestion of acting as a free American individual is offered by Taylor who asks her to embark with him on a Californian adventure, the ultimate location for freedom. Taylor had told her what to do with unwanted packages, and so she writes a confident "return" with thick marker pen to Bud Riplemeyer: "I am not choosing between men. I am caught between the promise of America and old world dutifulness" (240).

Feminist Strategies

> Despite our desperate, eternal attempt to separate, contain, and mend, categories always leak.
>
> Trinh T. Minh-ha, *Woman, Native, Other*[12]

The author interrogates the narrative of assimilation and feminism by taking into consideration the struggle that subaltern women have to undergo in the First world. However her claims can be bigger than her results. Mukherjee isolates, in fact, a particular figure from the Indian reality and forges her into the subject she needs to validate her transformative American model. The author does not take into account the communal aspect of Indian identity but selects *apropos* her subject as already characterised by inherent distinctiveness. In doing this, the quick passage towards individualisation is made possible for Jasmine.

Jasmine is particularly beautiful, with inborn aristocratic traits, intelligent and capable of learning the tricks of survival. In America she is recognised and marked as special, distinctive. Lillian Gordon strikes the chord of her difference "You're a very special case, my dear. I've written that to my daughter, so don't hesitate to call her" (134-35).

The authorial voice shifts in position between Jasmine's inherent nobility, that distinguishes her from other immigrants (therefore she can escape a future as a cleaner or paid nanny) and her naiveté as a Third World immigrant. These passages make *Jasmine* a rather American novel, and Mukherjee tries very hard to exploit the resources of Asian exoticness to succeed and to verify the American dream.

American prescriptive feminists have labelled *Jasmine* as not emancipatory enough because the character is too effeminate and passive. Mukherjee retorted, calling them "imperialists." According to her, Western feminists do not understand the implications for the gendered Indian struggle, and they impose instead their vision of how an emancipated female subject should act, despite her background and ethnicity. Mukherjee's idea of a militant Third World position is more radical than "middle class Ms Gloria Steinem" (she states in an interview with Maya Jaggi in *Bazar*, 1990). Her idea of integration, mongrelisation and fusion implies the transformation of Jasmine's different identities, none of which can be wiped out, but all exist contained and metamorphosed in the new other. Therefore in the constant politics of renaming, which is Mukherjee's leading device for showing the multiplying of identities, an element will remain unchanged and fixed.

From Jyoti the village girl in Hasnapur, to Jasmine the city woman, to Jazzy the undocumented immigrant, to Jase the Manhattan nanny, to Jane the Iowan woman who centres the story, the "J" will represent the element of continuity within transformation. As Elizabeth Bronfen wrote:

> This "J" serves as a signifier for the dialectic of a progressive engendering of identities as these bars any already existing identities, putting them under erasure without consuming them. In so doing, Mukherjee's novel traces the parameters of the narrative discourse available to the muted subaltern woman. Jasmine's dislocated Other speaks out of a self-conscious and

> self-induced effacement in the voice of a resilient, and incessantly self-refashioning hybridity.[13]

This is the "J," the aspect which will affect American society, all the men and people around her, that will cause their irreversible transformation. America has transformed Jasmine, but she has transformed America too.

> Then there is nothing I can do. Time will tell if I am a tornado, rubble-maker, arising from nowhere and disappearing into a cloud. I am out of the door and in the pothole and rutted driveway, scrambling ahead of Taylor, greedy with wants and reckless from hope (241).

These concluding lines release the tension, which runs like a red thread throughout the novel, between Jasmine's predicted fate and her desire to escape and transform it. Balancing between her fate and her will, the astrologer's premonition will reappear recurrently in the novel as a *Leitmotiv*. From the first page when her future will be read as a widow and exile until the last page when Jasmine says:

> Watch me reposition the stars, I whisper to the astrologer who floats cross-legged above my kitchen stove (240).

Jasmine's fate does not differ from that predicted by her astrologer, she will indeed be widowed and exiled, but in America these cultural referents assume a completely new function, of empowerment and multiplication. The "*porousness* of my days" (211) helps Jasmine towards self-fashioning in an upward movement within American society. However some critics have been highly unsatisfied with Mukherjee's use and abuse of the rhetoric of migrancy to support Jasmine's class mobility. Her fairy tales are far from being representative. Susan Koshy argues for example that:

> Mukherjee's celebration of assimilation is an insufficient confrontation to the historical circumstances of ethnicity and race in the United States and of the complexities of diasporic subject-formation.[14]

Mukherjee's protean feminist text overlooks important categories such as that of class and caste and how these categories interrelate to other axes of gender, ethnicity and age both in India and on the new American frontier. Mukherjee's main characters are middle class Indian women, but this implication is left unspoken and creates the assumption that every woman is granted the same possibility of upward mobility.

Mukherjee[15] distances herself from mainstream Western liberal feminists since their "tools and rhetoric" cannot be applied "wholesale and intact" to the situation of "some non-white, Asian women." However while Mukherjee sketches her character as self-fashioning, autonomous and self-determining "she is deeply complicit with some of the underlying assumptions"[16] of mainstream feminism.

Despite being personally unconvinced by Mukherjee's feminist strategies I do not agree with Koshy's statement. As Mukherjee has tried to demonstrate, more or less successfully, the relation between Third World strategies of survival and First World emancipatory declarations are neither separate nor exclusionary. It is in their interpenetration, which can result in paradoxical and conflictual outcomes, that Mukherjee's revisionist discourse should be placed. Asian women use all the tools they have to succeed, and this can be detected from the boldness characteristic of Punjabi communities of emigrants, to feminine devices such as beauty and passive attitudes, to the embrace of Western feminist self-assertion strategies.

However it is in her indication of positioning within the structure of dominance that I think Mukherjee's characters are flawed. In that respect they remain flat, without introspection or real believable fusion between origin and point of arrival. As such Mukherjee leaves the frontier of arrival open. Often the success and mobility of Jasmine is confused by readers with her agency and assertiveness, whereas the novel often highlights how much she is still a prey of her fate. Taylor decides to move West to California, and Jasmine just joins in, but does not plan it herself.

> Mukherjee's writing celebrates assimilation or whether this celebration reveals a positive attitude toward immigration. The question is, how is assimilation constructed in her texts?[17]

Chandra Mohanty has criticised Western feminism for constructing a monolithic image of the Third World women as "ignorant, poor, uneducated, tradition-bound, domestic, family oriented, victimised etc..." while implying a self-representation of white women as more modern and sexually emancipated. What is created is the Western standard as the norm and referent versus Third World standard as "Other"[18]

In this regard Mukherjee's position is highly disputable. Because of her narrative reversions she presents the backwardness of the status of women in Punjab through an identification with Westernised ideas. These originate from her locating the narration and, therefore the language of emancipation, in Iowa, a cross location which functions as a trope for the transformations which have already taken place.

Mukherjee unconsciously recreates a split between an idea of feminism as applied to Third World conditions and an idea of feminism applied to Third World migrant subjects in a Western society. She therefore reproduces the objectification mentioned by Mohanty by portraying Jasmine's singularity (and therefore with inborn requisites to become a successfully developed emancipated subject in the West) as compared with other anonymous village women, backward and doomed to oblivion. As Koshy writes:

> The celebration of Jasmine's singularity is dependent on flattening out the subjectivities of other nonwhite women whom she encounters and identifies with, but from whom she is carefully distinguished.[19]

Jasmine's exceptionality is developed at the expense of other non-white characters who are homogenized as "Other" and objectified as victims:

> all over our district, bad luck dogged dowry less wives, rebellious wives, barren wives. They fell into wells, they got run over by trains, they burned to death heating milk on kerosene stoves (41).

This discourse constructs the Third World as a monolithically oppressive society where resistance and rebellion is impossible. Mukherjee becomes trapped by the formulation of her own discourse. If there is no escape for Hasnapuri women, Jyoti escapes through extraordinary means, because of her mission of committing *sati* in front of Prakash's aspired University in Florida. This narrative trick is insufficient to justify Mukherjee's claim of forwarding a situated and historically bound notion of feminism as applied to Asian women. Her fictional imagination takes over and in constructing her mythography of "making it" in the *tabula rasa* that is America, Mukherjee emphasises the fabulistic pattern of the romantic heroine rather than carefully identifying the shifts in the development of identity as centred around a well-articulated notion of race, caste and class.

Jasmine becomes only "special" and "exotic" for Americans and different from other racialised women. As Lillian Gordon tells her "Jazzy, you don't strike me as a picker or a domestic.... You're different from these others" (134). Jasmine is set apart from a monolithic alterity, she is distinguished and destined to success with respect to other migrant workers.

Mukherjee operates the transformation of Jasmine's identity according to two main master's discourses, the first relative to colonial oppression (technology, the mastering of English and migration should deal with it) and the second one to patriarchal oppression (by becoming multiple selves, seductive and transformative). Jasmine uses the various tools provided by her male partners, adapts her identity to the role she is expected to fulfil then dishevels the master's house, moves on, and proceeds with her self-realization by acquiring new master's tools.

> I have had a husband for each of the women I have been. Prakash for Jasmine, Taylor for Jase, Bud for Jane, Half-Face for Kali (197).

Jasmine's power is indicated in her restlessness to keep changing shape and houses. The master discourse cannot trap her in any definite and finite location and self. In this transmigratory mythology, the self which is fluid and accumulative can be killed and endlessly reincarnated, and this strategy defies both the patriarchal and the colonial logic.

However, Mukherjee is not transformative in her gendered and ethnicized representation since she uses clichés and stereotypes to create a postmodern text for the West and an improbable mythological tale of an escaping princess for India: rampant individualism with an exotic tinge. What Mukherjee lacks is thinking through difference according to which "neither the totalitarian effacement of difference nor the delirious celebration of a limitless and ever-proliferating "in-difference" take place.[20] With her celebrating of postmodern geography and free-floating identity the novel *Jasmine* plays with the subject who is in a non-position, everywhere and nowhere at the same time, consuming differences and creating mobile identities.

The most important particularity of Mukherjee's strategies is her use of language. The characters speak in a fancy, hip American slang, fuse registers and styles and convey the unique voice of American's multiple idioms. However, Mukherjee flattens the category of difference by making most of her characters—with ostensibly different backgrounds, itineraries, and histories—speak all the same "hip, jumped-up, word jazz."[21] Nonetheless, as Pfeil adds, "the tonal and stylistic equivalence of these voices is, paradoxically, their most salient feature."[22]

Despite the declaration of discontent Mukherjee's postcolonial assimilatory manifesto is a text where the emphasis on pleasure and agency (jouissance) challenges the images of fragmentation and victimisation that are usually projected on those who are perceived as the other by the hegemonic subject. It is for this that Mukherjee's book must be praised. Despite its pitfalls and limits of essentialism the novel shows that the road to America is open. This exuberance of immigration makes the text worthwhile despite its controversial aspects.

Multicultural Identity

In order to position Mukherjee's discourse of assimilation within American multiculturalism it is useful to briefly discuss here Peter McLaren's article, "White Terror and Oppositional Agency: Towards a Critical Multiculturalism."[23] In this article McLaren distinguishes three forms of multiculturalism. These refer to the way in which race and ethnicity are mapped out in the cultural construction of difference or sameness.

The first form is defined by McLaren as "Conservative Multiculturalism." It indicates the white groups who do not question their whiteness as an ethnic category but position other ethnicities and minority groups on a lower ladder of civilisation. For the purpose of multiculturalism this implies that the integration of different groups by the dominant hegemonic group takes place at the expense of their specificity. The hegemonic group forwards, in fact, a common culture where the colonialist and imperialist ideology still dominates. This implicates that the various ethnic groups are "add ones" to the dominant white culture. With reference to the specific case of the United States, to give an example, this entails the negation of an education in Spanish to the detriment of the Hispanic community, but which is in favour of an English and Anglo-Saxon form of integration.

The second form of multiculturalism indicated by McLaren is termed as "Liberal multiculturalism." This vision defends the natural equality existing among white and other communities. However, as McLaren explains, the social and educational opportunities necessary for competing in the capitalist marketplace are not the same. Liberal multiculturalism erodes, therefore, into an ethnocentric and universalising humanism. The legitimising norms which govern the substance of citizenship are, in fact, identified most strongly with Anglo-American political communities.

The third form considered is "Left-Liberal Multiculturalism," which emphasises cultural differences, and suggests that the stress on the equality of races only erases the importance of the cultural differences between races which are responsible for different behaviour and social practices. The backdrop to this approach is the exoticisation of "Otherness' and a nativist trend to locate differences into a primeval past of cultural authenticity. This tendency to essentialise difference—by ignoring the historical and cultural situatedness of difference—runs the risk of requiring a definite identity as starting point before a dialogue can be undertaken. Therefore, people can be trapped in a constructed identity on the basis of their ethnicity, gender or class without taking into account how personal experience has developed within the ideological and discursive complexities of its formation.

Identity is constantly being produced through a play of differences linked to, and reflected by, shifting and conflicting discursive and ideological relations, formations and articulations. As Joan Scott writes, "experience is a subject's history. Language is the site of history's enactment."[24] Therefore, identity politics must be placed within a more complex tracing of relations and influences which are based on hegemonic relations and on non-defined and fixed knowledge. Hegemonic Western cultures are usually not perceived as specific to any particular ethnicity and they are hegemonic precisely because they are able to represent themselves effectively as neutral and universal.

Following this position McLaren moves towards a fourth position which entails a radical understanding of the concept of difference. With "Critical Multiculturalism" he wants to stress the central task of transforming the social, cultural, and institutional relations in which meanings are produced. If conservative and liberal multiculturalism stress "sameness," and the left-liberals stress difference, they create a false opposition, because both perspectives are based on an essentialist logic. In both cases identity is presumed to be autonomous and self-contained. Critical multiculturalism starts from the notion of differences as constructed between and among groups. Critical multiculturalism interrogates the construction of difference and identity in which the working of power and privilege are analysed, examining how structures of exclusion are still at work despite the declaration of equality among differences.

If we follow this classification to analyse how Mukherjee represents assimilation in *Jasmine* then we have to admit that she skips around different forms of multiculturalism, holding to only one constant pattern that is that of individualisation. Mukherjee forwards a conservative multiculturalism when she elects Jasmine as a special case, as an elected immigrant who fulfils the right requirements to be assimilated within the dominant white model of American society "you are a very special case, my dear" (135). Jasmine shows the capacity to transform and to adapt in order to survive and to acquiesce to the role already written for her.

> I wanted to become the person they thought they saw: humorous, intelligent, refined, affectionate. Not illegal, not murderer, not widowed, raped, destitute, fearful (171).

However, at the Hayes' Jasmine has to adapt to that democratic idea that she is as worthy as they are, as cultivated and articulate. This idea of liberal multiculturalism sees no differences among human beings:

> Taylor didn't want to change me. He didn't want to scour and

sanitize the foreignness. My being different from Wylie and Kate didn't scare him. I changed because I wanted to (185).

Jasmine's efforts to improve herself open the question to which standard and for whom must this improvement be performed. Jasmine says, "for herself," and here enters that leading concept of Mukherjee: individualism. Only if you detach yourself from your traditional heritage and fixed familiar bonding can you have a chance at success. Individualism, hence, is an illusion that is upheld by projecting cultural specificity exclusively on others. And therefore Jasmine becomes unique, different and special in order to fulfil her path towards individualisation.

She plays her exotic card to conquer the various men, and she uses modesty and naiveté in order not to infuriate the women whose men she steals, but to win them over as well: "Karin, Bud's ex called me a gold digger" (195) or "Taylor loves you," Wylie said, "but you must know that" (182). With Bud Ripplemeyer there is an evident case of left-liberal multiculturalism since he falls for Jasmine because of her "otherness": "Bud courts me because I am alien. I am darkness, mystery, inscrutability. The East plugs me into instant vitality and wisdom. I rejuvenate him simply by being who I am" (200). Differences are necessary for the construction of identity and within the notion of left-liberal multiculturalism, differences are emphasised and fixed into a static notion of alterity. No one investigates what constitutes Jasmine's Indianness. In America, Lillian Gordon tells her, people know only walking and speaking American. If you divert from this assumed majority then you will qualify as other-than-American. Lillian Gordon carries out her humanitarian mission under the flag of conservative multiculturalism inciting Jasmine-Jazzy's rapid integration.

However, Jasmine survives in America and guarantees her upward mobility not through purely playing by the rules but also by making strategic use of her difference as Asian in order to acquire maximum visibility and privileges. For such acceptance of Left-liberal Multiculturalism Mukherjee has been criticised for having essentialised both the notion of Indianness and of Americanness into coded and prescriptive categories. India is fate, immobility, oppression; America is rewriting your destiny, change and empowerment. Mukherjee assumes in her novel that there is only one way to be American, that is to say, by asserting one's own individuality, centering the others around the self.

We can also identify forms of what McLaren defines as Critical Multiculturalism, since the historical and situated difference of Jasmine's Indianness hinders her from preceding unencumbered in her path towards self-emancipation. When she sees Sukhwinder, the Sikh terrorist in Central Park, she knows her past has come to reclaim her, that she cannot shake off her previous role despite the promise of Americanness. Therefore her identity is relational in the sense that only by maintaining her American environment can she assert a certain kind of identity whereas in other situations her construction will be immediately demolished. Mukherjee does not ignore the exclusionary structures of power that are still at work within swinging equality discourses. At a certain point Jasmine remarks: "I wish I had known America before it got perverted" (201), implying that the American dream of a happy melting pot had lost its magic and the different immigrant communities were competing with one another, often with fatal consequences. Whether that pure America ever existed is not Mukherjee's concern, it is in the perversion that imbalances within the power structure are revealed.

The democratic people, the Hayes, who are so fond of her are really interested in "other" cultures and have exquisite collections:

> The apartment was stocked like a museum. Wylie and Taylor weren't simple acquisitors ... Some of them [art pieces, S.P.] seemed offensive to blacks or women or red Indians. There were slave auctions posters from New Orleans in 1850 ...; old color prints celebrating the massacre of an entire Indian village down to the last baby; a poster of a naked woman with parts of her body labeled choice, prime, or chuck, as in a butcher shop (174).

The "minor" cultures are represented not only as "other" but they are clearly objectified with violence, exploitation and commodification. This is part of the making of America, part of the American dream and identity. However, by letting Jasmine-Jase be part of the American dream the Hayes compensate for the exploitation upon which their prosperity is based and make Jasmine-Jase complicit with the hegemonic group. This intersection of historical responsibility is rendered more apparent when Jasmine visits Wylie's new lover's apartment:

> He had been to India several times as a guest lecturer in Delhi, as a World Bank consultant, as a U.S. government aid officer. He spoke Hindi passably and owned so many Indian paintings and tapestries that his living room looked to me like a shop or an art gallery. His wife was an Africa specialist, so the walls were hung with spears and masks that competed with mirror-work cloths and Moghul miniatures (184).

There is obviously not only a commodification of the Third World as exotic and interesting but also a need, almost artificial, to equalise the values of other cultures to America, or even to reduce them to a symbolic world, that is that of art through which the Third World is reduced to fetishes and token figures. These decorate the modern American apartment of "politically correct" people, Americans who do really care for the rest of the world and do have humanitarian positions within the capitalist structure of exploitation. Stuart works as an aid officer for the US, covers an international function for the World Bank and knows enough about other cultures not to be an exploiter, but, in contrast, he became a treasurer.

In his article "The Post-colonial and the Postmodern" Kwame Anthony Appiah[25] offers an analysis of the marketing of African art works in American museums. The selection of pieces for a show at the Center for African Art in New York clearly demonstrates through a politics of inclusion and exclusion how "Africa" is made for the American postmodern world. David Rockfeller the art collector "who would never surely criticise sculptures from other ethnic groups in terms of [his] own traditional criteria" (Appiah 1992: 222) tries to assimilate the pieces "between considerations of finance, of aesthetics and decor. In these responses, we have surely a microcosm of the site of the American in the contemporary—which is, then, surely to say, postmodern—America" (Appiah 1992: 223). Appiah's comments on African art within Western collections unveils the hegemonic colonial structures which are still at work despite the postmodern, postcolonial equalisation of all cultures. I will quote Appiah extensively since he offers a clear picture of the concept of multiculturalism in its historical shifts:

> The incorporation of these works in the West's world of museum culture and its market has almost nothing, of course, to do with postmodernism. By and large, the ideology through which they are incorporated is modernist: it is the ideology that brought something called "Bali" to Artaud, something called "Africa" to Picasso, and something called "Japan" to Barthes. [This incorporation as an official Other was criticised, of course, from its beginnings: Oscar Wilde once remarked that "the whole Japan is a pure invention. There is no such country, no such people."] What is postmodernist is Vogel's muddled conviction that African Art should not be judged "in terms of (someone else's) traditional criteria." For modernism, primitive art was to be judged by putatively universal aesthetic criteria; and by these standards it was finally found possible to value it. ... For postmodernisms, by contrast, these works, however they are to be understood, cannot be seen as legitimated by culture—and history—transcending standards (Appiah 1992: 239).

If modernism regarded primitive art as part of a universal aesthetic code postmodernism has erased the hidden relations of power between dominant and dominated cultures through a politics which sees culture disentangled by its historical context. Therefore equalising cultures by abstracting them in order not to deal with "difference" and "otherness" but by assimilating it into the dominant pattern of commodification.

Such reasoning is relevant to Jasmine who functions as an exotic artwork to be integrated into an American multicultural pluralism. Like the Hayes' paintings and Stuart's valuable collection, she enters a marketplace where she can be commodified according to her "financial, aesthetic and decor" applicability in a Western environment. Mukherjee's resistant discourse, however, requires that the Western environment cannot be the same once it has been in touch with Jasmine, that her tornado, rubble-maker nature affects identity construction both ways. It is by emphasising this quality to confront and subvert the concept of Americanness that Jasmine has an agency and is empowered. Bud's inherent racism leads him to acquire an Asian wife and an adopted Vietnam refugee as a son, to be deserted by them both, the undermining of his American dominance and values symbolised by his becoming crippled and having to live in a wheelchair.

Jasmine has moved progressively away from the conservative multiculturalism "walk American" of Lillian Gordon, to the Liberal multiculturalism of the Hayes "you don't have to change" to a left-liberal multi-culturalism in which her difference is enhanced in Iowa. The conclusion is an attempt to represent critical multi-culturalism with her decision to move on and to leave everything behind, everything that was erased by her tornado.

However the asymmetrical power structures are not really explored by Mukherjee, which prevents us from seeing the novel as an act of critical multiculturalism. She has sketched more general traits to open the discussion on multiculturalism. With these general traits she has stumbled on essentialisations, not really thinking through difference and identity and by using existing categories which were appealing and comprehensible to the West. She has not created an alternative representation of agency and pleasure, but a representation of the subjects' consent to hegemonic representations of transnational and multicultural reality, Mukherjee has explored this consent as a two-sided alteration/infection. Furthermore by following the path of consent to hegemonic structure she has made her "minority text" extremely successful opening the discussion on subaltern migrant identity to a wider audience and stimulating further representations.

NOTES AND REFERENCES

1. Michael Connell, Jessie Grearson and Tom Grimes, "An Interview with Bharati Mukherjee," *Iowa Review* 20.3 (1999): 7-32, 26-27.
2. Mukherjee, *Bazar* 1990.
3. V.S. Naipaul, *The Overcrowded Barracoon* (Middlesex: Penguin, 1976) 30-31. First published by André Deutsch, 1972.
4. V.S. Naipaul, *The Overcrowded Barracoon* (1976) 24. A different, but connected issue on language and imposition of landscape stereotypes has been widely debated by the French speaking Martinican critic and writer Aimé Césaire who worked for the cultural and artistic decolonization of the Caribbean by editing a journal with René Menil *Tropiques: Revue Culturelle* (1941-45) and by publishing other important works such as *Discours sur le*

Colonialisme (1955). In the article "Aimé Césaire's Subjective Geographies: Translating Place and the Difference it Makes" Indira Karamcheti reports Suzanne Césaire's manifesto for Martinican poetry. In an issue of *Tropiques* Suzanne Césaire criticised the colonial's implications of Martinican literatures for its use of exoticization and stereotypical tropicalism (paradoxically enough for a journal called *Tropiques*) calling it "Literature of the hammock, literature of sugar and vanilla. Tourism literature [...]. The hell with hibiscus, frangipani, bougainvillea. Martinican poetry will be cannibal or will not be." Choosing hibiscus, frangipani and bougainvillea as metonyms for exoticism both Aimé and Suzanne Césaire emblematically represent the problematic, also explored by V.S. Naipaul, of translating a place such as the Caribbea with the language inherited from the colonizer. In *Between Languages and Culture: Translation and Cross-Cultural Texts*, eds. Anuradha Dingwaney and Carol Maier (Pittsburgh: University of Pittsburgh Press, 1995).

5. Mukherjee, *Bazar* 1990.
6. Malashri Lal, *The Law of the Threshold* (Shimla: Indian Institute for Advanced Study, 1995). In her article on Bharati Mukherjee Lal discusses the subject of the threshold in Mukherjee as a "timely example of how far the Indian woman's periphery may be extended beyond her home" (145) to the point of downgrading her Indian heritage and affiliations strenuously emphasizing her American citizenship and illustrating the credo of immigrant writing as a "maximalist" act.
7. Bharati Mukherjee in Timothy Brennen, *Salman Rushdie and the Third World: Myths of the Nation* (London: Macmillan, 1989).
8. See the already mentioned Malashri Lal from the University of Delhi, but also Sunanda Mongia from the University of Varanasi and Sherine Upot from the University of Calicut for their readings of Mukherjee from the Indian point of view.
9. Gayatri C. Spivak, "Imperialism and Sexual Difference," *Oxford Literary Review* 8:1-2 (1986): 234.
10. For further illustration see Sandra Ponzanesi, "Marginalia: Rearticulating Subaltern Studies Across System Divisions" which appeared in *Thamyris* 5.1 (Spring 1998) and which reviews the important text edited by T.V. Sathya Murthy, *Region, Religion, Caste, Gender and Culture in Contemporary India*, vol. 3 (New Delhi: Oxford UP, 1996) with a detailed account of India's separatist movements.
11. Judie Newman, *The Ballistic Bard: Post-colonial Fictions* (London: Arnold. 1995).
12. Trinh T. Minh-ha, *Woman, Native, Other: Writing Post-coloniality and Feminism* (Bloomington: Indiana UP, 1989).
13. Elizabeth Bronfen, "A Sense of Strangeness: The Gender and Cultural Identity in Bharati Mukherjee's *Jasmine*," *Baetyl* 2 (1990): 79.
14. Susan Koshy, "The Geography of Female Subjectivity: Ethnicity, Gender and Diaspora," *Diaspora* 3.1 (1994): 69.

15. Connell et al 7-32.
16. Koshy 70.
17. Koshy 76.
18. See Chandra Talpade Mohanty, "Under Western Eyes: Feminist Scholarship and Colonial Discourse," *Third World Women and the Politics of Feminism*, eds. Chandra T. Mohanty, Ann Russo and Lourdes Torres (Bloomington: Indiana UP, 1991) 51-80.
19. Koshy 78.
20. Fred Pfeil, "No Basta Teorizer: In-Difference to Solidarity in Contemporary Fiction, Theory, and Practice," *Scattered Hegemonies: Postmodernity and Transnational Feminist Practices*, eds. Inderpal Grewal and Caren Kaplan (Minneapolis: U of Minnesota P, 1994) 225.
21. Pfeil 201.
22. Pfeil 201.
23. David Theo Goldberg, *Multiculturalism*: *A Critical Reader* (Cambridge: Blackwell, 1994).
24. Joan Scott, "Experience," *Feminists Theorize the Political,* eds. Judith Butler and Joan Scott (New York: Routledge, 1992) 34.
25. Kwame Anthony Appiah, *In My Father's House*: *Africa in the Philosophy of Culture* (London: Methuen, 1992).

7

The (Un)making of Saladin Chamcha: Rushdie's Subversion of the *Bildungsroman*[1]

SHAUL BASSI*

"I am Born." This is the title of the first chapter of *David Copperfield*, and in a good four of our six novels *Tom Jones*, *Jane Eyre*, *David Copperfield* and *Great Expectations*, the heroes' childhood, if not always their birth, is granted an emblematic and lasting prominence. It is the first of the many differences between the English "Bildungsroman" and the continental one (Franco Moretti 1987: 182).

It is significant that many of the postcolonial novels that chart [the] process of *Bildung* for the individual self and the nation ... begin with a death rather than with the more conventional birth of the *Bildungsroman* protagonist (Lima 1993: 441).

"To be born again... first you have to die": death and birth traverse each other in the opening of Salman Rushdie's *The Satanic Verses*, as the two protagonists Saladin Chamcha and Gabriel Farishta fall from the sky after the explosion of their airplane and land unharmed on the shores of Britain.

The encounter between postcolonial authors and *Bildungsroman* was almost inevitable: no genre could better serve the purpose of narrating complex hybrid cultural legacies and negotiate within them new forms of identity (Lima 1993: 433, 440). And yet this encounter was vitiated by an original sin: in the classical Victorian

*University of Venice, Venice, Italy.

novel of apprenticeship, the success of the European hero depended on the riches accumulated in the colonies at the expense of the natives (Said 1994: 73ff).

The death to which Maria Helena Lima refers in our opening quotation depends on the state of impoverishment and devastation in which the "triumph" of the West has left the colonies. This denounces the radical difference between European and postcolonial space. The former is a space of possibilities (of which the colonies are an ideal extension), where the hero, albeit facing numerous vicissitudes, is free to construct his fortunes and his self. In the postcolonial space, deprived of its resources and left in dire social and political conditions, one can optimistically aim at reconstructing.

The Rushdian incipit, with its fantastic non-death which turns into a rebirth, seems to combine the English and postcolonial models. Pursuing this hypothesis, I would like to read the story of Saladin Chamcha as a dialogue between the writer and the tradition of *Bildungsroman*, on the basis of the precious typological and morphological observations on the English novel of education by Franco Moretti in his seminal study of this genre (1987; 1999).

In the revised Italian edition, Moretti responds to those who have criticized the euro- and male-centrism of his analysis by simply admitting to the limits of his own competence and, more crucially, drawing precise historical and geographical boundaries for the *Bildungsroman* as he intends it. A genre which he considers quintessentially European and "declared impossible" by the outbreak of World War I (1999: xiv-xv, 257). I argue that thanks to the postcolonial time-lag of modernity theorized by Homi Bhabha (1994: 246-56), Chamcha starts as a belated follower of the Western promises of the *Bildungsroman* and ultimately fails because his world is no longer that of Dickens or Thackeray.

Let us begin by summarizing the facts of Saladin's life before his fatal fall in the linear form of the Victorian novel, piecing them together from the narrator's flashbacks.

Salahuddin Chamchawala was born in Bombay around the middle of the 20th century, together with Independent India. His childhood is marked by his domineering father, a rich nationalistic philanthrope who exerts a rigid control over his son, as when he confiscates some money that the boy had found by chance or when he catches him, quite literally, with his pants down.

Salahuddin then develops an intense hatred for his environment and dreams of escaping to London, which in his imagination is the capital of riches and the antithesis of the squalid and vulgar Bombay. One day the thirteen-year old boy is sexually harassed, and the feeling of shame which prevents him for disclosing the event projects him even closer to his longed-for destination.

The dream comes true when the father offers him to educate in England. He escorts him to London and unexpectedly returns him the subtracted money but leaves him to support himself on his own. The impact with British school takes the shape of a kipper, a mysterious fish that will keep Salahuddin occupied for ninety minutes, without any of his new schoolmates coming to his aid.

Despite everything, his determination brings him over high school and college, and, save some sporadic homecomings that simply allow his frail mother to witness disconcertedly the transformation of his estranged son, he becomes a true Englishman. Eventually Salahuddin Chamchawala truns into Saladin Chamcha, adopting a name which is more compatible with English phonetics. To put down deeper roots in his new homeland, he also takes the final, logical step: Saladin marries an English woman, Pamela Lovelace.

Saladin's inveterate Anglophilia, far from being a simple childish eccentricity, is the late fruit of that project of social engineering devised by the British in 19th-century India. To mediate between them and the masses, otherwise not controllable, they aimed at creating a class of people who were supposed to be, in the famous words of T. B. Macaulay, "Indian in blood and colour, but English in taste, in opinions, in morals, and in intellect" (cit. in Kalinnikova 1982: 2). Saladin's name is itself significant, as Rushdie explained in an interview a long time before the publication of the novel:

> Colloquially, a *Chamcha* is a person who sucks up to a powerful people, a yes-man, a sycophant. The British Empire would not have lasted a week without such collaborators among its colonized peoples. You could say the Raj grew fat by being spoon-fed. Well, as we all know, the spoon-feeding ended, or

at least ceased to be sufficiently nourishing, and the British left. But the effects of the Empire linger on (1982: 8).

The England admired by Saladin is surely a mythical England, an idealized image of the "mother land" created *ad hoc* for the subjects of the Empire. It has been amply demonstrated how English literature was used to transmit to the Indian higher classes the main Western and Christian values, where the teaching of the Bible would have offended the religiousness of Hindus and Muslims. It is not by chance that its first academic appearance took place in Bengal, before it was introduced at London University College (Viswanathan 1989; Rajan 1992; Chandra 1992).

It is at this point that I would like to venture the hypothesis that Saladin may have been a reader of English novels of education, and that he may have tried to model his life on their exemplary plots: he leaves the paternal house, suffers a stern education made harsher by financial hardship, but finally finds an English job and takes an English wife.

If things went like in Dickens's books (on his presence in *The Satanic Verses* see Hennard Dutheil 1999: 63-79), the wedding would sanction the accomplishment of the education, it would constitute that "'pact' between the individual and the world," that "metaphor for the social contract" that guaranteed to the Victorian hero familial and economic stability (Moretti 1987: 22). Events for Saladin, however, take a very different route. The bankrupt of the marriage represents a check of the project of *Bildung* that Saladin had been cultivating since adolescence and his acting and dubbing career follows the ups and downs of show business.

Many postcolonial narratives relate how many immigrants become disillusioned with their European experience and return home to rediscover their native culture. Saladin seeks relief from his existential crisis in a trip to Bombay, where a group of friends and an extemporaneous lover try to win him back to his Indianness. But this temporary homecoming solves none of his personal dilemmas: the Great Socialization which the *Bildungsroman* promises and promotes (Moretti 1999: 258) is no more possible in India than in Britain. Saladin heads back to London, embarking on the plane which will be blown up by Kashmir separatists.

Upon his landing to Britain after the fall, Saladin is arrested as illegal alien and brutalized by the police. He then undergoes a strange metamorphosis that turns him into a goatish monster and causes his internment in a sinister clinic for "mutants." After taking part in a collective getaway, he finds shelter in the attic of a London café, run by a family of Asian immigrants. Onlyeth their help and at the end of a long interior travail will Saladin be able to repossess his human semblance.

The main thesis of this essay is that in this postlapsarian stage, Rushdie deconstructs Chamcha's English "apprenticeship" manipulating and deforming many of the founding elements of the classical novel of formation, demonstrating how and why they cannot apply to the postcolonial individual.

This may sound as an anachronistic operation, since the 19th-century *Bildungsroman* had already been reconfigured by successive traditions (suffice to think of early 20th-century Avant garde). The crucial difference lies in the fact that the previous models of *anti-bildungsroman* expressed a lack of confidence in the idea of progress inherent in the original. So their (anti-)heroes traversed life without learning, without advancing, remaining at the point where they had started, which still was a relatively privileged social position (Moretti 1999: 257ff). This possibility is not available to the postcolonial subject, for reasons that a detailed list of Rushdie's deformations will clearly show.

Youth. Youth is the age that the *Bildungsroman* elects to key moment of life and "symbolic form of modernity" (Moretti 1999). For Saladin, youth turn out to be the age of utopias and false promises when he endorses values that will miserably fall apart when he is forty.

History. The great historical events, from the French Revolution to the 1848 uprisings, were always marginal in the plots of novels of education, exorcised or alluded to grant to the hero safe unlimited space for his (self-)exploration (Moretti 1987: 12). On the contrary, history tracks Saladin down: the terrorist attack by the Kashmir separatists sucks him in the whirlpool of Indian politics and starts his misadventures. The inextricable link between individual and History is at the centre of Rushdian narrative since *Midnight's*

Children, whose protagonist is born "handcuffed" to History. A metaphor which suggests the violent enforcement of the law which we will presently discuss.

Mobility. The classical European hero was mobile by definition and his movements took the form of "travel and adventure, wondering and getting lost, 'Boheme' and 'parvenir'" (Moretti 1987: 4), in any event a necessary and often desired exploration. Postcolonial mobility means migration, exile, escape from war and persecution. Saladin falls from the sky, is transported in a prison-van, is interned in a special clinic, is involved in a getaway, and finally secluded in a small café. As much as the classic hero is master of his own destiny, Saladin remains wholly subordinate to it until he breaks the spell of his idealized *Bildung*.

The Law. Moretti has observed that the law dominates the horizon of English novels of education, which "do not simply state that everyone 'has a right' to justice; they maintain instead that everyone, in fact, *receives* justice" (1987: 213). The happy ending is always sanctioned by a tribunal which acknowledges the identity of the hero, his social status and usually bestows on him a substantial unexpected inheritance. The Law that manifests itself to Saladin after his landing is a brutal and violent police force that arrests, beats, jails him, and, above all, refuses to recognize him as a "citizen" because of his ethnic difference. When he tries to identify himself as the star of a popular TV show—"Don't any of you watch TV? Don't you see? I'm Maxim. Maxim Alien.'—a policeman replies: "So you are. And I am Kermit the Frog" (140).

This episode bears out the observation of Hannah Arendt, for whom the western notion of human rights depends on citizenship and does not apply to those individuals (refugees, immigrants, illegal aliens) who fall outside the parameters of the nation state and precisely for this reason would most require protection from violations (1975: 267-302).

Metamorphosis. In the English novel "conservation" seems to be the most important value and its centrality "generates an equally inevitable repugnance to change" (Moretti 1987: 8). Chamcha, whose assonance with Kafka's Samsa rings a loud intertextual bell, is subject to the most radical form of change: physical metamorphosis. He turns into a sort of satyr with horns, hooves and an embarrassingly big phallus. This example of Rusdhie's often misinterpreted "magical realism" (Bassi, 1999) foregrounds the vulnerability of the body to the modern disciplinary power of the state.

The Villain. The theme of metamorphosis is connected to another distinct feature of the English novel, where "[b]etween the insipid normality of the hero, and a stable and a thoroughly classified world, no spark will ever flash" (Moretti 1987: 200). Hence the need of a *villain*, an antagonist who comes from the outside to break the social order by embodying all its negative values (Frankenstein, Dracula, Mr. Hyde, etc.). Saladin, who dreamt of being the hero, finds himself in the role of its opposite. He ends up representing the quintessential villain of the society he had idealized: devilish, bestial, lascivious, stinking, sensual—a creature which embodies all the western stereotypes of the ethnic Other. After all he has the name of an ancient foe of the West: "when the French general Gouraud entered Damascus in 1920, he proceeded immediately to the tomb of Salah al-Dîn al-Ayoubi, who had defeated the Europeans in the Third Crusade, and announced gloatingly: 'Nous revoilà, Saladin!'" (Kabbani 1986: 5).

The Narrator. The traditional Victorian narrator was heterodiegetic, omniscient and lavishly offered psychological and moral judgments on his characters. He "awaited" them as a member of the society in which they were gradually integrating. The narrator of *The Satanic Verses* is somehow kin to this antecedent, at least in his self-confidence: "I know the truth, obviously. I watched the whole thing. As to omnipresence and -potence, I'm making no claims at present, but I can manage this much, I hope" (10). But for a paradox which is solely apparent, he is much less sure of his own identity as demonstrated in his first aside: "Who am I? / Who else is there?" (4); and a few pages later: "Who am I? / Let's put it this way: who has the best tunes?" To understand oneself, the narrator, seems to suggest, one has to interrogate one's relationship with others and with language.

Identity. In a way all the previous themes merge in the grand theme of identity, since the *Bildungsroman* is the story of an identity in the making. Lukacs asserts that "the novel tells of the adventure of interiority; the content of the novel is the story of the soul that goes to find itself, that seeks adventures in order to be proved and tested by them, and by proving itself, to find it own essence" (1978: 89). This definition, written as part of Lukacs's response to World War I—which for Moretti marks the end of the *Bildungsroman*—endorses the notion of an *essentialist* subject who believes in "secure authorial intention, individual autonomy, integral self-determination, and universal law" (Barney 1993: 360). A subject for whom language is an instrument to *express, describe* and *comment* the world.

Many of these assumptions are echoed by Saladin when, on the verge of his crisis, he recites to himself a litany of his vacillating principles:

> I am a real man, he told the mirror, with a real history and a planned-out future. I am a man to whom certain things are of importance: rigour, self-discipline, reason, the pursuit of what is noble without recourse to that old crutch, God. The ideal of beauty, the possibility of exaltation, the mind. I am: a married man. But in spite of his litany, perverse thoughts insisted on visiting him (135-36).

Modernist and postmodernist literature, philosophy and psychoanalysis have deconstructed this ideal self-piece by piece, and Rushdie wittily captures many of the issues of the post-structuralist critique of the subject that reached its peak in the 1980s. Man has no essence, being less a unity than a field of conflicting forces; he is never identical because it is continuously reinvented in each new horizon where he is placed; he considers himself as universal without perceiving his own social, ethnic, sexual and cultural relativity and situatedness; he is never external to the world and therefore cannot judge it objectively. His memory does not retrieve the past in a transparent and fluid manner but processes and edits it into a narrative form and his language shapes, influences and produces his perception of the world. His identity, in short, is not self-defined but interpellated by ideology and guided, if not controlled, by the various dispositives of power of society and the state.

In his first portrait of the character, Rushdie curiously weaves together the two rival conceptions of the self.

> Mr Saladin Chamcha had constructed this face with care—it had taken him several years to get it just right—and for many years now he had thought of it simply as *his own*—indeed, he had forgotten what he had looked like before it. Furthermore, he had shaped himself a voice to go with the face... (33).

An *invented* and *constructed* identity is impressed in Saladin's conscience as if it had always been lodged there as "true self." Later the reasons for this operation are clarified:

> A man who sets out to make himself up is taking on the Creator's role, according to one way of seeing things; he's unnatural, a blasphemer, an abomination of abominations. From another angle, you could see pathos in him, heroism in his struggle, in his willingness to risk: not all mutants survive. Or, consider him socio-politically: most migrants learn, and can become disguises. Our own false descriptions to counter the falsehoods invented about us, concealing for reasons of security our secret selves (49).

Following another classic model such as *Tom Jones*, three women characters are made to represent three interpretations of the dilemma of identity. The English wife Pamela, chronically depressed, is incapable of thinking herself out of her identity which is static, self-referential and evokes the collective crisis of the 1960s generation. As soon as she has learned of his husband's death, she jumps in the arms of a friend, committing (unknowingly?) that adultery which was inconceivable in the English *Bildungsroman.*

At her antipodes stands Zeenat Vakil, a successful Indian doctor, a warm, positive character who attempts to reconcile Saladin with India. "Tonight ... we cracked your shell" (56), she tells him after a night of love. Her rhetoric is that of the "true [Indian] self" around which a fictitious personality has calcified and needs to be removed.

The third woman is Mimi Mamoulian, who is a colleague of Saladin. Mimi, who is Armenian and Jewish, is the perfect migrant who has learnt to accept her own condition with irony and with no apparent conflicts. When half-jokingly she suggests that they should get married, Saladin responds: "You're Jewish.' ... 'I was brought up to have views on Jews.'" She retorts: "So I'm Jewish,' ... 'You're the one who's circumcised. Nobody's perfect'" (60). Saladin is obsessed by self-definition which also consists in rigidly discriminating between self and other, and the Jew is Other both for Christians and Muslims. Mimi's quip reveals to him that a sign of that alterity which he strives to keep at distance is marked on his very body. Shortly after, that feared alterity will swallow him completely turning him into a monster.

The theme of identity surfaces in the pivotal episode of the clinic for mutants, where Saladin meets the Manticore. Borges informs us that the manticore is an anthropophagous creature, with the head of a tiger and three rows of teeth (Borges-Guerrero 1966). Here such bloodthirsty animal appears as a victim of the system who can explain his metamorphosis in these terms: "'They describe us,' the other whispered solemnly. 'That's all. They have the power of description, and we succumb to the pictures they construct'" (168). In this Foucauldian nightmare, forces that transcend the individual can control him to the extent of modifying his very body and turning him into a monster. Moretti describes the rising presence of institutions in the *Bildungsroman*, which gradually erode the space of the individual (1999: 258). Here the institution encroaches the very borders of the human body in an instance of that biopolitics which has characterized the 20th century and culminated in the Nazi concentration camp (Agamben 1995).

But stressing the fact that such a process can occur only if the victim cooperates, the Manticore leaves a decisive opening for the freedom of the individual to determine his own fate.

After fleeing from the clinic, Saladin finds refuge in the Shaandaar Café, a peripheral B&B run by an immigrant family from Dhaka. This may be one of the *neutralized spaces* which, according to Moretti, are the background of education novels (1999: 258). We may say that the European dinner gives way to the Asian breakfast, as the ritual that allows the individual to find his way in life.

The father Muhamad Sufyan is a former teacher who emigrated for political reasons. He loves to quote from Darwin, Apuleius, and above all Ovid and Lucrece, with their opposing ideas on metamorphosis and identity (276). It is at once an ironical and realistic that the high culture from which the young protagonists of the *Bildungsroman* would take their intellectual nourishment, is preserved in postmodern London by an Asian teacher demoted to coffeehouse owner. Sufyan's adolescent daughters, who wear blue-jeans and speak a disarticulate slang, represent a new generation for whom ethnic and other differences are flattened in the new urban mass culture. They are not shocked by Saladin's beastly appearance: "It's just we've been thinking, know what I mean, and well it'd just be awful if you weren't, but you are, 'course you are, so that's all right," (Mishal). "Brilliant...Magic. You know. *Extreme*" (Anahita) (258). Is this an instinctive spirit of tolerance or the endemic inability of distinguishing between simulation and reality of the MTV generation?

On the backdrop of Saladin's captivity, London is shaken by violent social and ethnic turmoil, the last aftermath of colonialism which now reverberates in the Western metropolis.

Deemed dead, betrayed by his wife, imprisoned in an animalesque body, Saladin has to reconsider his values:

> I am by nature an inward man, he said silently into the disconnected phone; I have struggled, in my fashion, to find my way towards an appreciation of high things, towards a small measure of fineness. On good days I felt it was within my grasp, somewhere within me, somewhere within. But it eluded me. I have become embroiled, in things, in the world and its messes, and I cannot resist. The grotesque has me, as before the quotidian had me, in its thrall. The sea gave me up; the land drags me down (260).

Interiority, a cardinal value in the *Bildungsroman*, turns out to be a chimera. Saladin then yields to his own condition of impure, hybrid, mutable and grotesque being: "*I am*, he accepted, *that I am*" (289). Recuperating this Biblical phrase, Rushdie also reverses the notorious words of Iago ("I am not that I am," *Othello* 1.1.64), the proto-bourgeois and proto-racist character who builds his own identity in contrast to the "barbarian" Othello.[2]

According to the philosophers Lakoff and Johnson "A large part of self-understanding is the search for appropriate personal metaphors that make sense of our lives.... The process of self-understanding is the continual development of new life stories for yourself" (1980: 233). More recently, Antal Borbely has offered psychoanalytical support to this view: "when individuals are able to integrate strong emotional experiences, they do so with increased recourse to metaphorical processes," which are opposed to "idiomatic, rigid analogical thinking" (1998: 930). We could paraphrase these observations by saying that Saladin initially made his identity depend analogically on the narrative and rhetorical patterns of the *Bildungsroman* and only when is he able to conceive alternative metaphors, to translate his own mind, he finds a way out of the translational state of his body and regains his human form.

Home. The traditional hero would leave his home in search of himself only to find that the "truth" was just in what he had left behind, and so he would return there. How come, then, that after having subverted the main parameters of the *Bildungsroman*, *The Satanic Verses* closes with the most classical homecoming and Saladin's reconciliation with his dying father?

The answer perhaps lies in the non-definitive nature of this homecoming, which does not mark the reintegration of the hero in his place of origin and the subsequent fetishization of ethnic identity. The return is an unavoidable stage because one needs to come to terms with his own roots, but Saladin does not find in Bombay any ultimate truth. After his father's death, his friend Zeeny exclaims "Let's get the hell out of here," and Saladin answers "I'm coming" (547). These are his final words in the novel.

Writing about "literature and life" Gilles Deleuze suggests that

> Sanity as literature, as writing, consists in inventing an absent people which is needed. It pertains to the fabulating function to invent a people. One does not write with his memories unless he makes of them the collective origin or destination of a people to come, still buried under its betrayals and repudiations (1993: 14, my translation).

Saladin Chamcha represents a world to come, born of the death of the Empire, out of a cataclysmic clash of civilizations, a world made of cultural fragments that struggle to find a new balance in the age of globalization.

A late epigone of David Copperfield, Chamcha walks the road of the *Bildungsroman* in reverse, moving from the illusion of an autonomous and self-sufficient subjectivity to the recognition that every individual is enmeshed—even though by no means powerless—in our modern disciplinary society.

The deformation of the *Bildungsroman* by Rushdie may be another chapter of the project theorized by Homi Bhabha:

> the postcolonial translation of modernity rests in its performative, deformative structure that does not simply revalue the contents of a cultural tradition, or transpose value 'cross-culturally.' The cultural inheritance of slavery of colonialism ... is to introduce another locus of inscription and intervention, another hybrid, 'inappropriate,' enunciative site (1994: 241-42).

Where Saladin would have gone after leaving his house in Bombay and where Rushdie would have gone after *The Satanic Verses* in his exploration of postcolonial identity are questions whose significance has been dramatically changed by the *fatwa* against the writer.

NOTES

1. An earlier version of this essay was published in Italian as "*The Satanic Verses* come romanzo di (de)formazione," in *Anglistica e...: metodi e percorsi comparatistici nelle lingue, culture e letterature di origine europea.* Volume I: *Transiti letterari e culturali. Atti del XVIII Convegno dell'Associazione Italiana di Anglistica, Genova*, edited by Giuseppe Sertoli and Goffredo Miglietta, Edizioni Università di Trieste, Trieste, 1999.
2. Saladin's statement is followed by the word 'Submission,' which may stand for the acceptance of the new condition but is also the translation of 'Islam.' An allusion to another fundamental component of Saladin's identity which we can now only mention in passing.
3. Cfr. Lima 1993: 454. From a postcolonial perspective the house offers "an illusion of coherence and safety based on the exclusion of specific histories of oppression and resistance and on the oppression of differences even with oneself." B. Martine C. T. Mohanty, cit. in Lima, 1993: 439.

WORKS CITED

Agamben, Giorgio. 1995. *Homo Sacer*. Torino: Einaudi.

Arendt, Hannah. 1975. *The Origins of Totalitarianism*. London: Harcourt, Brace and Company.

Barney, Richard A. "Subjectivity, the Novel, and the *Bildung* Blocks of Critical Theory." *Genre* 26 (Winter): 359-75.

Bassi, Shaul. 1999. "Salman Rushdie's Special Effects." *Coterminous Worlds: Magical Realism and Post-Colonial Anglophone Literature*. Eds. Elsa Linguanti et al. Rodopi, Amsterdam & Atlanta: Cross/Cultures. 47-60.

Bhabha, Homi K. 1994. *The Location of Culture.* London: Routledge.

Borbely, Antal F. 1998. "A Psychoanalytic Concept of Metaphor." *International Journal of Psychoanalysis* 79: 923-36.

Borges, Jorge Luis-Monica Guerrero. 1966. *Manual de zoologia fantastica*. Mexico: Fondo de Cultura Economica.

Chandra, Sudhir. 1992. *The Oppressive Present: Literature and Social Consciousness in Colonial India*. Delhi: Oxford UP.

Deleuze, Gilles. 1993. *Critique et clinique*. Paris: Minuit.

Hennard Dutheil de la Rochère, Martine. 1999. *Origin and Originality in Rushdie's Fiction*. Bern: Peter Lang.

Kabbani, Rana. 1986 *Europe's Myths of Orient.* London: Pandora Press.

Kalinnikova, Elena J. 1982. *Indian-English Literature: A Perspective*. Ghaziabad: Vimal Prakashan.

Lakoff, George-Mark Johnson. 1980. *Metaphors We Live By*. Chicago: U of Chicago P.

Lima, Maria Helena. 1993. "Decolonizing Genre: Jamaica Kincaid and the *Bildungsroman.*" *Genre* 26 (Winter): 431-59.

Lukács, György. 1978. *The Theory of the Novel*. London: Merlin Press.

Moretti, Franco. 1987. *The Way of the World: The Bildungsroman in European Culture*. London: Verso.

Moretti, Franco. 1999. *Il romanzo di formazione.* Rev. Ed. Torino: Einaudi.

Rajan, Rajeswari S. 1992. *The Lie of the Land: English Literary Studies in India.* Delhi: Oxford UP.

Rushdie, Salman. 1982. "The Empire Writes Back with a Vengeance." *The Times* 3 July.

Rushdie, Salman. 1988. *The Satanic Verses*. London: Viking.

Said, Edward. 1994. *Culture and Imperialism*. London: Vintage.

Viswanathan, Gauri. 1989. *Masks of Conquest*: *Literary Study and British Rule in India*. New York: Columbia UP.

8

Rushdie's Un-Indian Music: *The Ground Beneath Her Feet*

CHRISTOPHER ROLLASON*

> "This book[1] is not a novel about rock'n'roll, but an attempt to respond to the evolution of world culture in the last half-century."
>
> (Rushdie to *Le Monde*, 1999[2])

Prologue

In 1968, from the symbolically radical location of the French capital's *rive gauche*, no less a critic than Roland Barthes proclaimed the death of the author.[3] Following on from the "death of God" announced by Nietzsche close on a century before, the iconoclastic Gallic philosopher laid the "Author-God" to rest,[4] arguing that the literary text henceforth belonged not to its writer but to its readers, who now had the right to interpret its words multiply and at will: "the birth of the reader comes at the price of the death of the Author."[5] This gesture ushered in an era of text-centered, anti-intentionist, anti-biographical criticism, the underlying tenet being that the reader's dynamic appropriation and rehandling of the text necessitated no reference whatever to the details of the writer's life.

Twenty-one years later, in Tehran on 14th February 1989, the death of the author, or, at least, of one individual author, was decreed in a rather less symbolic fashion by Ayatollah Khomeini: "[...] the author of the book entitled *The Satanic Verses*, which has been compiled, printed and published in opposition to Islam, the

*17 Avenue Foch 4EME, 57000 Metz, France.

prophet and the Qur'an, as well as those publishers who were aware of its contents, have been declared [...] those whose blood must be shed,"[6] Khomeini thus unwittingly countered Barthes' anarchic radicalism with a stern return to tradition. The English translation of his fatwa seems to imply that a text—in this case, Rushdie's novel—has only one meaning ("opposition to Islam") and is "compiled" by its author with a single intention that is totally consonant with that one meaning; and that the author bears full responsibility for his or her text—a responsibility that may light an unfortunate author all the way to dusty death. The Shi'ite cleric's edict unleashed a battle of the books—indeed, a war that involved not two but three texts—*The Satanic Verses*, the Koran, and his own fatwa. Few observers noticed a certain curious detail—the incontrovertible circumstance that the Ayatollah could not, when he made his ruling, possibly have read *The Satanic Verses*, a book which then existed only in English, a language in which he could not have handled a complex and allusive postmodernist novel. Similarly, only a minority of the neo-Zhdanovite,[7] pro-censorship lobby in Britain who subsequently demanded the banning of Rushdie's novel had actually read it—though that small matter did not stop them calling for its suppression in the name of political correctness, in an epidemic of moral absolutism worthy of their Puritan forbears. It appeared that Roland Barthes' notion of an infinitely fecund text, permanently reinterpreted by its readers, was in serious danger of succumbing to a rigid, theocratic notion of a text which, imbued with a single, self-evident, and authorially signified "meaning," manifests itself in identical fashion to all, readers and non-readers alike.

Another decade passed, and while Khomeini was now dead, Salman Rushdie was still alive. Political correctness had continued its advances in the West, but no OECD country, with the predictable exception of Turkey, had banned *The Satanic Verses*—not even Britain, despite the best efforts of certain politicians on the left.[8] In 1999, Rushdie published *The Ground Beneath Her Feet*, a novel in which he visibly aims to revisit the theme of the death of the author—this time, by drinking from the wellsprings of Western culture, from the Greco-Roman tradition and the myth of Orpheus, the archetypal poet-musician. For that tale ends with the spilling of a poet's blood: Orpheus is killed by a vengeful band of would-be followers. Such is the mythical destiny around which Rushdie has consciously woven this new fiction, ten years on from the fatwa.

1

From this point on, I shall return to Barthes, as far as is still possible today, and endeavour to read and interpret *The Ground Beneath Her Feet* with only incidental reference to the fatwa or to Rushdie's personal life, although I shall take due account of certain of the author's opinions, as expressed in articles and interviews, as well as of his other literary works. As the French critic Guy Astic stressed in 1996, "the Indo-British writer is not an individual defined by a single work, nor is he just the face of a fatwa [...] we have to examine Salman Rushdie's work as a whole."[9] I shall take it as axiomatic that a literary text is to be read primarily as text—as a piece of writing that exists in dialogue with other texts, as well as with the wider series of texts surrounding it that we know as history—a history that, obviously, does not exclude Khomeini's edict or the PC lobby's burn-it-and-ban-it campaign, but also ranges far deeper and wider in time and place, transcending all such narrow ideological concerns.

The Ground Beneath Her Feet (hereinafter referred to as *GF*) is based on what might be called a literary-musical conceit: the reader is asked to suspend disbelief and accept the notion that—to quote Rushdie himself, from an interview with the Madrid daily *El País*—"the world's two most famous rock stars are both Indian,"[10] Rushdie's two fictional stars are Ormus Cama, born into an old Bombayite Zoroastrian family in 1937, and Vina Apsara, born in the US in 1944 to an Indian father and a Greek-American mother, raised there till her parents die in 1956, and then sent "home" to India. She and Ormus, then aged nineteen, meet in a Bombay record shop. The two migrate in the 60s to London, where they form the group VTO (the reader never learns what those initials stand for) and achieve stellar success. Ormus writes the lyrics; both sing. The two megastars fall in and out of love, move to the US and go on notching up super platinum sales worldwide through the 70s and most of the 80s, in VTO until the group breaks up and afterwards as solo artists. After Vina's death in 1989, in an earthquake in

Mexico, Ormus carries on, despite increasing psychological instability, until one winter's morning when a crazed woman fan kills him in New York. The whole saga is narrated in the first person by another Bombayite, Rai Merchant, an internationally known photographer of secular Muslim origins who bears within himself a second, secret identity as Vina's occasional non-platonic confidant.

One of the distorting effects of the *Satanic Verses* controversy has been to cast Rushdie as a writer defined essentially in relation to Islam. This is, in reality, only partially the case if we consider his fictional work as a whole. *Shame*, certainly, is a novel about Pakistan, and the protagonists of *Midnight's Children* (hereinafter *MC*) and *The Satanic Verses* (hereinafter *SV*), and, indeed, the narrator of *GF*, are of Muslim origin, albeit secularised to a greater or lesser degree. However, it is far more illuminative to view Rushdie less as a product of Islam than as the chronicler in fiction of the Indian subcontinent in the twentieth century—and of that subcontinent's relations with the wider world.

Rushdie's fictional production thus far may be roughly classified into two modes, magic-realist and fantastic, with the former predominating. His first novel, *Grimus* (1975), set in the imaginary location of Calf Island, is cast in the fantastic mode throughout, and he revisits that dimension in the central part of *Haroun and the Sea of Stories* (1990) and in the final section of *The Moor's Last Sigh* (1995; hereinafter "*Moor*"), whose nominal Spanish setting reads more like an arbitrary dream-world. For the rest, Rushdie's writing is magic-realist with the main emphasis on the realist component, located either wholly or mostly in the Indian subcontinent and with the explicit presence of real, if partially distorted historical events. This is the pattern established in *MC* (1981) and repeated in *Shame* (1983), *SV* (1988), and the first three-quarters of *Moor*. The subcontinent is narrated, not as a closed-in, autarkic universe, but in its dynamic interaction with the rest of the world—with the West and beyond—from the colonial period through Independence and Partition to the era of globalisation: *MC*, *Shame* and *Moor* all range in chronology from the Raj-era early twentieth century to the actual time of writing, a pattern which is repeated in *GF*. The action of *MC* takes in India, Pakistan and Bangladesh, and while not straying topographically outside the subcontinent, introduces British and American colonials and expatriates; *Shame* focuses on Pakistan but includes episodes in Britain; *Moor* is set in its first three sections in India, again including turn-of-the-century colonials in its cast, before spiraling out at the end to an invented Spain. A somewhat different logic is followed in *SV*, which, based squarely in the contemporary world and centred on Indian characters, situates the bulk of its action in London, with forays to Bombay and, briefly, to Argentina, while also, crucially, featuring a series of dreams: some located in an Indian village, others—as, notoriously, even the book's non-readers know—set in a simulacrum of the Hejaz in the time of the Prophet; while the short stories collected in *East, West* (1994), read in order, take the reader from the subcontinent to an Asian émigrés' London. In all Rushdie's fictions other than *Grimus* and *Haroun*, invented characters coexist with historical figures; the latter appear either under their own names or disguised and satirised but still clearly recognisable (the Gandhis in *MC*, the Bhuttos and Zia Ul-Haq in *Shame*, Bal Thackrey in *Moor*). All in all, Rushdie's fictional production prior to *GF*, taken as a whole, may be read as constituting an imaginative model of the Indian subcontinent within twentieth-century history, a latter-day Asian equivalent, albeit on a smaller scale, to what Honoré de Balzac did for nineteenth-century France in his monumental *Comédie Humaine.*

GF follows the pre-established pattern—up to a point, and with significant divergences. The two protagonists and the narrator are, as before, Indian, or at least half-Indian, while Rushdie pays obeisance to his own previous work by discreet use of the device (again harking back to Balzac) of recurring characters: the Englishman William Methwold, who plays a key part in *GF*, has walked in from *MC*, and Homi Catrack, also from that novel, and Aurora Zogoiby, from *Moor*, are resurrected for bit-parts. In terms of fictional chronology, *GF* begins, like its predecessors, in the Raj of the early twentieth century; in narrative sequence, however, it opens in 1989, in Guadalajara, Mexico, with the earthquake and Vina's dramatic disappearance, before shifting back, in reverse mode, to the characters' Indian past. The bulk of the novel does, however, approximately observe an linear chronology, with the notable circumstance, new in Rushdie, that halfway through the action moves definitively to the West—to Britain, then the US—with virtually no subsequent revisiting of the subcontinent (Vina, Beatles-like, spends a brief spell in a ashram;[11] a planned tour of India by Ormus falls victim to a government ban[12]). The East-West alternation model of *SV* has been ditched in *GF*, in favour of a sequential model: the reader watches East being replaced by West as the epicenter.

2

This change in spatial priorities has been admitted by Rushdie himself, with specific reference to Bombay, the city which has been so important to his writing in the past. Bombay, or as we now have officially to call it, Mumbai (the recent, ideologically-motivated change of name was actually predicted by Rushdie himself, in his quasi-historical account of the Hindu-particularistic "Mumbai's Axis" movement in *Moor*) has played a part in his work which may be compared to that of Paris in Balzac. *MC* opens with the narrator, Saleem Sinai, declaring: "I was born in the city of Bombay [...] in Doctor Narlikar's Nursing Home on August 15th, 1947,"[13] *SV* ends with Saladin Chamcha's return to the Maharashtrian metropolis: "He stood at the window of his childhood and looked out at the Arabian Sea";[14] the narrator of *Moor*, Moraes Zogoiby, laments the decline of his once-latitudinarian home city into shallow sectarianism: "Bombay was central; had always been. [...] now barbarism was standing at our gates. O Bombay! Prima in Indis! Gateway to India! Star of the East with her face to the West!"[15] Of course, other contemporary Indian or "Indo-Anglian" writers as well as Rushdie have centred their fictional imaginings around Bombay-Mumbai: notable examples include Anita Desai's *Baumgartner's Bombay* (1988), Vikram Chandra's *Love and Longing in Bombay* (1997), and, indeed, the best-selling Shobha Dé's Bollywood saga *Starry Nights* (1991). However, the city returns in Rushdie's pages with a special insistence, as the symbol of a specifically Indian version of multiplicity, tolerance and (in the subcontinental sense) cosmopolitanism; as Roshan G. Shahani put it in 1994, "Bombay's infinite variety, its paradoxes and contradictions [...] mirror and account for the heterogeneous presence and the polyphonous voices of the 'Bombay writers'"[16]—among whom Shahani highlights

Rushdie, for whom the city "had encapsulated this country's multicultural diversity and its secular ideology."[17] In *GF*, we find Rushdie re-treading the city's streets—indeed, Rai Merchant's father turns out to be an amateur Bombayologist: "Bombay. Don't ask. I could pass any exam you care to set [...] My father liked digging into place names, so allow me to inform you, just off the top of my head, that Chinchpokli is 'tamarind hollow' and Cumballa Hill is named after the lotus flower and Bhendhi Bazaar is situated where once the ladies'-fingers grew."[18] In the end, however, this evocation of Bombay comes over as a valediction, as the centre of gravity of Rushdie's world shifts (irrevocably?) to the US: Rushdie, indeed, has said as much, in an interview with Laura Miller in the on-line magazine *Salon*:[19] "I think I really have said what I had to say about that city, and I don't want to repeat myself [...] I think I've done it." Whether this apparent abandonment of his subcontinental roots for the glittering surfaces of globalisation makes for a real gain is an open question. Shahani states that "by writing about Bombay, writers like Rushdie have charted anew the cultural map of the world;"[20] it remains to be seen if those who cut loose from India can still keep their bearings or read that global "cultural map" with their old acuity.

3

Throughout *GF*, Rushdie deploys his customary artillery of literary, historical and intellectual references, from Karl Marx and Charles Baudelaire through to William Faulkner and Jorge Luis Borges, but, at the same time, gives centre stage to a form of popular or mass culture, namely rock music. His reasons for choosing this theme are no doubt multiple. One is that as a long-standing rock'n'roll fan (from the moment when, as a Bombay adolescent, he bought a much-prized copy of Elvis Presley's 45 rpm record "Heartbreak Hotel"[21]), he has an expert's knowledge of the field. Another may be, as Carla Power hypothesised in *Newsweek*, the circumstance that Rushdie can himself be considered "a household name [...] literature's first global celebrity—as famous as a pop star."[22] In addition, there are partial precedents in his earlier work. Specifically subcontinental popular-cultural forms are present in *MC*, where Saleem's sister, the "Brass Monkey," becomes, as

Jamila Singer, a highly-regarded popular vocalist in post-independence Pakistan, and another of Saleem's relatives works in the Bollywood film world; while in *SV*, Gibreel Farishta is one of India's greatest celluloid heartthrobs, and, indeed, the all-too-controversial dreams that haunt him when he undergoes psychiatric treatment have the unfortunate star imagining himself playing the lead role in a filmic reinterpretation of the founding years of Islam.

If we step outside the subcontinental mass-cultural orbit and enter that of the West, we discover a fair number of rock-music allusions in Rushdie's writing prior to *GF*. In *Grimus*, one of the main characters is called Bird Dog, after an Everly Brothers hit from 1958: "When I was your age I went into the town, she said, and listened at a window outside an eating-place. There was a singing machine there. It sang about a creature called a bird-dog, clever, fiendish.."[23] An article of 1990 on the novelist Thomas Pynchon (reprinted in the essay collection *Imaginary Homelands*) features the phrase "days of miracle and wonder," which comes from "The Boy in the Bubble," a song by Paul Simon from his *Graceland* album of 1986.[24] In "The Courter," the concluding story of *East, West* (1994), the narrator, an Indian adolescent growing up in London in the 60s, listens avidly to rock'n'roll on the radio, and, in an ironic detail, confesses: "London, W8 was Sam Cooke's country that summer. Another Saturday night [...] I was down with lonely Sam in the lower depths of the charts [...] How I wish I had someone to talk to,/I'm in an awful way"[25]; it so happens that Cooke's hit, "Another Saturday Night," returned to the charts in the 70s, in a cover version by Cat Stevens—a Anglo-Greek singer who later abandoned international stardom, converted to the Muslim religion, changed his name to Yusuf Islam and [...] became a particularly virulent defender of Khomeini's fatwa.

To mention Cat Stevens in this way is not purely anecdotal, for it is this kind of surprising connection that illuminates the globalised nature of culture today. Rushdie, as an émigré writer with a foot in both Eastern and Western worlds, is himself clearly both product and exponent of that globalisation; and that phenomenon affects, not only (and as is notorious) mass culture, but high culture too. If both high and mass culture now operate on a planetary scale, their inevitable interaction can only become more intricate and more complex. In this context, a prominent aspect of Rushdie's writing in *GF* is his endeavour, on the level of the text, to confer a degree of solidity and credibility on that rock music world which some Olympian intellectuals would dismiss as, always and necessarily, innately trivial and insubstantial. Rushdie explained his position to *Le Monde* on 1 October 1999: "Most pop music is purely intended to make money and then disappear. [...] But if you take the other end of pop music, the best of the last forty years [...] you have to take it seriously,"[26] similarly, in the *Salon* interview he stated: "I wanted to take this [rock'n'roll] world and treat it seriously as a vehicle to examine our life and times."[27] With this in view, he adopts two main strategies: the dignification of his subject through the Orpheus myth; and the incorporation of a rock'n'roll sensibility into the texture of his writing, via wholesale quotation from song lyrics.

4

To take the second-named strategy first, a close reading of Rushdie's text reveals a remarkable density of song references. Song titles, album titles, individual lines and phrases from songs: all abound in this book's pages. Some are quoted au pied de la lettre, others are reshaped; some are attributed to their historical authors, some are deliberately misattributed, others still are left unflagged. To these real or modified-real song texts should be added the imaginary lyrics of Ormus Cama's songs, extracts from which are "quoted" at length. The heterogeneous nature of these quotations and allusions fits in with Rushdie's general method in *GF*: throughout, literary texts and authors, historical events, etc., are alluded to with a magpie eclecticism that by no means always recognises the dictatorship of fact. In Rushdie's reordered universe, John and Robert Kennedy are killed together by the same Palestinian gunman;[28] Britain's Labour government sends troops out to Vietnam;[29] and The Garden of Forking Paths is not an imaginary novel existing only in Borges' story of that name, but a real book, Vina's "favourite nineteenth-century novel."[30] The same rewriting of history applies to the novel's rock'n'roll world. The song "Feelin' Groovy" is attributed not to the real Paul Simon and Art (Arthur) Garfunkel, but, punningly and absurdly, to an invented duo of the real (but female) Carly Simon and the non-existent Guinevere Garfunkel.[31] Again, we are told that in a series of "solidarity concerts" held circa 1974 to protest Ormus' threatened deportation from the US, "Dylan, Lennon, [Janis] Joplin, Joni [Mitchell], Country Joe and the Fish turn up to sing for Ormus,"[32] although, even had Ormus Cama really existed, one of those artists, Ms Joplin, could hardly have turned up, as she had died of an overdose in 1970.

The song micro-texts that are embedded in Rushdie's macro-text, wherever they stand on the real-to-imaginary spectrum, are clearly offered as an integral part of this novel's global textual project—and, as such, call for detailed elucidation. Their presence is already announced in the book's chapter-headings: chapter 10, "Season of the Witch," takes its title from a 60s song by Donovan, and the title of chapter 13, "Transformer," is also the name of a Lou Reed album from 1972. The rock-generation singer-songwriters whose words or titles are quoted, straight or askew, across Rushdie's text include Paul Simon, Joni Mitchell, Carole King, Randy Newman, Tom Waits and, notably, Bob Dylan (in view of the central issues it raises, I shall consider Rushdie's use of Dylan in a separate section[33]). To cite examples, the phrase "the hissing of summer lawns"[34] is the title of a 1975 album (and song) by Joni Mitchell, while "I feel the earth move under my feet"[35] quotes the title and first line of a 1972 song by Carole King. At one moment, Vina and Ormus (accurately) quote, paraphrase and dissect Randy Newman's song " Sail Away," also from 1972.[36] At another, Vina puts on a disc: "This is the CD she plays: Rain dogs, the honky-tonk blues as reinvented and growled out by Lee Baby Simms. She starts singing along with Simms, long and slow, and the hair rises on my neck. Will I see you again/on a downtown train."[37] Here, rock fact and fiction intertwine: the lines Vina sings are slightly misquoted from "Downtown Train," a song which indeed appears on an album called *Rain Dogs* (spelt thus), released in 1985 not by the non-existent Lee Baby Simms, but by Tom Waits.

On occasion, Rushdie steps back in time to raid older songwriting traditions. Vina recalls the blues singer Ma Rainey ("I go back a century to ugly Ma Rainey preaching Trust No Man"[38])—but gets her chronology wrong, since the historical Rainey flourished in the 1920s; and when Ormus declares: "Like a mole in the ground I will root this mountain down," his words are virtually a direct quotation from the traditional song "I Wish I Was A Mole in the Ground," recorded in 1928 by an obscure Appalachian folk-blues singer, Bascom Lamar Lunsford.[39] The text even once quotes from the repertory of French-language chanson, with a pun ("she was predictably called the pornographer of the phonograph"[40]) which must have come from Georges Brassens' song of 1958 "Le Pornographe" ("J'suis l'pornographe/Du phonographe/Le polisson/De la chanson"). Despite these instances, however, the great majority of Rushdie's song quotations and references are to Anglo-American lyrics of the 60s and 70s.

5

Nonetheless, if Rushdie's musical vision is largely bound to a particular time, place and genre, he still wishes to claim universality for it: and here his reanimation of the Orpheus myth comes into action. The reader may not object to being reminded of the story, in the refined form which it eventually assumed in the ancient world and which has provided the "Orpheus template" for later generations in the West. Orpheus is the archetypal poet and musician of the Greco-Roman world, begotten by the god Apollo, himself famed for his prowess on the lyre, on Calliope, the Muse of epic poetry. Orpheus' haunting voice and plangent lyre had the power to subjugate nature: as Shakespeare put it centuries later, he "made trees/And the mountains that did freeze/Bow themselves when he did sing."[41] Soon after the poet's marriage to Eurydice, his young bride died from a snake-bite as she was fleeing the unwanted advances of Aristaeus, a bee-keeper. The inconsolable Orpheus went down into Hell to get her back and charmed the powers of the underworld into accepting his outrageous demand, subject to one condition: he must walk out of Hell ahead of her, and must not look back till both of them were safely within the sunlight. He looked back at the very last minute and lost her forever. Inconsolably mourning his twice-lost bride, he vowed never to touch a woman again. This incurred the wrath of the Maenads, the crazed women devotees of the god Dionysus, and one day, feeling provoked beyond endurance, a band of them seized on the recalcitrant poet and tore him to pieces. They cast his limbs and head into the river;

and yet the severed head went on singing. The Muses gathered his remains and buried him; the gods placed his lyre in the stars as a constellation. The martyred poet lived on posthumously into recorded history, as the inspirer of a devotional cult, whose initiates were called the Orphics; at some point in the sixth to fourth centuries BC, there emerged from their circles the "Orphic hymns," a set of panegyrics to the gods which remain extant today.

Only two full versions of this legend have come down to us from the ancient world, both by Roman poets—Virgil in the *Georgics* (29 BC; Book Four),[42] and, later, Ovid in the *Metamorphoses* (8 AD; Books Ten and Eleven).[43] There is a very clear latter-day summary by the American Thomas Bulfinch, in *The Age of Fable*[44] (1855), and a more speculative modern synthesis, with analytic commentary, by Robert Graves in *The Greek Myths*[45] (1955). I shall use Virgil's version—the one essentially followed by Rushdie—as my reference point. Although Orpheus is most certainly a figure of Greek origin, associated with Thrace, no complete account of his story by an ancient Greek writer has survived; passing references appear in, for instance, Euripides' *Alcestis* (438 BC)[46] and Plato's *Symposium* (c. 370 BC).[47] Euripides speaks of "the Thracian inscriptions/Written down from the voice of Orpheus,"[48] a handful of these have survived, as have eighty-seven Orphic hymns. This material, all written in Greek, has recently been collected in a French translation, carefully edited by Jacques Lacarrière; only one of the hymns, however, actually mentions the legendary poet's name (as a putative "signature" in the last line,[49] and none tells his story. Graves, while underlining Orpheus' status for the ancients as "the most famous poet and musician who ever lived," notes that "Eurydice's death by snake-bite and Orpheus's subsequent failure to bring her back into the sunlight figure only in late myth."[50] This view is confirmed by Lacarrière, who calls the Eurydice episode as it stands in the *Georgics* (with Aristaeus and the serpent) a "fable invented by Virgil," adding that "the name of Eurydice, as Orpheus' wife, appears only very late in ancient literature" and noting that "Plato and Euripides knew the myth of Orpheus' descent into hell in search of his wife, but did not name her."[51] Virgil's canonic version of the story seems even to be an afterthought—a bypath from the main highway of the *Georgics* (essentially a poetic treatise on agriculture), an interpolation into a digression which may have been dictated less by literary choices than by political events in the Rome of Augustus.[52]

The Orpheus-Eurydice story, with its long history of reverberation across Western culture, seems then, ironically, to have appeared in its now-familiar form almost by chance. Lacarrière does, however, stress Orpheus' key importance to the ancients as the archetype of the artist as initiate, a human in intimate contact with the forces of death and darkness:

> What assured Orpheus his glory and eternity in Greece (and later in the West) was [...] the power he was believed to have of exorcising death by his songs, the power that allowed him to descend alive into hell and then return. Having been able to confront and conquer the darkness, he came to symbolise the initiate, the master of the beyond, the messenger of immortality [...] the poems, the music, the message of Orpheus [had the role of] awakening humans, revealing their true selves by opening up before them the path to immortality.[53]

Across Rushdie's text, references to the Orpheus myth come thick and fast, starting with the novel's very title (which suggests the ground trembling beneath Eurydice's feet as she descends into hell) and the holographic lyre on the front dust-jacket of the British edition. Rushdie appears to see his musician protagonists as manifestations of the Orphic principle of the indestructibility of music; in the *El País* interview, he declares: "the myth of Orpheus tells us that you can kill the singer, but not the song."[54] The Ormus-Vina saga is preceded by an epigraph from Rainer Maria Rilke's *Sonnets to Orpheus* (1923)—"Once and for all/it's Orpheus when there's singing";[55] Virgil's "extraordinary" version of the myth is summarised;[56] Plato's commentary, too, is paraphrased, with Orpheus seen by Rai Merchant as "the singer with the lyre or, let's say, guitarist—the trickster who uses his music and wiles to cross boundaries";[57] on stage, after Vina's death, Ormus impersonates Orpheus as part of his act;[58] even his recording studio in New York is baptised "the Orpheum."[59]

Unfortunately, it may be seriously doubted whether very much is achieved by these and the numerous other textual references to the Virgilian myth. The analogy between the Ormus-Vina and Orpheus-Eurydice pairs proves, on closer inspection, to be at best rather forced, and at worst downright vague. Ormus is, certainly, a celebrated musician like Orpheus, but Vina too is a musician—a role which Eurydice is not known to have filled. Vina's earthquake death, however spectacular, scarcely resembles Eurydice's: on her last night in Mexico, she dreams, it is true, of a serpent, but it is the god Quetzalcoatl, "the plumed serpent,"[60] and Raúl Páramo, the ephemeral partner with whom she spends that night, is no Aristaeus-like unwanted admirer, as the relationship, if superficial, is clearly consensual ("she had surrendered herself to this nobody ... had selected him more or less at random from the backstage throng"[61]), and her intimacy with Ormus is by then over. Ormus, does, for a long time after Vina's decease, do his utmost to deny it, but his refusal to accept reality comes over as a near-pathological delusion, not a hero's endeavour to reverse nature's law ("they could see how hard he was trying to get there, maybe some world through a gash in the air, some variant dimension where Vina was still alive"[62]). His denial of death takes on, with this notion of a "variant dimension," a science-fictional aspect which, strangely, has Rushdie returning to the somewhat dubious experimental mode of *Grimus* ("The pain is caused by one's first experience of the Outer Dimensions. Suddenly universe dissolves, and for a fraction of time you are simply a small bundle of energy adrift in a sea of unimaginably vast forces"[63]). The reader will, however, search in vain for an episode that might approximate to Orpheus' descent into hell and his attempt to undo his consort's death; Ormus heals his wounds with generalised denials, searching for substitute Vinas, and bringing fake Vinas on stage. Finally, the Indian star meets his end, not from a group of frustrated would-be admirers, but a single demented fan, "a tall dark-skinned woman with red hair gathered above her head like a fountain"[64]: this could perhaps be a solitary Maenad, but the violent death and the assassin's gender still provide only a sketchy and incomplete parallel with the fate of the Thracian bard.

All in all, if Ormus does in any substantive sense resemble Orpheus, it can only be insofar as the text presents him as the artist-initiate, nourishing his creativity at the fount of dark, mysterious forces—a daemonic element which comes to the fore in the paranormal communication which the patient reader is asked to believe Ormus maintains with his dead twin Gayomart, the alleged ghostly inspirer of some of the most celebrated Anglo-American songs of the 60s. This "Gayomart conceit," which will be looked at in detail below, will itself prove to be far from unproblematic; the alert reader has no choice but to ask whether Rushdie's much-vaunted "rewriting" of the Orpheus myth is in reality little more than a forced, arbitrary and far-fetched set of doubtful part-analogies.

6

If the Ormus-Vina musical couple ostensibly derive part of their energy from the Orpheus-Eurydice dyad, the story does not end there: other analogies, far more recent, also populate the narrative. Those addicted to the *roman a clef* school of criticism have, predictably, had a field day trying to train spot which Anglophone rock stars Ormus and Vina might be modelled on. In so dense and allusive a text, both can only be composite figures, not fictionalisations of singer X or Y; nonetheless, a brief consideration of possible models does have its interest, as it may help understanding of the precise nature of the cultural hybridation that Rushdie appears to be propounding in this novel.

For a start, neither is modelled on an Indian singer: I shall return to this point below, in the discussion of "world music," but it may be stressed here that only one rock artist of (ultimately) South Asian origin has ever achieved international stardom, and that was the late Freddie Mercury, the lead singer of Queen, who is mentioned in the novel[65] but whose music Rushdie has explicitly said he detests.[66] Mercury was, in fact, born Farrokh Bulsara in Zanzibar in 1946, to parents who were British subjects but had their roots in Bombay's Zoroastrian community, and spent most of his childhood in Bombay before moving to Britain in 1963: this circumstance may, despite Rushdie's views on Queen's music, have provided a hint for the Ormus idea. Reviewers have tended to see Ormus as a cross between Presley (a raw talent manipulated by the rock business), Lennon (threatened with expulsion from the US; murdered by a psychopath) and Dylan (poet laureate of modern music).[67] Those three giants of twentieth-century song clearly are all there behind Ormus, and I shall examine the particularly important Dylan connection in some detail in the next section.

The case of Vina is actually more problematic: the genius and originality of Presley, Lennon and Dylan is beyond doubt, but Rushdie's fictional diva seems only to have been compared by the reviewers to certain women artists of undoubted commercial projection but zero musical value, whose names are not even worth mentioning. There is repeated stress across the text on the extraordinary quality of Vina's voice ("she was a great river, which could bear us all away"[68]), and it may seem best to conclude that she stands for a female creative principle which has never quite manifested itself in rock music in the shape of a truly talented woman singer as world-famous as Lennon or Presley. Possible models do exist, in the shape of US women singers who have had such a voice: two candidates might be the late Laura Nyro, of Italian-American origin, and the Mexican-American Linda Ronstadt—both remarkably gifted vocalists in full control of their material, and both hyphenated Americans like Vina, but neither of whose trajectories especially resembles hers. Rushdie himself, in the *Salon* interview,[69] half-suggests Grace Slick, the full-throated lead singer of the 60s group Jefferson Airplane, but again the analogy is not close. A more intriguing possibility surfaces at the beginning of the novel, when, just before the fatal earthquake, the reader learns for the first time of "that celestial voice of hers, that multiple-octave, Yma Sumac stairway to heaven of an instrument."[70] Yma Sumac was a Peruvian singer who claimed to be a lineally-descended Inca princess and achieved major US and international success in the 50s; as a curious intertextual aside, it may be noted that one of her songs bore the title "Earthquake,"[71] while one critic of the time wrote of her four-octave voice: "There is no voice like it in the world today [...] It soars into the acoustic stratosphere, or it plumbs sub-contralto depths of pitch with equal ease."[72] This connection, if developed, could have helped make Vina-the-voice something less of an all-American phenomenon, but, regrettably, Rushdie's text does not—as will be shown below—develop this "world music" dimension to its full potential. For the most part, his Ormus and Vina are stuck firmly within the Anglo-American rock-music mainstream.

7

One key influence on the figure of Ormus remains to be considered, which leads the reader into areas other than rock'n'roll pure and simple, and that is the question of Rushdie's singer-songwriter's resemblances to Bob Dylan. The Jewish-American Dylan (born Robert Allen Zimmerman in 1941, into a family which had left Odessa—then in Russia, now in Ukraine—in 1875) is, beyond doubt, both the most celebrated and the most talented example of the modern singer-songwriter. Dylan's work eludes the category of songwriting pure and simple, to trespass boldly on the terrain of literature: his close associates have included not just fellow popular musicians but writers like Allen Ginsberg and Sam Shepard, his song texts have been subjected to sustained and detailed literary analysis,[73] and he is the only practitioner of the singer-songwriter genre to have been proposed (in 1997, 1998 and 1999) for the Nobel Prize for Literature—a distinction which, indeed, he shares with Salman Rushdie.

Dylan's presence in *GF* is undeniable: Rushdie explains in the *Salon* interview that he wanted to honour rock'n'roll with its "best-case portrait: Bob Dylan," adding:

> Dylan is very important to me because I think along with Paul Simon, he is probably the greatest songwriter [...] other than Lennon and McCartney [...] of the last many decades. I remember first hearing early Dylan when I was still at boarding school in England and being astonished. I'd never heard anyone write like that in a song, this fantastically impressionistic but also savage writing, which was completely complemented by his phrasing and his voice.[74]

Dylan is certainly one of the models behind Ormus: in the *Le Monde* interview, to his interlocutor's assertion that "the character of Ormus borrows a lot from Dylan," Rushdie replies: "If you want to invent a rock God, there are only a limited number of models!"[75] Indeed, several references to Dylan appear in Rushdie's earlier work; the songwriter's influence on the novelist has been pointed out in a critical study, the French-language volume *Salman Rushdie* (1996) by Marc Porée and Alexis Massery.[76] In *The Jaguar Smile*, Rushdie's documentary record of his visit to Nicaragua in 1986, he tells how an acquaintance informs him he has visited Mobile,

Alabama—upon which, confesses Rushdie, "Dylan started to sing 'Stuck inside of Mobile' in my head."[77] Dylan reappears in the 1990 essay on Thomas Pynchon (mentioned earlier with reference to Paul Simon), which contains a direct quotation of the songwriter's celebrated line from 1963: "The answer is blowin' in the wind."[78] Most intriguingly, in no less a novel than *SV*, Saladin Chamcha attends an event at the Brickhall Friends Meeting House, London, at which "a pretty young British Asian woman with a slightly-too-bulbous nose and a dirty, bluesy voice was launching into Bob Dylan's song, I Pity the Poor Immigrant."[79]

Given these antecedents, it is neither surprising nor fortuitous that the text of Rushdie's rock'n'roll novel should, on close examination, yield up a whole rich vein of Dylan references, analogies and quotations. Dylan's name appears in *GF* all of three times, all in the book's American section; in the most significant of these, Ormus' ever-more spectacular shows are described as precursors of "the whole multiple-image videorama which is now the staple fare of stadium rock but in those days gave people the kind of shock Bob Dylan did when he went electric" (this is a historically correct allusion to Dylan's electric performance at the Newport Folk Festival in 1965, which famously offended the folk purists).[80] In addition, the text of *GF* reveals a good sixteen Dylan quotations/allusions, culled from eleven different songs. By no means all are openly sourced by Rushdie/Rai, but they give Dylan, all in all, a denser and more copious textual presence in this novel than any other songwriter can claim. The first, implicit allusion comes as early as the earthquake episode: "It [the town] had acquired the quality of brokenness, had become kin to the great family of the broken: broken plates, broken dolls, broken English, broken promises, broken hearts";[81] here, Rushdie is echoing Dylan's "Everything is Broken," from 1989: "Broken bottles, broken plates, broken switches, broken gates/Broken dishes, broken parts, streets are filled with broken hearts." The 1965 song "Mr Tambourine Man" supplies a quintessentially sixties reference when, in the heady incense-and-patchouli atmosphere of Antoinette Corinth's London boutique, we are told that the owner is, in true psychedelic fashion, "disappearing down the smoke rings of her mind" (Dylan's line is "take me disappearing through the smoke rings of my mind");[82] while Rai posthumously names Vina "Death-Vina, the sad-eyed lady of the broken lands,"[83] in a clear reference to "Sad-Eyed Lady of the Lowlands," Dylan's epic song of 1966.

Further Dylan song-references are scattered all across the novel.[84] However, the most significant of these allusions—if not the most conceptually successful—are those to "Blowin' in the Wind" (1963), no doubt the Dylan composition best known to the general public. This song's title phrase—cited earlier, as we have seen, in the 1990 Pynchon essay—crops up three times in Rushdie's text,[85] but the most venturesome instance is in the bizarre "Gayomart episode." This, as already noted, is built around the notion that, in and around 1960, a whole series of what were to become major hit songs of the 60s in the West were "really" (!!) composed in Bombay by Ormus Cama, acting on the supernatural promptings of his dead twin Gayomart. These "songs from the future," the reader is impudently informed, included "Blowin' in the Wind":

> At first Ormus played only the songs he had half learned from Gayomart in his dreams, singing those strange vowel sequences of his that made no sense to anyone, or fitting nonsensical words to them that utterly undermined the mysterious authority of the dream-music [...]." The dancer is glowing with her sin. The gardener is mowing with a grin [...]," [...] one thousand and one nights later, "Blowin' in the Wind " hit the airwaves in its authentic version [...] and whenever one of Gayomart Cama's melodies burst through from the world of dreams into the real world, those of us who had heard them for the first time in garbled form in a Bombay villa on the old Cuffe Parade were forced to concede the reality of Ormus' magic gift.[86]

This conceit of Rushdie's must be considered as, at best, problematic. It may seem, on the face of it, a liberating gesture to create a reshaped world in which a song like "Blowin' in the Wind" had origins that were not just Orphic, rising up from the depths of the "world of dreams," but Asian too—as if, through the workings of a "magic gift," Indian culture could stake out a claim of authorship in the new global popular culture that came into being in the West in the 60s. However, there is the small question to be considered of the real origins of Dylan's song. The fact is that Dylan based "Blowin' in the Wind" on a nineteenth-century song called "No More Auction Block," in which a fugitive slave who has escaped to Canada celebrates his new-found freedom; in 1978, he told a journalist: "I took it off a song called 'No More Auction Block'—that's a spiritual, and 'Blowin' in the Wind' has the same feeling."[87] There was, then, already a verified historical input into Dylan's song from a non-WASP source; given which, why did Rushdie feel the need to give it a contrived and fantastical origin in Bombay? The reader is entitled to ask whether the "Gayomart conceit," applied to this and other 60s songs, actually has, in its sheer arbitrariness, the effect of trivialising those songs, instead of underscoring their claims to universal significance.

Beyond the specific textual allusions, the reader is invited to see Ormus the songwriter as some kind of fictional Dylan. His career exhibits certain resemblances to Dylan's: Rushdie's star is removed from public view in 1967 by a near-fatal car crash[88] which recalls Dylan's motorcycle accident of 1966; and, later, he takes obsessively to non-stop touring ("For most of 1994 and 1995 he lived exclusively in the world of the tour [...] Rio, Sydney, London, Hong Kong, Los Angeles, Beijing"[89]), mirroring the "Never Ending Tour" that has occupied a large part of Dylan's energies almost constantly from 1987 to the present. As for Ormus' lyrics, their "perceived anti-establishment contents" are, we are told, expressed through a throng of chaotic images: "street entertainers, card-players, pickpockets, wizards, devils, union men, evil priests, fisherwomen, wrestlers, harlequins, vagabonds, chameleons, whores, eclipses, motorbikes and cheap dark rum."[90] For Rai, "Ormus Cama was the greatest popular singer of all, the one whose genius exceeded all others [...] a golden troubadour the jouncy poetry of whose lyrics could unlock the very gates of Hell; he incarnated the singer and songwriter as shaman and spokesman."[91]

All this seems reasonably close to Dylan, at least to certain phases or facets of his career (the anti-establishment position, the troubadour-shaman-spokesman role); Ormus' images and characters, too, resemble their counterparts in the real Dylan songbook. Dylan's work of 1965-1966, notably, offers evil ecclesiastics (the "jealous monk" of "Desolation Row"), vagabonds ("It's All Over Now,

Baby Blue"), fish trucks ("Visions of Johanna"), sex industry workers ("Just Like Tom Thumb's Blues"), an eclipse ("It's Alright, Ma [I'm Only Bleeding]"), a "motorcycle black Madonna two-wheeled gipsy queen" ("Gates of Eden"), and even a bottle of "Jamaican rum" ("4th Time Around"). Ormus might thus appear to have a goodly part of Dylan in him.

An unfortunate problem occurs, however, when Rushdie's text shifts from the evocation of Ormus' lyrics to their (fictional) reproduction. It is difficult to see how these productions, as given, could possibly be thought to come up to the exacting standards of modern poetic song laid down by Dylan. Two examples of Ormus' alleged compositional gifts, as "quoted" in the text, should suffice: "The earth begins to rock and roll, its music dooms your mortal soul, and there's nothing baby nothing you can do"[92]; and again: "Now I know she's kinda crazy and a little too much, but I'm hopin' for the strokin' of her lovin' touch, and I'm really not insistin,' but if we were tongue twistin,' what a twistin' good time it'd be."[93] Against these specimens, it should be enough to quote two examples of Dylan's songwriting, without further qualitative comment: "When you wake up in the mornin,' baby, look inside your mirror/You know I won't be next to you, you know I won't be near/I'd just be curious to know if you can see yourself as clear/ As someone who has had you on his mind" ("Mama, You Been On My Mind," 1964); and: "Footprints runnin' 'cross the silver sand/ Steps goin' down into tattoo land/I met the sons of darkness and the sons of light/In the border towns of despair" ("Dignity," 1994). The reader may justifiably ask whether Rushdie himself really thinks there is any particular merit in Ormus Cama's lyrics, or whether their "reproduction" is, to quote Dylan's words from "Desolation Row," "some kind of joke" ....

8

Whether or not Ormus and Vina come up to the musical standards of their real Western counterparts, a further question has to be asked concerning Rushdie's claim to have subversively rewritten rock history by inventing two Indian megastars: what, in fact, is Indian about these two—apart from their origins? What, if any, are the specifically Indian elements behind these twain's meteoric careers? The reader will search in vain for any but the most superficial references to any subcontinental musical tradition, be it erudite, folkloric or popular. In *SV*, Rushdie did include a stray mention of the "hindi-pop" scene in London;[94] this is probably a reference to British bhangra (an urbanised version of traditional Punjabi dance music), or to the then-budding "techno-Asian" school—but if Rushdie, as he may do, knows anything about either genre, *GF* finds him keeping that musical knowledge remarkably close to his chest. In recent years in both Britain and the US, fusions of Indian and Western genres have produced interesting and listenable new popular-music hybrids, in the work of artists such as London's Talvin Singh[95] and Sheila Chandra,[96] or the Gujarat-born, California-resident female vocalist Shweta Jhaveri;[97] such musical hybridation might seem in tune with Rushdie's own oft-declared belief in cultural mixity and miscegenation,[98] but there is precious little evidence of any such synthesis in VTO's arch-Western music.

Vina Apsara's professional name, it is true, designates a South Indian instrument (vina) and a mythical female dancer (apsara); but in the music of VTO's heyday any Asian musical influences are minimal. Ravi Shankar gets a brief, rather superficial allusion, when Ormus names him to an ignorant Briton as an example of a famous Indian;[99] but the great Shankar, friend of the Beatles and Yehudi Menuhin, is, as he never ceases to remind the Western press,[100] an Indian classical musician who would not qualify as a direct influence on exponents of more demotic genres. Early on, we are told of Vina: "The music of India, from northern sitar ragas to southern Carnatic melodies, always created in her a mood of inexpressible longing. She could listen to recordings of ghazals for hours at a stretch, and was entranced, too, by the complex devotional music of the leading qawwals."[101] There is, alas, no input into VTO's music from these early influences. They remain promising hints that are never developed: the ghazal and qawwali genres both straddle the subcontinental classical/popular divide, raising possibilities of ground-breaking hybrids and crossovers, and the most famous qawwal of modern times, Pakistan's Nusrat Fateh Ali Khan, actually worked with the British rock musician Peter Gabriel on recordings that fuse devotional tradition with state-of-the-art technology. Jamila Singer from *MC*[102] might have had a word to say here, too, but unfortunately in *GF* Rushdie seems to have forgotten her legacy. Ormus, very late in his career and after Vina's death, does at last begin to integrate something of his origins into his music, evolving towards a "techno-Asian" style: "the tabla rhythms and sitar and yes vina riffs pushed through his sequencers along with pure synthesised sound";[103] but this mutation is little more than a hint, coming so close to the end. VTO's music, and, therefore, the greater part of both Vina's and Ormus' musical production is, from the textual descriptions and the sources and analogies named, clearly a textbook case of mainstream Anglo-American 60s/70s stadium rock, bereft of any "Asian" input other than the two stars' national origins and the piece of trickery that is the "Gayomart conceit."

9

Vina, nonetheless, in the final, solo, stage of her career, does develop artistically, away from mainstream rock and towards something more resembling "world music." Again, though, Rushdie's treatment of a potentially interesting theme proves disappointingly superficial. The term "world music," in the sense that emerged in the late 80s and 90s, deserves some elucidation here. "World music" may be approximately defined as either: traditional-based music from anywhere in the world that makes use of modern recording technology, distribution systems, etc., rather than remaining "ethnic" in a purist sense; or: a fusion of traditional-based musical idioms from more than one culture. Philip Sweeney, compiler of the *Virgin Directory of World Music*, defines the term as "world popular and roots music from outside the Anglo-American mainstream";[104] Ian Anderson, editor of *Folk Roots*, the British magazine that has done much to promote the concept, speaks of a form of cross cultural musical dialogue that "has greatly helped international understanding and provoked cultural exchanges."[105] Outstanding exponents of "world music" in the first sense include Khaled, an Algerian singer based in Paris who performs in both Arabic and French,[106] and Senegal's Youssou N'Dour, who has been described as "Africa's most successful musician [...] thanks to [whom] Senegal is becoming more [...] Senegalese,"[107] and has said that "if a Senegalese musician played a synthesiser or an electric guitar, it became a Senegalese instrument."[108] In the second sense, among the best-known examples are Paul Simon's *Graceland* album of 1986, made largely in collaboration with South African musicians; and the Buena Vista Social Club project, which has engendered a CD (1997) that has sold over 2 million on the global market, as well as a critically-acclaimed film by Wim Wenders (1999), and involves the Californian guitarist Ry Cooder and an agglomeration of superb Cuban musicians, some of them septuagenarian or even nonagenarian, whom Cooder's musicological researches helped re-emerge from obscurity.[109] Essentially, the notion of "world music" entails an openness to musical dialogue and cooperation on a footing of cultural equality, whether the collaborators are all from third-world or "exotic" backgrounds or, as in the Buena Vista case, hail from both sides of the first/third world divide.

The world music phenomenon is a viable contemporary alternative to the commercial excesses of today's mass-consumption Anglo-American music, and Rushdie certainly seems to be aware of its existence. His familiarity with Simon's *Graceland* is clear, since he has, as already noted, quoted elsewhere from one of that album's songs. Rai-the-narrator himself notes that one of the possible meanings of his own name is—Algerian rai music, the genre of which Khaled is the best-known exponent: "And in another part of the world, Rai was music. In the home of this music, alas, religious fanatics have lately started killing the musicians. They think the music is an insult to god, who gave us voices but does not wish us to sing, who gave us free will, rai, but prefers us not to be free."[110] A rai star, Cheb Hasni, was, indeed, assassinated by fundamentalists in Oran, birthplace of the genre, in September 1994;[111] and the word rai, associated by Rushdie with free will, derives, according to the music critic Ken Hunt, from the Arabic for "opinion."[112] These narratorial insights, of course, approximate the risks facing Algerian performers to Rushdie's own predicament, but, alas, no more is made of the possible connections by either Rai or Rushdie. Nor can it possibly be said of the novel's Indian stars that they send western listeners back to Indian music, as has happened in reality with Buena Vista Social Club and Cuban music (as Ibrahim Ferrer, one of the Buena Vista artists, has rather bemusedly declared:

"There is all this music in America and Europe and they come to Cuba for our sound"[113]). The VTO stars' musical trajectory, from Bombay to New York, is, surely, quite the reverse.

Both Ormus and Vina do, admittedly, push their later careers somewhat away from mainstream American rock and more in a world-music direction. One of the later incarnations of VTO is characterised by "un-American sounds" added by Ormus: "Cuban horns," "Brazilian drums," "Chilean woodwinds," "African male choruses," and even "the holy passion of the Pakistani qawwals." The very excess of this hyper-eclectic pot-pourri, however, suggests less a tribute to world music than a superficial travesty of it, while the Ormus/Vina vocal combination clearly remains as American as ever: "more Righteous than the Righteous Brothers, Everlier than the Everlys, Supremer than the Supremes."[114] After VTO finally split, Vina, in 1988, tours Latin America, showcasing self-penned songs with a new backing band ("her three demented Brazilian percussionists and her pair of duelling Argentine guitarists who threatened to end each performance with a knife fight").[115] Here too, the concession to world music does not go beyond the superficial, either on Vina's part (the old VTO hits are still at the heart of her repertoire) or, indeed, Rushdie's: there is no reason why the intentness of Brazilian percussion, with its roots in African ritual, should be dismissed as "demented," while the concept of "duelling guitarists" (based on a pun on "duel" in the twin senses of musical and physical combat) merely replicates a stereotype of Argentine violence which, if acceptable in a Buenos-Aires born writer like Borges, from Rushdie's pen seems a tired, second-hand cliché. The conclusion seems inevitable that Rushdie has missed a golden opportunity, fluffing the challenge of a sustained literary engagement with the world music phenomenon. We could have had an Indian Buena Vista Social Club; what we get is VTO, playing born-in-the-USA rock'n'roll while laying claim to an Asian "authenticity" that derives from literary sleight-of-hand alone.

10

The critical response to Rushdie's rock-generation odyssey has been mixed. As a novelist (and not just a *cause célèbre*), its author has, among people who read books, a formidable reputation to live up to. Anita Desai, looking back on *MC* in 1995, declared: "It was a very ambitious and bold book. And [...] it led to a whole generation of young writers and gave them the confidence they might not have had otherwise. He can be said to have set free the tongues of the younger writers—a tremendous influence upon their work."[116] Of *SV*, considered as a novel, the Franco-Algerian political scientist Sami Naïr wrote in 1989: "The interpretation of *The Satanic Verses* could be multiplied indefinitely: but this novel is so rich that no such reading could exhaust its meaning [...] This is the birth of a great—of a very great writer."[117]

By no means all reviewers found *GF* up to the standard of Rushdie's earlier fictional production. A representative sample of reviews from various countries suggests an approximately equal three-way breakdown between the eulogistic, the ambivalent and the disappointed or downright hostile. In the first category, Hermione Lee, in the London *Observer*, praised *GF* as "a very exciting novel, hugely ambitious and original," full of "true Rushdiean boldness"—a book "about the making and the meaning of myths," in which "the Orpheus and Eurydice myth gets turned around and upside down";[118] while *Newsweek*'s Carla Power lauded it as "a book about the way we live now," remarkable for its "mythic scope, epic stretch and huge intelligence."[119] In France, *Le Monde*'s reviewer, Raphaëlle Rérolle, read Rushdie's tale as celebrating "the force of dream and imagination" and affirming "music and its power" against "the violence of those who oppose it";[120] conversely, in *Libération* Antoine de Gaudemar found it a "metaphoric and finally pessimistic novel," an indictment of our times in which the musical protagonists are "unreal beings, abstract icons, toys in the hands of a ruthless system and a fiercely volatile public opinion."[121]

A more ambivalent note was struck by the *Economist*, whose reviewer noted the "familiar mix of magical realism, dazzling verbal display, self-conscious fictionality, and allusion," but found the novel rather amorphous: "Designed to mimic the theme of cultural overload in its construction, its narrative shape is on the verge of constant collapse."[122] Similarly, *Time*'s reviewer, Paul Gray, while praising the "energy, intelligence and allusiveness" of Rushdie's writing, concluded that "the parts of this novel seem greater than the whole."[123] Perhaps most tellingly, in *La Quinzaine Littéraire*

Marc Porée (co-author, as noted above, of a substantial critical study of Rushdie),[124] found *GF* vitiated by a culpable dose of superficiality, deriving from an excessive fixation on the cult of celebrity ("Has he really striven to de-sacralise Islam [...] only to end up legitimating a latter-day version of the sacred?"), and drew attention to the un-Indianness of Ormus and Vina as musicians: "The idea of having Indian rockers as the main characters succeeds only imperfectly [...] the aficionado inevitably imagines these characters in the skin and the features of stars from the English-speaking world," before nonetheless concluding that the book "may be redeemed if we recognise its extreme darkness, the darkness of a world living on the edge."

Adverse views of Rushdie's novel included one from Italy and two from his native South Asian world. The novelist and critic Silvia Albertazzi, in her review in the Italian magazine *Pulp*, found *GF* markedly inferior to its author's earlier work, simultaneously over-superficial and over-complex: Rushdie, she complained, has "chosen to break with the methods of the Indian oral tradition—stories grafted on to one another, Chinese box-like, spiralling, to be swallowed all together—in favour of a more linear narrative," while "the novel gets tangled up in its own excess of stimuli, metaphors and sets of symbols, losing, above all, its sense of the link with history—hitherto one of the strongest points of Rushdie's narrative." The same critic concluded that nothing in the text justifies the alleged genius of Ormus and Vina, adding the judgment that "Ormus' song texts are of an exasperating banality beneath their rhetoric."[125] C.J. Wallia, writing on the *India Star* website, dismissed the book as a "muddled melodramatic novel," objecting to its "repeated inflictions of mindboggling mythological references" and "long pontifical soliloquies on death and art";[126] while the novelist Pankaj Mishra, in a violent critique first published in the Delhi magazine *Outlook*, accused Rushdie of producing a novel replete with "cartoon-like simplicities," "empty bombast," "pseudo-characters" and "non-events," which is not a critique but a symptom of the processes at work in today's world—and of using "secular radicalism" as a pretext for an uncritical and politically suspect eulogy of "American pop culture."[127]

From the reviews quoted, whatever their evaluation of Rushdie's novel, there emerges a consensus that one of its key themes is the economic and cultural process that has come to be known as globalisation. The critics also recognise that Rushdie's narrative and stylistic strategies—the use of mythology, the East-to-West sweep of the tale, the multi-layered allusiveness—represent an attempt, successful or otherwise, to create a fiction that will adequately reflect that process of globalisation and offer the reader certain possible responses to it. None of the critics cited has, however, looked in detail—as I have tried to do in this study—at those elements in the book (the non-use of the Orpheus myth, the failure to engage creatively with "world music") which fail to satisfy in this respect, and thus cast doubt on the validity and usefulness of Rushdie's social critique; and only Porée has drawn attention to the un-Indian nature of the novel's music, surely one of its most unsatisfactory paradoxes. Nonetheless, the strictures which Wallia and Mishra lay at the door of Rushdie's actual writing in this novel seem less justified than the more substantive faults identified: the allusive density of the text shows beyond doubt that Rushdie has put an enormous amount of work into this novel and has enriched it at the textual level with a wealth of ideas and information accumulated from his enormously wide reading and his own very specific interaction with history. Whether all this knowledge and effort has given birth to a genuinely useful fable for our times is another matter.

11

Globalisation is a knife that cuts both ways—threatening universal, US-dominated standardisation and the annihilation of cultural diversity, yet also opening up, through the Internet and its limitless resources, unprecedented possibilities of expression, communication and solidarity. The question is whether Rushdie's novel offers an adequate fictional representation of this dynamic contradiction. Certainly, his characters inhabit a world in continual flux, subject to endless shocks and mutations—as symbolised by the earthquake metaphor, and as self-consciously and repeatedly registered in the text: "if the world itself were metamorphosing unpredictably, then nothing could be relied upon anymore";[128] "Instability, the modern condition, no longer frightens them; it now feels like possibility."[129] The reader may ask, however, whether Rushdie's Asian protagonists do not end up as largely passive victims of US mass culture—a victimhood disguised only rhetorically, by the box-of-tricks strategy of the "Gayomart conceit." Large parts of the book's second half seem merely to replicate the hollowness of the one-dimensional creations of the entertainment industry, the self-validating procession of surfaces which Rushdie's text itself, in a metalingual flourish of doubtful profundity, calls "that zone of celebrity in which everything except celebrity ceases to signify."[130] It is also disappointing to find the East-West relationship embodied in this novel's narrative structure in such a linear fashion. Instead of East and West alternating, what we get is East in the first half, replaced by West in the second. As far as "Indo-Anglian" writing is concerned, the true continuators of the complex "East-West" narrative structure which Rushdie superbly deployed in *SV* would appear to be not Rushdie's own later novels, but such works as Vikram Chandra's *Red Earth and Pouring Rain* (1995)[131] and Amitav Ghosh's *The Calcutta Chromosome* (1996)—both novels in which a dense, intricate narrative, snaking back and forth in time and place, reflects an awareness of world history and culture in their sheer density which is, sadly, lacking in *GF*.

In 1994, Rushdie closed the final story of *East, West* with a proud declaration of neutrality between East and West—a pregnant manifesto of neither-norness and both-andness, of hybridity and cultural miscegenation:

> I, too, have ropes around my neck, I have them to this day, pulling me this way and that, East and West, the nooses tightening, commanding, choose, choose [...] Ropes, I do not choose between you. Lassoes, lariats, I choose neither of you, and both. Do you hear? I refuse to choose.[132]

Five years later, he chooses to conclude *GF* with the vignette of a New York child:

> Tara's got hold of the zapper. I've never got used to having the tv on at breakfast, but this is an American kid, she's unstoppable. And today, by some fluke, wherever she travels in the cable multiverse she comes up with Ormus and Vina [...] they're just going to go on singing.[133]

Whether this peroration marks Rushdie's final choice of "West"—not just over "East," but, perhaps more significantly, over his earlier, challenging choice of cultural hybridation—whether closing this novel with a child's ersatz journey into the "cable multiverse" means that our novelist has lost the plot, has finally given in to the seductions of transatlantic mass culture—whether the literal death of the author threatened by the fatwa has led to the spiritual death of the author we once knew: all these are enigmas to which only the future, and Rushdie's own future writing, can provide an answer.

Rushdie's sea of stories has certainly not dried up, but it does seem to have become a trifle shallow. My prediction is that *GF* will live less as a rock'n'roll epic than as pure text—in the mercurial play of the words on the page, in the allusive density and resourcefulness of Salman Rushdie's protean, spell-weaving, still-alert writing. It is, however, an open question whether a fiction that relies so heavily for its impact on textual scintillation can, ultimately, allow either writer or reader to gain a full, intelligent grasp on the dynamic and dangerous complexities of today's ever-shifting, globalised cultural universe.

NOTES AND REFERENCES

1. Salman Rushdie, *The Ground Beneath Her Feet* (London: Jonathan Cape, 1999). Hereinafter referred to as *GF*.
2. Salman Rushdie, interview with Bruno Lesprit ("Salman Rushdie, enfant du rock"), *Le Monde* 1 October 1999 (review section): VI.
3. Roland Barthes, "La mort de l'auteur" [1968], *Le bruissement de la langue: Essais Critiques IV* (Paris: Seuil [Collection Points], 1984).
4. Barthes 67.
5. Barthes 69.
6. Ayatollah Khomeini (quoted), Malise Ruthven, *A Satanic Affair: Salman Rushdie and the Rage of Islam* (London: Chatto & Windus, 1990) 112.
7. For Zhdanov, see George Steiner, "Marxism and the Literary Critic," *Language and Silence* (1967; Harmondsworth: Penguin, 1969).
8. For the campaign against *The Satanic Verses* in Britain, see Ruthven 4; Marc Porée and Alexis Massery, *Salman Rushdie* (Paris: Éditions du Seuil, 1996) 129-36.
9. Guy Astic, "Rushdie, écrivain laïc? ," *La Règle du Jeu* 18 January 1996: 60.
10. Salman Rushdie, interview with John Carlin ("El guardaespaldas de Rushdie"), *El País Semanal* 9 May 1999 <http://www.elpais.es>.

11. Rushdie, *GF* 404-407.
12. Rushdie, *GF* 555-57.
13. Salman Rushdie, *Midnight's Children* (1981; London: Picador, 1982) 9.
14. Salman Rushdie, *The Satanic Verses* (London: Viking, 1988) 546. Hereinafter referred to as *SV*.
15. Salman Rushdie, *The Moor's Last Sigh* (London: Jonathan Cape, 1995) 372.
16. Roshan G. Shahani, "Polyphonous Voices in the City: Bombay's Indian-English Fiction," *Bombay: Mosaic of Modern Culture,* eds. Sujata Patel and Alice Thorner (Bombay: Oxford UP, 1995) 104-105.
17. Shahani 110.
18. Rushdie, *GF* 60-61.
19. Salman Rushdie, interview with Laura Miller ("A touch of vulgarity"), *Salon* 16 April 1999 <http://www.salonmag.com/books/int/1999/04/16/rushdie/index.html>.
20. Shahani 112.
21. See Rushdie, *Le Monde* interview; Rushdie, interview with Antoine de Gaudemar ("Star Traque"), *Libération* 30 September 1999: 48.
22. Carla Power, "Rock'n'Roll Rushdie," rev. of *GF*, *Newsweek* (international edition) 19 April 1999: 71.
23. Salman Rushdie, *Grimus* (1975; London: Paladin, 1989) 18-19.
24. Salman Rushdie, "Thomas Pynchon" (1990), *Imaginary Homelands: Essays and Criticism 1981-1991* (1991; London: Granta, 1992) 352. A second Paul Simon reference occurs in the same essay (353): "Paul Simon's girl in New York City who calls herself the Human Trampoline, bouncing into Graceland " (this is a paraphrase of lines from "Graceland," the title song of Simon's 1986 album of the same name).
25. Salman Rushdie, "The Courter," *East, West* (1994; London: Vintage, 1995) 196-97.
26. Rushdie, *Le Monde* interview: VI.
27. Rushdie, *Salon* interview.
28. Rushdie, *GF* 225.
29. Rushdie, *GF* 266.
30. Rushdie, *GF* 351.
31. Rushdie, *GF* 267.
32. Rushdie, *GF* 402.
33. See section 7 below.
34. Rushdie, *GF* 492.
35. Rushdie, *GF* 349.
36. Rushdie, *GF* 330-31.

37. Rushdie, *GF* 459.
38. Rushdie, *GF* 336.
39. Rushdie, *GF* 375.
40. Rushdie, *GF* 385.
41. William Shakespeare, *Henry VIII*, III-I, 3.
42. Virgil, *Georgics* [29 BC], trans. into English prose by H. P. Fairclough, Virgil, *Eclogues. Georgics. Aeneid 1-6* (Cambridge, Mass.: Harvard U.P [Loeb Classical Library], 1916; rev. ed. 1999); *Géorgiques*, trans. into French verse by Jacques Delille [1769], Virgil, *Bucoliques. Géorgiques*, ed. Florence Dupont (bilingual French/Latin edition) (Paris: Gallimard [Folio], 1997).
43. Ovid, *Metamorphoses* [8 AD], trans. into English prose by Mary M. Innes (Harmondsworth: Penguin, 1955) 225-27, 246-48.
44. Thomas Bulfinch, *The Age of Fable* [1855] (London: Dent [Everyman's Library], 1912; rep. 1948) 190-99.
45. Robert Graves, *The Greek Myths* (1955; rev. ed., 2 vols., Harmondsworth: Penguin, 1960), vol. 1, 111-15; see also Simon Hornblower and Antony Spawforth, eds., *The Oxford Companion to Classical Civilization* (Oxford: OUP, 1998) 504-505.
46. Euripides, *Alcestis* [438 BC], trans. Philip Vellacott, *Alcestis/Hippolytus/ Iphigenia in Tauris* (Harmondsworth: Penguin, 1953; new ed. 1974), lines 357-62.
47. Plato, *The Symposium* [c. 370 BC)], trans. as *The Banquet of Plato* by Percy Bysshe Shelley [1818], Shelley, *Selected Poetry, Prose and Letters* (London: Nonesuch Press, 1951) 821-80 (for Orpheus, see 831).
48. Euripides, lines 968-69.
49. Jacques Lacarrière, ed. and trans., *Orphée: Hymnes. Discours sacrés* (bilingual French/Greek edition) (Paris: Imprimerie nationale, 1995). Hymn 59 in this volume ("Aux Moires" / "To the Fates") concludes with the line: "Thus ends this ode to the Fates, composed by Orpheus."
50. Graves 111, 115.
51. Lacarrière, introduction 17, 18.
52. According to Florence Dupont in her 1997 preface, the second half of the fourth book of the *Georgics* originally consisted of a panegyric to the general Caius Cornelius Gallus. However, between Virgil's first and second editions, Gallus had committed suicide after falling out of favour with Augustus, and therefore, says Dupont, "Virgil did not hesitate to replace Gallus by Orpheus" (19). This version of the poem's history is, however, disputed by other modern scholars.
53. Dupont 7.
54. Rushdie, *El País* interview.
55. Rainer Maria Rilke, *Die Sonette an Orpheus* (1923); trans. by Charles Dobzynski as *Sonnets à Orphée* (bilingual French/German edition) (Paris:

Éditions Messidor, 1989). The passage quoted in Rushdie's epigraph is from Sonnet V, in a translation by M. D. Herter Norton.

56. Rushdie, *GF* 21-22.
57. Rushdie, *GF* 498.
58. Rushdie, *GF* 561.
59. Rushdie, *GF* 413 and *passim*.
60. Rushdie, *GF* 3.
61. Rushdie, *GF* 4.
62. Rushdie, *GF* 560.
63. Rushdie, *Grimus* 244.
64. Rushdie, *GF* 569.
65. Rushdie, *GF* 517.
66. Salman Rushdie, interview with Philippe Manoeuvre ("Mes disques à moi"), *Rock & Folk* September 1999: 20.
67. For instance, John Carlin, in the *El País* interview, sees Ormus "as a composite of Elvis, Dylan and Lennon."
68. Rushdie, *GF* 124.
69. Rushdie, *Salon* interview.
70. Rushdie, *GF* 8.
71. Yma Sumac, "Tumpa (Earthquake)" (written by Moisés Vivanco); issued on *Voice of the Xtabay*, 1950; CD reissue, "The Right Stuff" (Hollywood, CA), 0777-7-91217-2-4, 1996.
72. Glenn Dillard Gunn, *Washington Times-Herald* 1950; quoted in liner notes, *Voice of the Xtabay*.
73. See, notably, the 918-page study by Michael Gray, *Song and Dance Man III: The Art of Bob Dylan* (London: Cassell, 2000). I have myself published at length on Dylan (from 1998 to the present), in essays collected at the *Bob Dylan Critical Corner* website <http://www.geocities.com/Athens/Oracle/6752/magazine.html>.
74. Rushdie, *Salon* interview.
75. Rushdie, *Le Monde* interview; for Rushdie on Dylan, see also the *Rock & Folk* interview.
76. See Porée and Massery, 14-15, 115.
77. Salman Rushdie, *The Jaguar Smile: A Nicaraguan Journey* (London: Picador, 1987) 125.
78. Rushdie, "Thomas Pynchon," *Imaginary Homelands* 352.
79. Rushdie, *SV* 415. The reading of the song which Rushdie's text goes on to offer is rather dubious, but its discussion would take us outside the scope of this study; whether or not Dylan thought it an honour to have his name mentioned in *SV* is not recorded.

80. Rushdie, *GF* 425. The other Dylan references are: "Lennon, Dylan, Phil Ramone, Richards, these old men were still the giants along with VTO themselves" (435); and the invented benefit concert incident (402), as already quoted in section 4 above.
81. Rushdie, *GF* 17.
82. Rushdie, *GF* 286.
83. Rushdie, *GF* 491.
84. Further Dylan allusions in *GF* are to: "The Times They Are A-Changin'" (1964), 435; "With God On Our Side" (1964), 266 and 281; "She Belongs To Me" (1965), 269 and 500; "It's Alright, Ma (I'm Only Bleeding)" (1965), 239; "Like A Rolling Stone" (1965), 183 and 470—another song "attributed" to Gayomart!; "Lay Lady Lay" (1969), 322 and 500; and "Forever Young" (1974), 486. These, together with the four songs discussed in the text, make up eleven Dylan compositions echoed by Rushdie in this novel.
85. Rushdie, *GF* 274, 455.
86. Rushdie, *GF* 141.
87. Bob Dylan, quoted by John Bauldie, booklet notes, Dylan, *The Bootleg Series* volumes *1-3* (3-CD set), Columbia, 1991, 6.
88. Rushdie, *GF* 307.
89. Rushdie, *GF* 558-59.
90. Rushdie, *GF* 395, 102.
91. Rushdie, *GF* 89.
92. The "rock and roll/mortal soul" rhyme is taken over from a real song, Don McLean's Dylan-influenced "American Pie" (a hit of 1971).
93. Rushdie, *GF* 390, 416.
94. Rushdie, *SV* 291.
95. See Talvin Singh, *OK*, Island/Omni CID 8075/524 559-2, 1998; Pete Lawrence, "Tabla tastemaker," *Folk Roots* (January/February 1999) 22-29.
96. See Sheila Chandra, *Moonsung: A Real World Retrospective*, Real World CDR W77, 1999; Ruth Rosselson, "Return of the voice," *Folk Roots* (July 1999) 15-16.
97. See Shweta Jhaveri, *Anahita*, Intuition Music & Media INT 3509-2, 1998; Ken Hunt, "Khyal Creed," *Folk Roots* (June 1999) 34-35.
98. Rushdie speaks of cultural mixity and "métissage" in " L'entretien d'Arte," interview with Bernard-Henri Lévy, *La Règle Du Jeu* 13 May 1994: 28-29.
99. Rushdie, *GF* 284.
100. See, for instance, Eric Dahan, "Shankar, un grand classique" (interview with Ravi Shankar), *Libération* 6 July 1999: 30-31.
101. Rushdie, *GF* 122-23.
102. Cf. section 3 above.

103. Rushdie, *GF* 546.

104. Philip Sweeney, *Virgin Directory of World Music* (London: Virgin, 1991) ix.

105. Ian Anderson, "World Wars," *Folk Roots* (March 2000) 39.

106. For Khaled and the rai genre, see Tewfik Hakem, "L'inventaire Khaled-Mami," *World* (March/April 1998): 86-89; Ken Hunt, "Khaled Comfort," *Folk Roots* (October 1999) 26-27, 41.

107. Lucy Duran, "The Xippi Trail [Youssou N'Dour]," *Folk Roots* (November 1999): 20.

108. Anderson 39.

109. *Buena Vista Social Club*, collective CD produced by Ry Cooder, World Circuit/ Nonesuch 79478-2, 1997; Wim Wenders, dir., *Buena Vista Social Club*, Road Movies, 1999; see Nigel Williamson, "The Bolero Boy [Ibrahim Ferrer]," *Folk Roots* (June 1999) 28-29, and "Ry comments [Ry Cooder]," *Folk Roots* (July 1999) 20-27; cf. for a US perspective, Tom Moon, "The Cuban Invasion," *Rolling Stone* 2 September 1999: 29, 40.

110. Rushdie, *GF* 19.

111. See *World* (March/April 1998) 82.

112. See Hunt, "Khaled Comfort" 26. This etymology is confirmed by Sweeney, who explains how young Algerian singers "began to pepper their verses with the phrase 'Ha er-rai' or 'Ya rai,' meaning something like 'it's my opinion'" (9).

113. Ibrahim Ferrer (quoted), Williamson, "The Bolero Boy" 29.

114. Rushdie, *GF* 379.

115. Rushdie, *GF* 8.

116. Anita Desai, "A Sense of Detail and a Sense of Order: Anita Desai Interviewed by Lalita Pandit," Patrick Colm Hogan and Lalita Pandit, eds., *Literary India: Comparative Studies in Aesthetics, Colonialism and Culture* (Albany: State U of New York P, 1995) 163.

117. Sami Naïr, "Comment lire *Les Versets Sataniques*?," Esprit, (October 1989); reprinted in the collective volume *Pour Rushdie: Cent intellectuels arabes et musulmans pour la liberté d'expression* (Paris: La Découverte/Carrefour des Littératures/Colibri, 1993) 235. This volume in fact consists not of the contributions of 100 authors, but of 99 essays and one musical score (by a Moroccan composer) by a total of 226 authors, as one item is a collective letter in support of Rushdie signed by 127 Iranian intellectuals.

118. Hermione Lee, rev. of *GF*, *Observer* (review section) 28 March 1999: 11.

119. Power 71.

120. Raphaëlle Rérolle, rev. of *GF*, *Le Monde* (review section) 1 October 1999: VI.

121. Antoine de Gaudemar, "Rushdie, chaos tectonique," rev. of *GF*, *Libération* (review section) 30 September 1999: VII.

122. "Boy's toys," rev. of *GF*, *Economist* 15 May 1999: 13.
123. Paul Gray, "Ganja Growing in the Tin," rev. of *GF*, *Time* 17 May 1999: 62.
124. Marc Porée, "Rushdiessime," *La Quinzaine Littéraire* 16-31 October 1999: 5.
125. Silvia Albertazzi, "Salman Rushdie: *La terra sotto i suoi piedi*," rev. of *GF*, *Pulp* 20 (July-August 1999): 29.
126. C. J. Wallia, rev. of *GF*, *India Star*, 1999 <http://www.indiastar.com/wallia20.html>.
127. Pankaj Mishra, "Anatomy of an Anti-Novel," rev. of *GF*, *Outlook* 9 April 1999 <http://www.wish.u-net.com/roy/pm_rushd.htm>.
128. Rushdie, *GF* 184.
129. Rushdie, *GF* 487.
130. Rushdie, *GF* 425.
131. On Chandra's novel, see Christopher Rollason, "Entwining Narratives: Intertextuality in Vikram Chandra's *Red Earth and Pouring Rain,*" *Il Tolomeo* (Venice) IV (1998/1999): 108-113.
132. Rushdie, "The Courter," *East, West* 211.
133. Rushdie, *GF* 575.

9

Elizabethan Influences in Vikram Seth's *A Suitable Boy*

PIERPAOLO PICIUCCO*

A Suitable Boy, the novel of the records, was no small achievement in 1993 when it was first published. Its vast amount of work did not fail to impress critics and reviewers all over the world: "more than 8 lakh words kneaded in 478 sections of 19 parts in its 1347 pages weighing about fifteen hundred grams,"[1] counted a very daring commentator. Planned therefore also with the intent to overwhelm its reader, it is not a work lacking consistency. Written in a highly readable style, characters well-sketched, a very neat and natty (central) plot, it may look deceptively simple in its structure and content. But Vikram Seth wrote a monumental work which, although clearly set in a definite socio-historical context, makes direct reference to various elements and creates a new hybrid world.

Although many reviewers and critics have stressed Seth's Victorian taste for his tenacious determination to impose on his readers fully detailed descriptions of scenes and characters, he seems to be at least equally indebted to Elizabethan drama for a considerable number of parallelisms. The constant reference to the Elizabethan comedy as a structure to the whole novel is not a secondary aspect. Obviously, the emphasis on *The Twelfth Night* as a model is quite overt, since some of the major characters are even called to play a part in the representation of the Shakespearean

*Department of Foreign Languages, University of Turin, via S. Ottavio 19-10124 Turin, Italy.

play, which therefore functions as a *mise en abime* in the novel. Even though critics have not directly pointed out this cross-reference, in several cases their comments seem straightforward hints at the presence of such an aspect. Here is, for example, Shyam S. Agarwalla's view:

> one of the themes of this great novel is Mrs. Mehra, in search of a suitable boy for her dear daughter, Lata, and Lata's unconcern for the concern of her obsessional and hysterical mother. The medium is comedy.[2]

Although in this case Agarwalla does not restrict his analysis to a precise literary period, he later shows the parallels between the early fifties in India to the Shakespearean age:

> The early years of the Nehruvian age started with a bang, like that of the Elizabethan age of the sixteenth century, full of bubbling optimism, robust vitality and great expectations. One of the chief factors was the presence of leaders of proven integrity, the other being the continuation of the services of "steel frame" bureaucracy. Nehru had wide choice in choosing able and trustworthy counsellors. Like Elizabeth I, he had a heart but it was always ruled by his head [Agarwalla 33].

It may be thus tempting to analyse the common traits of these two distinct literary genres, in periods and places which could not be more different. We may begin by taking into consideration a very obvious, if not visible, element. Originally, in fact, some of the sections of the novel are mere transcriptions of theatrical text rather than fictional discourse. Apart from the cases in which Lata is rehearsing the comedy and talking to Kabir, this happens on various occasions; 5.15, 5.16 and 14.26, for instance, are cases in point. Presumably, the only other similar example of this peculiar kind of narration in Indian English fiction occurs in the final pages of Raja Rao's *The Cat and Shakespeare*, in a scene inside an office with the lead character Govindan Nair talking with other clerks.[3] Yet, the influence of the Elizabethan dramatist on the whole novel is indisputable since his name evidently features in the title itself of Raja Rao's work.

Another factor which both Shakespearean works and *A Suitable Boy* share is the characteristic vision of the natural course of life paralleled to the representation of a play. In Shakespeare, needless to say, this happens a number of times; in particular, in the *Twelfth Night*, it is Fabian who, addressing the audience, brushes this Shakespearean tenet up: "If this were played upon a stage now. I could condemn it as improbable fiction" (3. IV. 133-34). In Vikram Seth's novel the analogy life/play returns many times, too. Among the several instances, I would privilege section 12.13, where a dialogue between the masseur Maggu Gopal and his patient Pran Kapoor develops the concept of stage performance as a metaphor of life. It is the masseur who first indulges in Pran's palm reading with the following response: "It is written in your hand that your married life will be a comedy" (798). Pran's reply, a little later, is on the same wavelength: "'Really?' said Pran, interested, but rather fearful. 'Will my wife like this? I fear my life may become a comedy of the wrong kind.'"[4]

In a vein of offering cheap wise observations, the masseur closes the cycle by decreeing: "Family life with children is a comedy, both today, yesterday and tomorrow" (798).

Among the topics dearest to Shakespeare, and possibly one of the most celebrated, one cannot forget the representation of folly in its most ambivalent aspects: real and/or pretended. That is a theme Seth develops too, even though with less prominence than in the Elizabethan drama. Madness, in a pure Elizabethan fashion, is to be seen as a disease and, in the following quotation, it is juxtaposed with presumed madness. This is the case of Kabir's parents:

> When they were children, Kabir, Hashim and Samia had always, and rather proudly, declared their father to be slightly mad. It was clearly his eccentricity—or something aligned with it—that made respect him so much. But it was their affectionate, amusing and practical mother who had been afflicted with this strange visitation, so causelessly and so incurably (784).

In Shakespeare's plays madness is often related to love affairs and Seth seems very keen on portraying this situation, too. Maan's story exemplifies such a predicament in various circumstances: at first he does not hesitate to ruin his reputation to court his sweetheart Saeeda Bai and then he stabs his very dear friend Firoz—whom, he has only very recently saved from certain death—because blinded by jealousy. The case of Rasheed is far more illuminating. His fanatical passion for Tasneem leads him to commit suicide. This takes us to a further point. In both the cases, as David Myers suggested very aptly, the reader is confronted with a kind of general orientation on the writer's part that one may interpret the whole novel as a "manifesto against the passions in sexual love."[5] As a matter of fact, Lata's choice to marry Haresh and discard Kabir (Amit never had a real chance to be considered a good party) are discovered in a very revealing passage, which validates Myers' theory. We are here confronted with Lata's confession to Malati:

> If that's what passion means, I don't want it. Look at what passion has done to the family. Maan's broken, his mother's dead, his father's in despair. When I thought that Kabir was seeing someone else, what I remember feeling was enough to make me hate passion. Passionately and forever (1296).

Starting from these premises, Myers traces the parallel with *Twelfth Night*. Even though his theory does not take into consideration further affinities, one cannot but agree with it:

> It is not accidental that *A Suitable Boy* features Shakespeare's comedy in general and *Twelfth Night* in particular. The moral of *Twelfth Night* is the comic education of Malvolio, who falls outside the borders of social acceptability with his lack of ironic balance and his insane passion or idee fixe that he can win the sexual love of his mistress-employer and career-advancement at the same time. Malvolio pays a near-tragic penalty for his uncontrolled passion and is a microcosm of the moral theme of *A Suitable Boy* [Myers 97].

That, incidentally, is equally true of Seth's most recent novel *An Equal Music*. This is obviously one of Shakespeare's constants, too. Even though sex was one of the most privileged sources with which the dramatist could create misunderstanding and witticism and produce ironical situations in general, he never crowned passionate love at the end of his plays. On the contrary, it featured as a prime cause of evil in some of the most celebrated tragedies.

The deep secular component which regulated the overall moves of Elizabethan drama seems equally present in *A Suitable Boy*. If an ardent Neoplatonist principle moulded many Shakespearean heroes, one may easily trace vestiges of such an outlook in Vikram Seth, too. The choice of the Indian author to place his monumental work in the early Fifties, the period that immediately followed the horror caused by the Hindu-Muslim riots, overtly reveals that intent. Consequently, all characters who are religious fanatics are doomed defeat before the end of the novel. On the other hand, we are confronted with many cases of characters who cross the imaginary barriers of religious extremism. Significantly, they serve as positive examples. The instance of the friendship between Maan and Firoz, with the almost idyllic epilogue, is to be read in this perspective. The surprising finale is designed in order to be welcomed as a right—although there has been blatant violation of justice—measure by the reader. Moreover, that can be a compensation for Manesh Kapoor's political failure. To his credit, the narrating voice reports:

> Manesh Kapoor, though a Hindu, was well-known for his tolerance for other religions—his wife would have said that the only religion he was intolerant toward was his own—and was liked and respected among knowledgeable Muslims (620).

Moving on to the field of character analysis, the analogies become stricter and stricter. The "malcontent," to begin with, is a central figure and a distinctive specialty of Elizabethan drama. In *A Suitable Boy* there is much evidence to suggest that Amit is a manifest embodiment of such a cliché. The malcontent in Elizabethan drama is an outsider in the society he lives in, or a subaltern of somewhat higher level: he is an intellectual, a preceptor, a poor scholar or a poet. His melancholic disposition always distinguishes him from the common people.[6] Amit answers this description completely: he is a poet and his melancholic nature is quite evident. He is the author of "unhappy love poems in his first, very successful, volume" (939), while "his second volume showed a kind of philosophical resignation unusual in a man who was not yet thirty––and who was fairly famous" (939). It is significant that when he has the choice to go out with Lata, he takes her to Park Street cemetery and shows her the tombs of famous people buried in Calcutta. Like the most celebrated of Shakespeare's malcontents, Hamlet, Amit admits "I know I'm indecisive" (943) and in this way he reveals an earth-and-sky difference from Haresh, the chosen one, who somehow abounds in self-confidence: "Hamlet's indecisiveness irritated him" (599), reports the novelist's eloquent comment. Still more important, the malcontent in Elizabethan drama reflects the playwright's point of view and Amit, this is glaringly obvious, is the privileged mouthpiece for Seth's ideas. Compare, for instance, the case of Amit's answers to his readers at the end of his public reading of his poems at Berhampur Literary Society:

> "Why is it that you do not write in Bengali, your mother tongue?" asked a challenging voice. The young man who spoke appeared to be quite angry.
>
> Amit had been asked this question—and had asked himself this question—many times before. His answer was that his Bengali was not good enough for him to be able to express himself in the manner he could in English. It wasn't a question of choice. Someone who had been trained all his life to play the sitar could not become a sarangi player because his ideology or his conscience told him to. "Besides," Amit added, "we are all accidents of history and must do what we are best at without fretting too much about it. Even Sanskrit came to India from outside" (1253).

Moreover, as one reads a few biographical notes about the novelist, the parallel with Amit becomes undeniable: "his brother runs Buddhist meditational tours, and his sister, the youngest, recently married an Austrian diplomat."[7] Focussing on this aspect, A.K. Singh perceptively notes:

> Amit emerges as Seth's alter ego; the novelist has left enough clues in the course of his novel to prove it. Like his creator, who in spite of donning foreign degrees in economics, abandons them for creative writing, Amit prefers creative literary career to any job which he might have fallen upon with his degree in Law from London.[8]

Under such premises James Buchan's remark, "Why Lata—a sweet creation, if somehow forced, by the literary burden she's carrying, into speechlessness—chooses the suitor she chooses is not clear,"[9] completely loses substance: Myers could provide a first befitting answer, with his theory on the renunciation of passion as a higher moral code. Another possible solution takes into consideration the

Shakespearean thematic structure of the novel: Kabir cannot be chosen since he represents unrefrained passion while Amit, the malcontent, must follow the tradition by reaching the end of the play sentimentally unsatisfied.

Another central character in all Elizabethan drama is the fool, a witty, shrewd and wise figure who accompanies the protagonist (he is often the king's companion), and who is somehow closely associated with the malcontent.[10] In *A Suitable Boy* Kakoli, Amit's sister, overtly plays that role. She often speaks through facetious rhymes and she has a reputation for being able to reveal any truth: "Kuku can gurgle herself through any door; they're no obstacles to Kuku" (1099). Although Myers does not confine this role to Kuku alone, he underlines this aspect as he points out:

> [...] borrowed from Shakespeare is the character of the wise fool, who remains safely above the all too human passions, and who is perceived as possessing fragments of wisdom hidden in the nonsense of the continual joking. The rhyming couplets of Kakoli, and even of Amit as the protagonist Seth himself, may seem merely facetious, but they contain an attitude towards sexual passion especially which amounts to a sublimation of desire in wit (Myers 97).

Shakespearean influence in the creation of stereotyped characters in *A Suitable Boy* can be further exemplified by taking into account the case of the mirthful mistress' waiting-woman. In Elizabethan drama she is not called on to play a role of primary importance: she rather lives in the shadow of her mistress. Her specific purpose is to alleviate the tension in the plot whenever her mistress' intricate love affair appears to burden the atmosphere. She adopts a licentious conduct with several men at the same time, counterbalancing the dame's strictly regulated moral behavior. In Vikram Seth this role is played by Bibbo, Saeeda Bai's maidservant, "whose taste for both intrigue and gossip had caused enough damage already" (1228); she is overtly described as "a trouble-maker and a flirt" (804).

Last but not least, typical of Elizabethan comedy is the stratagem of sex-switching, which appears in *A Suitable Boy* camouflaged under various shapes. Manliness, in particular, plays a pivotal role in the economy of the novel. Lata, in fact, is called to decide which of the three different models of manliness she will marry. This notwithstanding, Seth seems to be interested in creating a third sex, a rather ambiguous or neutral area, neither male nor female. It must be stressed that this is a transitional epoch and Seth charges the historical context with the right weight: as the rampant Malati proudly exclaims: "This is a new age" (773). She explicitly refers to the early fifties, when Indian women's consciousness was awakened and emancipation movements took their first roots. It was a time when women's and wives' roles were re-examined; without losing their femininity they started to dedicate themselves to jobs and chores which had traditionally been the exclusive prerogative of the males. By hindsight, and with a mild mocking tone, Vikram Seth adds vigour to this historical representation and makes Veena a mouthpiece of these theories: "'Someday,' said Veena, 'this country will have a woman Prime Minister or a woman President'" (860).

The result is that the stereotyped conceptions of masculinity and femininity become blurred, interchangeable, ambiguous. In Shakespeare's *Twelfth Night*, it is Viola's disguise as Cesario which originates a series of contretemps. Referring to her misleading and equivocal situation, she sadly exclaims: "I, poor monster" (2. II. 34). It is significant, furthermore, that when she plans to alter her identity and invert sex she proposes to her friend the captain: "I'll serve this duke. Thou shalt present me as a eunuch to him" (1. II. 54-55), an observation which carries evident and ambivalent sexual connotations. This aspect acquires particular weight in *A Suitable Boy*. In a sequence of unimportant incidents, the author almost casually alludes to such a dubious predicament. That is, to begin with, the case of characters ironically playing the role of the opposite sex as if they were really acting on an improvised stage. This situation occurs at least twice in the novel: the reader first approaches the scene with Saeeda and Tahmina Bai clumsily jumping one on to the other and having fun while imitating men's lust and behavior with women. The episode has a "male" counterpart towards the end of the novel. This episode occurs a few nights before the wedding takes place and the narrator is talking here about Haresh:

> He stayed with Sunil Patwardhan, and the St Stephen's contingent gathered around him in the evenings to tease him

> and enact Scenes from Married Life. The vast Sunil was usually the shrinking wife (1334).

The parallels with similar scenes in Shakespeare's comedies is quite overt here.

Furthermore, *A Suitable Boy* courses through a series of ambiguous sexual situations with the major characters too. Three cases, in particular, call for closer scrutiny: Malati, Maan and Varun. The first, to begin with, is the dearest of Lata's girlfriends. She soon appears in a militant attitude towards the male sex. Vikram Seth is very keen on illustrating her case in psychological terms. As the reader first approaches Malati, he/she is informed about her saddening infancy. A series of coincidences seems to conspire to forge a strong opposition to the male sex in her personality. She has been brought up "almost entirely among women" (28) because both her two brothers and her beloved father had prematurely died: her father's demise, in particular, had left a void she would have tried to fill for the rest of her life. Hence,

> She also grew up as a sort of a boy—though not by any means like the tomboy her sister was—for a variety of reasons connected with her infancy: the direct gaze in her unusual eyes, her boyish look, the fact that the boys' clothes were at hand, the sadness that her parents had experienced at the death of their two sons (28).

Her critical stand against manliness in general is, though, fruit of irony on the part of the central consciousness on various occasions. Lata, whom we have reasonably motivations to consider one of Seth's most trusted mouthpieces, is the first to joke with her friend as the protagonist for the first time finds her quite well-disposed towards boys. Her remark ironically adopts the sex-switching technique to achieve its goal:

> "It's not all that easy for men to talk to us, you know," said Malati. "We shouldn't be so hard on them."
>
> "Malati defending the weaker sex!" said Lata. "I'd never thought I'd see the day" (48).

Another ironical comment the narrative voice reserves to her character occurs when she accidentally meets a man who invites her first to his hotel room (she unblinkingly accepts) and proposes to marry her to one of his five sons. She seems to misunderstand his proposal as she believes she has to marry all five brothers. The allusion to the story of Draupadi is overt and mocking. David Kinsley exposes the case of atypical female characters in Hindu mythology in these terms: "Several goddesses are cast in untraditional, 'masculine' roles that express unconventional, perhaps even experimental, thinking about sex roles."[11]

Maan is the second case in point. His character overtly (and sexually) subverts the notions of masculinity. At the beginning of the novel he is Saeeda Bai's passionate lover: his lust and desire seem irrepressible. That is far more remarkable since their relationship is overtly illegal. As the plot proceeds, anyway, he is the surprising protagonist of the homoerotic relationship with Firoz Nawab. The central consciousness disseminates more than one dubious hint as far as Maan's masculinity, as the common places generally identify it. Needless to say, this process is accomplished with finesse and a touch of irony. In two instances, the author in fact freely overturns the notion of masculinity by making a deliberate topsy-turvy use of the metaphor of the lotus flower and the bees. Since the homosexual relationship occurs much later, the two instances have flashforward function. In the first case it is Maan paralleling his dear friend Firoz to a lotus flower:

> "Don't interrupt," said Maan, throwing an arm around him. "If you were to go down into the garden, a good-looking, elegant fellow like you would be surrounded within seconds by eligible young beauties. And ineligible ones too. They'd cling to you like bees to a lotus. Curly locks, curly locks, will you be mine?"
>
> Firoz flushed. "You've got the metaphor slightly wrong," he said. "Men are bees, women lotuses" (20).

A little later the young Muslim lawyer promptly returns the joke to the Minister of Revenue's son.

> Firoz laughed. "Say that again. I can't believe it," he said. "Maan Kapoor, beau of Berhampur, at whose feet young women of good families, heedless of reputation, hasten to fling themselves like bees on a lotus, seeks the advise of the steely

and stainless Firoz on how to proceed in a matter of heart" (90).

The sexual ambiguity of Maan, as well as of Firoz, is therefore ironically advertised by reversing a classical poetic metaphor.

In addition, we must take into account Varun's case, too. Inversely from Maan, the development of his character completes an ascending curve. His initial passivity and subjection to his elder despotic brother Arun are so manifest that even his sister Lata feels the need to support him and encourage him to rebel against the tyrant. In contrast to all his other siblings, he seems be too introverted to have any relationship with the members of the opposite sex. Yet, much against any reasonable expectation at the end of the novel, "Kalpana Gaur gives him a sexual boost before his IAS interviews" (Myers 98); he passes his exams and thus it is she who makes him a successful man. It is at this time that Mrs. Rupa imposes her will on her younger son and declares: "You too will marry a girl I choose" (1343). The comment has a marked ironical connotation in that it clearly echoes the incipit of the novel. In that case, it was Lata to whom Mrs Rupa had peremptorily addressed the comment: "'You too will marry a boy I choose,' said Mrs. Rupa Mehra firmly to her younger daughter" (3). His condition is similar to that of his sister and it acquires far more mocking connotations if we take into account the fact that it comes at the very moment Varun has finally achieved self-confidence, and his maturity and virility have been successfully tested by the act of sex.

As a final note, one cannot forget that, although the novel is characterised by a variable focalisation, the central consciousness remains feminine, a technique which, incidentally, is once more adopted in Seth's most recent novel, *An Equal Music*. Vikram Seth therefore structures his fictional works using a sex-switching code, a choice quite rare in Indian English fiction by male authors.[12]

In conclusion, the studies of Vikram Seth's magnum opus must take into account his extraordinary ability to forge a fictional technique which contaminates various elements in terms of periods, genres, and characters. Nehruvian period freely mixes with Elizabethan age, dramatic and poetic discourse overlaps fictional narration and male and female identities are confused. In a very revealing passage, Lata overtly hints at this hybrid creation, and in a letter to her future husband Haresh, she writes: "I don't know if I'm myself or one of the Shakespeare's creatures" (912).

NOTES AND REFERENCES

1. A.K. Singh, "Vikram Seth's *A Suitable Boy*: a Critique," *Indian Fiction of the Nineties*, ed. R. S. Pathak (New Delhi: Creative, 1997) 11.
2. Shyam S. Agarwalla, *Vikram Seth's* A Suitable Boy*: Search for an Indian Identity* (Delhi: Prestige, 1995) 12.
3. Raja Rao, *The Cat and Shakespeare* (1971; Delhi: Orient, 1992) 73-75.
4. Vikram Seth, *A Suitable Boy* (1993; New Delhi: Penguin, 1997) 798.
5. David Myers, "Vikram Seth's Epic Renunciation of the Passion: Deconstructing Moral Codes in *A Suitable Boy*," *Indian Literature Today,* vol. 1, ed. R.K. Dhawan (Delhi: Prestige, 1994) 92.
6. For a more detailed description of the "malcontent," see W.J.D. Scott, *Shakespeare's Melancholics* (London: 1962).
7. Eugene Robinson, "A Tolstoy—on His First Try," *Washington Post Foreign Service* 1st May 1993.
8. Singh 19.
9. James Buchan, "A Foreign Country is the Past," *The Spectator* 27th March 1993: 31.
10. For a more detailed description of Shakespeare's Fools, see R.H. Goldsmith *Wise Fools in Shakespeare* (Liverpool: 1955).
11. David Kinsley, *Hindu Goddesses* (Delhi: Archives, 1987) 4.
12. Other cases in point are R.K. Narayan's *The Dark Room* and B. Bhattacharya's *Music for Mohini*.

10

The Discoverer Discovered: Amitav Ghosh's *The Calcutta Chromosome*

JOHN THIEME*

At first sight Amitav Ghosh may appear to be one of the burgeoning groups of post-Rushdie Indian novelists in English for whom globalization is an everyday fact of existence. He wrote his Oxford doctoral thesis on the history of weaving and the cloth trade between England and India in the nineteenth century; he lived in Egypt while researching material for *In An Antique Land* (1992), a personal memoir which is also an investigation of aspects of the medieval mercantile culture which extended from the Western Mediterranean to the Malabar coast;[1] and he has lived in New York, from which his most recent novel, *The Calcutta Chromosome* (1996) takes its departure-point, as its initial protagonist journeys around the world through the medium of a futuristic version of the World Wide Web.

Like such novelists as Naipaul, Rushdie, Desai and Mistry, Ghosh seems to move effortlessly across national frontiers—as Robert Dixon puts it, not inhabiting "a culture rooted in a single place, but a discursive space that flows across political and national boundaries, and even across generations in time" (9). Dixon's remark refers specifically to Ghosh's second novel, *The Shadow Lines* (1988), which takes the events that followed in the wake of Partition as its central subject, suggesting that the cartographical shadow-lines that divide Bengal are political fictions that nonetheless

*Professor of English/HSS, South Bank University, London SE1 OAA United Kingdom.

generate all-too-real murderous consequences. As I have put it myself, "'Shadow lines' are, however, far more than just the borders constructed by politicians. They are also the lines of demarcation that separate colonized and colonizer, present and past, self and image. Ultimately they are the signifying acts that construct notions of discrete identity [...]" (65-66). Ghosh projects a view in which the frontier that separates India from East Pakistan/Bangladesh is a "looking-glass border" (*Shadow Lines* 228) and in which complex affinities link the apparently dichotomized worlds of colonizer and colonized.

Such a view may, of course, be seen as suggesting that the Manichean binaries which certain postcolonial critics have seen as a prime characterizing aspect of colonial discourse are illusory rather than real since an underlying humanism prevails. Alternatively, it could be seen as a fictive equivalent of the hybridization model promoted by such postcolonial theorists as Homi Bhabha. However, both these readings are, in my opinion, mistaken, although I do wish to argue that Ghosh eschews the conventional postcolonial view of Manichean allegory for other reasons. Both run the risk of "dehistoricizing"—and "degeographizing"—cultural difference: the former through a glib, if comfortable, humanism; the latter through a tendency to use a global vocabulary to locate what constitutes colonial discourse, without adequate attentiveness to the social and historical specificities of the texts under discussion. While such specifics are themselves hybridized, the particular components (once again hybridized) that go into their making vary enormously.

My contention, which I should like to try to develop in relation to *The Calcutta Chromosome*, is that, far from being a diaspora writer whose global interests obscure social and ideological specifics, Ghosh is concerned to excavate a labyrinthine network of traces, which foreground such specifics, while making it clear that essentialist versions of national and regional cultures, such as those inherent in Orientalist discourses, are unsustainable. This paper also endeavours to discuss Ghosh's work in relation to the Subaltern Studies project[2] and to argue that *The Calcutta Chromosome* exposes the limitations of postcolonial theorizing, of the kind pioneered by Fanon and developed by Jan Mohamed, on the subject of Manichean allegory. Such theorists relocate Manicheism—a religious system that originated east of Suez and, when it moved westwards, threatened the medieval hegemony of the Catholic church in Western Europe—as a Western discourse. Augustinian theology deemed Manicheism a heresy, but in this re-reading it is wrested from its traditional position in Western Christian thought for revisionist purposes predicated on a dualistic model of a kind which traditionally would have been considered heterodox. Ghosh, I argue, engages closely with this orthodox Christian view and, in so doing, implicitly—and occasionally explicitly—offers a much more radical challenge to Eurocentric modes of thinking. While the theorists of colonial Manicheism see Europe as having developed binary systems of classification (in which the colonial partner is, of course, always the inferior in a two-way power relationship) Ghosh appears to subscribe to the view that Western discourse silences alterity by denying its very capacity for utterance. At the same time, despite his own location within the West, he slips the nets of Eurocentric classification through an approach which investigates the possibility of opening up a discursive space in which the notion of giving voice to the hitherto silenced subaltern is a viable imaginative possibility. Putting this another way: in Augustinian terms, he is propounding a heresy, suggesting that a Manichean counter-force, which threatens the cornerstone of Judeo-Christian thought and, I would argue, by extension, colonial discursive systems, may exist. Gayatri Spivak asks the question, "Can the subaltern speak?" All of Ghosh's work to date seems to have been directed towards wanting to answer this question in the affirmative, while recognizing that the recuperation of the voice of an indigenous culture which is assumed to have existed in parallel with colonial discourse, is a problem fraught with difficulties, partly because acknowledgement of the existence of such a culture could presuppose that such a domain had an autonomous, uncontaminated existence (and all the evidence—linguistic, archaeological, theological, etc.—suggests that cross-pollination and syncretism always occur when cultures come into contact); and also because colonial and other forms of elite historiography have effectively occluded subaltern narratives from the scribal records of societies.

The two main strategies which Ghosh employs to counter these difficulties are imaginative reinventions based on a bedrock of historical "fact" and a recurrent emphasis on the interactions occurring within both "Western" and "Eastern" cultures during the last millennium. His most "factual" work to date, *In An Antique Land*, and an essay which is subsumed within this text, "The Slave of MS. H. 6" (which originally appeared in the seventh volume of *Subaltern Studies*), blend anthropology, travel-writing, cultural theory and fiction to produce a possible rather than a supposedly authenticated account of subaltern history, as Ghosh pursues the fugitive traces of an eleventh-century slave to be found in the letters of the Jewish merchant who was his master. Meanwhile, the Ghosh persona in *In An Antique Land* and in another essay which was subsumed within the book, "The Imam and the Indian," is a social anthropologist doing fieldwork in Egypt, who discovers the migrant, unsettled nature of what he has taken to be settled, "authentic" cultures. *The Calcutta Chromosome* is more overtly fictive, but again it interweaves a network of traces—from the history of late nineteenth-century malaria research, theological movements generally deemed to be heretical in the West and slightly futuristic information technology *inter alia*—to provide the possibility of an alternative subaltern history, which exists in parallel with colonial history as an equally (or possibly more) potent epistemological system, albeit one which has traditionally operated through silence rather than articulation.

Such interweaving has been central to Ghosh's work from the outset. Its centrality in his Oxford doctorate fed into his first novel, *The Circle of Reason* (1986), which follows the fortunes of a young weaver who travels from his home village near Calcutta to work in the Gulf. The novel suggests that weaving is a diasporic activity that transcends national origins and unites worlds which have habitually been viewed as separate, and in so doing anticipates Ghosh's later contention in *In An Antique Land* that the medieval trade-routes functioned as a mobile inter-continental network that was largely unaware of Western Oriental/Occidental bifurcations. In *The Shadow Lines*, weaving is less literally central, but, as Dixon points out, it remains an "organizing figure" (9) in a text which challenges notions of the rootedness of place and in so doing subverts the rhetoric of English India. Putting this another way, *The Shadow Lines* operates through a poetics of migrancy, radically unsettling essentialist conceptions of both nation and subjectivity. So too does *The Calcutta Chromosome*, Ghosh's most powerful anthropological detective-story to date.

The main narrative of the novel involves a re-examination of the history of late nineteenth-century malaria research by a possibly deranged Calcutta-born man named Murugan (he is also known as Morgan) who works for an international public health company called LifeWatch and uses an Americanized slang register, which characterizes him as a diaspora subject. Murugan has had a life-long obsession with the history of malaria research, which has led him to the conviction that Ronald Ross, the British scientist who was awarded the 1902 Nobel Prize for Medicine for his work on the life-cycle of the malaria parasite which four years earlier had isolated how the disease is transmitted, was not a "lone genius" (57), a brilliant British dilettante who outstripped all of the contemporary scientists in the field. Murugan believes there is a secret history that has been erased from the scribal records of the colonial society and from medical historiography more generally. He has devoted himself to uncovering the hidden truth.

Murugan is first encountered through the mediation of another diaspora subject, Antar, a New York-based computer systems operator, who has been a former colleague of Murugan's and now works for an international water agency which has absorbed LifeWatch. In the opening chapter Antar comes across a fragment of an ID card on the screen of his computer and this sets him off on a quest to reconstruct the totality of the card and then the recent life-history of its missing owner. The owner turns out to be Murugan, a man whom Antar has interviewed a few years before—the novel is set in the near future—on behalf of LifeWatch, to try to dissuade him from a request to be transferred to Calcutta, at a greatly reduced salary, so that he can pursue his "notion of the so-called 'Other Mind': a theory that some person or persons had systematically interfered with Ronald Ross's experiments to push malaria research in certain directions while leading it away from others" (36). Murugan has been reported as missing; he has last been seen in Calcutta on August 21, 1995.

From this departure-point the novel uncovers its intricate network of traces, interweaving a number of parallel quest-stories which range from those of Ross and his late nineteenth-century medical contemporaries through to Antar's pursuit of Murugan through the resources of the Internet, which at this moment in the near future has already become considerably more sophisticated than it was at the time when the novel was published. In *The Calcutta Chromosome* the Web assumes much the same role as weaving in Ghosh's earlier work, functioning as a synecdoche for the interpenetration of cultures, which as I have indicated is central to all of Ghosh's writing. Antar's quest for Murugan leads the reader into a Russian doll-like assortment of other quests, which are gradually revealed to be interlocking narratives and which, to borrow Dixon's phrase again inhabit "a discursive space that flows across political and national boundaries, and even across generations in time." In this sense at least, *The Calcutta Chromosome*, which initially seems to be very different from *The Shadow Lines*, is exploring very similar terrain.

A single example of the novel's numerous interlocking narrative strands may help to illustrate how its linkages across time and space operate. On the day on which Murugan arrives in Calcutta, August 20, 1995, Phulboni, a famous writer, is being given an award to mark his eighty-fifth birthday. Receiving the award, Phulboni gives a gnomic speech about the power of silence. Like Murugan/Morgan, Phulboni has more than one name, more than one identity. His "real name" (27) is Saiyad Murad Husain; Phulboni is a pen-name. In his earlier life Phulboni has undergone a mysterious experience, when as a young recruit to a British company he was sent, in 1933, to a provincial town named Renupur. He has arrived by train at its deserted station, some distance from the town and in a landscape flooded by monsoon rains; and there, despite the stationmaster's attempts to persuade him to the contrary, he decides to spend the night in the signal-room. A night of terror ensues. Objects move as though controlled by some telekinetic agency. Phulboni falls asleep, awakes to discover that the signal lantern is no longer where he has placed it and then sees it some fifty yards down the railway track. Assuming that the stationmaster is carrying it, he follows it down the line, trips and narrowly averts being killed by a train which comes hurtling down the track at this moment, even though the line is a siding and no train is due. In fact the stationmaster has told him that the station has only ever been used once before. He appears to fall asleep again and wake up the next morning to find the stationmaster telling him that the lantern has not been moved. And then he appears to awaken again, just in time to throw himself out of the path of *another* oncoming train. This time the experience is "all too real" (279). Phulboni subsequently speaks to the train's stokers and engineers, who are horrified that it has been directed into the siding, which they say has not been used for thirty years and where the tracks are rusty, overgrown and full of debris. When Phulboni suggests that the stationmaster may have "pulled the switch by mistake" (279), the chief engineer of the train tells him there has not been a stationmaster at Renupur for thirty years.

The first part of this episode could well be explained away as Phulboni's fantasy or hallucination and the text is full of incidents which raise the possibility that those who experience them are Pynchonesque paranoid schizophrenics or fever-prone former malaria sufferers, experiencing recurrent bouts of delirium—Antar, Murugan and Ross have all contracted malaria at some point in their lives—but, as in Pynchon, there is a body of circumstantial evidence to suggest that the dangers faced by the text's questers are "all too real" and that a secret Manichean counter-force may be at large in the world. Rather more than thirty years previously, in 1894, an American scientist, Elijah Farley, who appears to have discovered that a sinister conspiracy is manipulating the experiments of Ross's Calcutta predecessor, D.D. Cunningham (also known as C.C. Dunn), has been reported as having vanished after disembarking from a train at Renupur. Like virtually everything else in the text the nature of this report is presented as unreliable: it takes the form of Antar's super-computer Ava's partly fictionalized reconstruction of a lost e-mail account of Farley's missing last letter, a letter which has itself mysteriously disappeared after Murugan has read it in a Baltimore library. Nevertheless it posits the possibility of a startling link with the Phulboni episode. In this episode the veteran guard of the train that has nearly killed Phulboni remembers a foreigner dying at Renupur in 1894 in an almost identical incident. At the time of the foreigner's death the sole occupant of the station was a young man named Laakhan. Laakhan (also known as Lutchman—the shifting nature of names is a clue to the text's central revelation concerning the Calcutta chromosome which still lies ahead) has been one of the assistants in Cunningham's laboratory, whose conspiratorial activities Farley appears to have discovered. Hence, at least according to one interpretation, the need to eliminate Farley. And by this point in the novel, which employs a Conradian battery of time-shifts, the reader knows that Laakhan/Lutchman has subsequently worked for Ross and there are also traces of his identity in a range of other contexts. He has a thumbless left hand and in the Phulboni episode, along with the evidence of poltergeist activity Phulboni has seen a mysterious imprint of just such a hand in the signal-box at Renupur. The elderly guard completes the story of what happened at Renupur in 1894 by telling Phulboni that, after the death of the foreigner, a stationmaster *was* found, an upper-caste man who regarded Laakhan and his misshapen left hand as worse than untouchable and attempted to kill him "by switching the points and leading him before a train" (281), only to suffer the fate he has intended for Laakhan himself—a third instance of a narrowly averted or actual death of this kind.

In some ways this third instance is the most interesting, though it is narrated in a more summary fashion, since it provides the most obvious case of a subaltern figure exercising power, even if this figure remains voiceless, an antagonist rather than a protagonist in the text's storytelling process. There will be a fourth trace of the Renupur station motif towards the end of the novel, which I will return to before concluding.

What Farley has discovered is that Cunningham's work on the mosquito parasite is being hampered by assistants he has picked up at Sealdah railway station in Calcutta: notably Laakhan and a woman, who in the text's imaginative reconstruction of these events is named Mangala. She appears to be both the high priestess of a secret medical cult offering a cure for syphilis and the brain behind the discoveries that will eventually lead to Ross's winning the Nobel Prize. So Ghosh's narrative discredits the Western scientist and instates an Indian female subaltern in his place.

Murugan's research leads him to the conclusion that Mangala and her associates are hindering Cunningham's research so that he will be replaced by Ross, whom they can use as a vessel for their discoveries. These discoveries are, however, concerned with far more than a malaria cure. They involve a counter-epistemology, which promises a form of immortality through the erosion of Western conceptions of discrete subjectivity, through the dismantling of the shadow-lines that construct notions of autonomous selfhood. This perhaps explains the text's recurrent destabilizing of notions of fixed identity by giving characters more than one name. Mangala's discovery of the means by which malaria is transmitted has come about as a by-product of her real research interest. Working outside the straitjacket of Western empirical methodologies, she has been attempting to evolve "a technology for interpersonal transference" (106), a means of transmitting knowledge "chromosomally from body to body" (107). In Murugan's view the relationship between Mangala's counter-science and that of conventional scientists such as Ross is analogous to the relationship between "matter and antimatter [...] rooms and ante-rooms [...] Christ and Antichrist and so on" (103). So, if one accepts Murugan's thesis, there is the possibility of a subaltern Manichean force which, though it operates through silence and secrecy, is at least as powerful as Western logocentrism. In this respect the novel is strongly reminiscent of Pynchon's *The Crying of Lot 49* (1966), where the protagonist finds traces of an alternative communications network, which appears to have been functioning in America—and prior to this in Renaissance Europe—as a hidden, but omnipresent Manichean system. Whether such a conspiracy exists or whether it is simply the product of a paranoiac's fantasizing is the central debate in *The Crying of Lot 49* and the novel concludes with this question left unanswered.

In one sense *The Calcutta Chromosome* is equally open-ended. Towards the end Antar receives information about Murugan's disappearance. He, too, has taken a train to Renupur and so it seems as though he may have suffered the fate of Farley and the stationmaster who has attempted to kill Laakhan. However, towards the end Ava, Antar's computer, locates him in the Department of Alternative States in Fort William, Calcutta; he has become a psychiatric patient. At this point Antar himself is feverish as a result of a recurrence of his malaria. So both the main interpreters of the evidence are, from one point of view, extremely unreliable. But, then, all of Ghosh's work suggests that the imaginative, fictive reconstruction of subaltern experience is the only way in which it can be rendered. Hence his blurring of the boundaries between anthropology and fiction. If one admits that fictive invention can operate in this way, then the reliability of the centres of consciousness who are experiencing the action ceases to be such a serious issue.

This is not to suggest that Ghosh engages in a playful postmodernist relativism, however. What *The Calcutta Chromosome* forces its readers to engage with is the possibility of an alternative historiography, in which traditionally disempowered subjects prove to be the real puppet-masters. The counter-science cult led by Mangala can only operate through silence—Phulboni's disquisition on the power of silence on his eighty-fifth birthday is the single passage which (paradoxically?) articulates this[3]—but the fictive reconstruction in which Murugan, Antar and ultimately Ghosh engage subverts the hegemonic dominance of Western logocentrism all the same. And this has implications for readings of colonial and postcolonial cultural practices that emphasize Manichean allegory. According to Jan Mohamed such allegory is a Western discourse which constructs binary oppositions in which the colonial subject is always the inferior partner in a two-way power relationship. But orthodox Augustinian theology, which is the lynch-pin of Western Christianity, regards Manicheism as a heresy because it propounds dualistic modes of classification. It is a heresy because it allows evil to exist in the world as a counter-force to good, whereas the orthodox position denies evil any such autonomous existence. Since God is omnipresent, evil can only be the privation of good. So postcolonial critics whose concern with the construction of alterity leads them to suggest that Western colonialism habitually operated in terms of Manichean classifications are in fact proposing a model which is at odds with the dominant view of Manicheism in European thought. Of course, Western attitudes may have changed in the late Victorian heyday of Empire, but the popular postcolonial version of Manicheism still distorts because it obscures the fact that classic Western discourse has been monistic not dualistic. Manicheism is more accurately characterized as an Eastern challenge to the exclusiveness of Western discourses which deny the other's capacity for utterance.

Ghosh engages with Manicheism in an altogether more complex and historically grounded way than the postcolonial interpreters of Manichean allegory. He only mentions it as such on one occasion in the novel (214). This is in a passage about the archaeological excavations of a woman who has been a devotee of a "Society of Spiritualists" that flourished in Madras at the same time as the Theosophical Society, which with its Gnostic beliefs was itself a late nineteenth-century challenge to Western monism. However, the Society is led by a woman who is seen as Madame Blavatsky's "arch-rival" (207) and her disciple, the Hungarian Countess Pongrácz, whom Antar appears to have met during his early life in Egypt (5-7), has become an advocate of the teachings of Valentinus (the Alexandrian-born Gnostic philosopher who took dualistic religious beliefs to Rome in the second century A.D.), as well as an excavator of archaeological traces of dualistic systems—Nestorian[4] as well as Manichean. Like the Countess Pongrácz, Ghosh discovers fragments of suppressed heterodox systems; and the novel's repeated emphasis on Silence provides a reading of the subaltern which suggests that a figure denied a voice by hegemonic cultures and deemed heretical in Christian thinking could exist as a viable power-player in his and, in this case even more, her own right.

The Calcutta chromosome and the possibility of effecting the "interpersonal transference" of knowledge occupies a central role in this investigation, since such transference would erode the barriers between elite and subaltern classes, between the purveyors and the recipients of knowledge. Everything about Ghosh's novel seems to be working towards this end. Structurally it moves between multiple stories and characters; and the near-repetition of variant forms of the same situation, such as the Renupur station episode, also works to dismantle the notion of discrete essentialist versions.

In addition to all this, there is a final twist in the narrative, which takes the investigation of epistemological relationships into yet more subtle territory. Throughout the text readers are made aware that the borderline between discoverers and those who are discovered is an extremely porous one. Ross appears to be a discoverer who makes a revolutionary advance in the science of microscopy, but it seems he has been discovered and controlled by Mangala and her followers. Murugan investigates the secret history of malaria research and is in turn investigated by Antar. The last two chapters of the novel complicate and extend this pattern even further. On August 21, 1995 Murugan follows the final stages of his trail with a magazine journalist, Urmila Roy, another quester who has been prominent throughout the novel. His thesis involves the belief that the counter-science cult is absorbed with "interpersonal transference" as part of a long-term strategy based on the notion that "to know something is to change it" (104). Towards the end the novel appears to be moving towards some kind of apocalyptic revelation and one wonders whether Murugan is about to become a victim or an initiate of the cult. Such ambivalence is, of course, central to *The Calcutta Chromosome*'s procedure and its unsettling of the shadow-lines between elite and subaltern subjects. Nevertheless there is a fresh surprise in the penultimate chapter when Murugan tells Urmila that *she* is the "chosen" (306) one of Mangala's contemporary incarnation and asks her to promise, "that you'll take me across if I don't make it on my own" (305). Urmila's investigations have played a significant part in Murugan's detective-work, but hitherto she has not seemed to occupy a central role in the process of discovery. Now Murugan sees her as having such a role and explains:

> You see, for them the only way to escape the tyranny of knowledge is to turn it on itself. But for that to work they have to create a single perfect moment of discovery when the person who discovers is also that which is discovered (306).

The final chapter provides an even more startling instance of a discoverer who is discovered. The text returns to Antar who, in his New York apartment with his super-computer, appears to be the ultimate discoverer of meaning within the novel. As the figure who frames the rest of the narrative, he alone seems to stand outside the multiplicity of other narratives, immune from the possibility of complicity in conspiracy. But he too is a feverish investigator and the final chapter undermines the possibility of exempting him from the process of "interpersonal transference" that has engulfed all the other main characters. He now begins to think that Ava's stumbling upon Murugan's ID card—the opening moment of the novel—has not, after all, been an accident; and the web of correspondences expands even further, as two of his New York friends who have seemed to be no more than incidental extras in the frame-narrative, are absorbed into the visual images of Murugan's last day in Calcutta which Ava is projecting for him. Another discoverer finds himself discovered.

As one closes *The Calcutta Chromosome*, there is perhaps yet one more inference to be drawn from the novel. In erasing the distinction between discoverers and the discovered, Ghosh has also demonstrated the unsatisfactoriness of making rigid distinctions between storytellers and listeners. Nobody, the suggestion seems to be, is exempt from history or from playing an active role in the *historiographical* process. So perhaps the ultimate discoverer who is discovered by the novel is the reader. *The Calcutta Chromosome* has invited its readers to play the role of hermeneutic detective, to piece together its numerous clues to arrive, if not at a solution, at least at a possible version of meaning. The final insistence that all the investigators within the text are implicated in the material they are investigating leaves the novel's readers having to consider the possibility that they too are caught in the conspiracy of history. Or, to put this another way, the conclusion suggests that readers have not been playing the role of passive subalterns, but rather, as makers of meaning, empowering themselves through the *silent* agency of reading. For adherents of reader response theory such a discovery will come as nothing new, but the novel's contribution to such debates remains a highly distinctive one, because it provides a site which combines a re-reading of fashionable postcolonial theorizing about Manichean allegory with this dismantling of the Manichean binary of writer and reader.

NOTES

1. I.e. involved a nexus of connections which bears little correspondence to the East-West "imaginative geography," which Said talks about in *Orientalism* (1978) or to post-Enlightenment European mappings of nation-states.
2. My argument takes its point of departure from Robert Dixon's article "'Travelling in the West': The Writing of Amitav Ghosh," to which I am particularly indebted. Dixon points out Ghosh's links with the Subaltern Studies project (9 ff.)
3. Why Phulboni survives the Renupur station experience, while Farley and the stationmaster appear to have died, is not made clear, but his later espousal of the gospel of Silence suggests that he has become a devotee of Mangala's cult and raises the possibility that he may be a subject of "interpersonal transference."
4. Nestorian doctrine insists on the distinctiveness of the human and divine aspects of Christ.

WORKS CITED

Dixon, Robert. "'Travelling in the West': The Writing of Amitav Ghosh." *The Journal of Commonwealth Literature* 31.1 (1996): 3-24.

Ghosh, Amitav. *The Circle of Reason*. London: Hamish Hamilton, 1986.

——. "The Imam and the Indian." *Granta* 20 (1986): 135-46.

——. *The Shadow Lines*. London: Bloomsbury, 1988.

——. "The Slave of MS. H. 6." *Subaltern Studies* 7: *Writings on South Asian History and Society*. Eds. Partha Chatterjee and Gyanendra Pandey. Delhi: OUP, 1992.

——. *In An Antique Land*. London: Granta, 1992.

——. *The Calcutta Chromosome*. London: Picador, 1996.

Jan Mohamed, Abdul. *Manichean Aesthetics: The Politics of Literature in Colonial Africa*. Amherst: U of Massachusetts P, 1983.

——. "The Economy of Manichean Allegory: The Function of Racial Difference in Colonial Literature." *Critical Inquiry* 12.1 (1985): 59-87.

Pynchon, Thomas. *The Crying of Lot 49*. Philadelphia: J.B. Lippincott, 1966.

Said, Edward, *Orientalism*. New York: Pantheon, 1978.

Thieme, John. "Passages to England." *Liminal Postmodernisms: The Postmodern, the (Post-)Colonial and the (Post-)Feminist*. Eds. Theo D'haen and Hans Bertens. Amsterdam and Atlanta: Rodopi, 1994. 55-78.

11

"A certain will of assimilation": Arundhati Roy, the Syrian Christians, and the Naxalites

ALESSANDRA CONTENTI*

With all its word play and sensational sex, Arundhati Roy's *The God of Small Things* poses a highly serious question about civil rights in India and the persistence of cruel forms of social injustice, of discrimination against human beings who happen to be born in the wrong section of society. As the novel seems to imply, the postcolonial era and Independence have not mended ancient wounds, such as poverty and the persistence of unsociability, in spite of Mahatma Gandhi's relentless campaign. The story shows how a Paravan, an untouchable, in the modern state of Kerala, a little more than 20 years ago could still be murdered shamelessly, denied the right to a trial, and to a basic human dignity.

To a western reader raised in the Christian tradition, the novel is all the more striking for its being set among Christians, a milieu that appears at once strangely familiar and yet bizarre with macroscopic moral aberrations; with all their Christianity—the Syrians of India claim to descend from Thomas, one of the twelve apostles—yet they find it natural to perpetuate the shameful institution of untouchability.

Justice and humanism are trampled upon in a number of ways in different societies; to understand this particular form of injustice, we must divest ourselves of our idea of Christianity, and connect

*Università RomaTre, Italy.

the story narrated by Roy with the actual culture from which it derives, and with a community with a particular history; this culture survived for almost two thousand years in India but in order to do so it underwent adaptations and transformations. This work is a partial attempt to follow up those transformations to the present day, in connection, of course with Roy's novel.

The Syrian Christians in India seem to have been, since the beginning, quite a thing of their own; their history, probably as old as Christianity itself, began in the legendary days of Thomas the Apostle, hence the name of St. Thomas Christians. A group of these, escaping from religious persecution, landed and settled down in Malabar, starting a community where the modern state of Kerala is—a land of temples and churches; they became rich and respected and well acculturated (although never assimilated) into the local milieu. A historian writes:

> Most of the Syrians today [...] consider themselves to be the descendants of the Apostle's first converts [ ] it is also certain that the first communities date from very early times indeed [...] in 239 A.D. there were already groups in existence [...] towards the end of the 4th century they were reinforced by another groups of immigrants who had travelled under the leadership of Thomas Cana, a wealthy merchant trading, in pepper and ginger [...] the last group established themselves at Quilon in 823.'

Until the beginning of Portuguese colonization the Syrian former immigrants consisted of communities residing in the ports. These foreign traders had established themselves permanently in Kerala by then and as the extant documents indicate, occupied a powerful position in key sectors of Kerala's economy, foreign trade, spices, salt, sugar and oil; apparently they dealt with all kinds of goods and even had a monopoly over commercial transactions "their group had the responsibility to collect custom duties."[2]

As to their social connections, apparently "the Syrian groups enjoyed" since the beginning "an extremely high status..."[3] which they retained in later periods. Having arrived in Malabar in subsequent immigration waves, they had established themselves in that region before the arrival of the Brahmins themselves, who, although more numerous, do not seem to have attempted to weaken their community; instead they accorded to the Christian Church and to the Christians who formed it, the same privileges as those belonging to a Brahmin temple; in other words a status equivalent to that of the highest places in the hierarchy of the time. The Brahmins "whose status resided on the manipulation of symbolic products and the rejection of any activity of secular nature, had no reason to oppose mercantile activities"[4]; besides, the Syrians could afford to be generous to the Hindu temples.

The Syrian Christians proudly held on to their identity, while acquiring a prestigious role in the local society: "They became an important trading community in Malabar," writes K. J. John,[5]

> they have become almost a part of Kerala's Hindu social order and it appears that they maintained the ecclesiastical connections with the Persian Church to safeguard their trading interests (a large part of the pepper trade was in their hands); they developed and grew in power, influence and number until our days.[6]

A historian relates that up to 1700 they had "lived through 16 centuries with no worse problems than those involved in maintaining their existence as a merchant group first in a society based on lineage relations, then in a caste society."[7]

A constant presence in Malabar history, the Syrians today (along with other Christians) represent 20% of the local population; they are socially active and have contributed in making the life standard in Kerala one of the highest in all of India. "In 1921 half the number of those literate in English belonged to this group."[8] Today they run schools of different levels for boys and girls; in Kottayam Catholic Syrians alone run fourteen primary schools, three secondary schools for boys and two for girls.

Their women enjoy a high degree of emancipation: the first woman to obtain a BA degree in law in Kerala in 1909 was a Syrian Christian (Mary Roy, the novelist's mother is quite probably one of those emancipated women; having led for 30 years a relentless campaign for women's rights, "as a lawyer she fought against the Christian inheritance law, winning a landmark Supreme Court verdict that granted Christian women in Kerala the rights to their parents' property").[9]

Recently the Syrians have invested in new plantations especially rubber, and from the 1920 onwards, the fields of finance and foreign trade once more became familiar to them[10]; in 1921 eleven banks out of fifty were Syrian.

The cultural heritage of the Syrians was recently brought to the world's attention by Arundhati Roy's hugely successful *The God of Small Things*, a novel that exposes certain racist attitudes of that community (into which the author herself was born); the novel illustrates, as it were, the present state of the Syrian Christians in Kerala, their evolution and corruption, and finally their substantial assimilation into Indian society. Implicitly it deals with the metamorphoses they underwent in order to survive and keep their privileges in a Hindu country, run by a Communist government, while being all along a community that has not ceased to proclaim its cultural difference (with a slight presumption of superiority).

It is not my purpose to deal with the autobiographical value of *The God of Small Things,* although one cannot overlook the fact that the author herself belongs to the community of the Syrian Christians, that the pickle factory in the story, Mammachi's creation, exists in real life, and that the heroine is to a large extent modelled upon the figure of Roy's mother, a sharp and an extremely intelligent woman, divorced, with two children; Mary Roy herself has not denied the points of contact between her biography and the story of Ammu.

This discussion's main concern is, however, to try and offer a cultural explanation for the main theme of the novel, the murdering of Velutha, an untouchable, by the Ayemenem police (with the unspoken support of the whole community) for daring to make love to Ammu, a Christian woman. The theme echoes a classic novel of the 1930's another story of a young untouchable, Bakha, humiliated and beaten in the marketplace, for having inadvertently brushed against a Brahmin in the street. Fortunately, in that classic story— M.R. Anand's *Untouchable,* 1935—a charitable Muslim, passing through the bazaar with his ox-cart, gives a welcome lift to the frightened boy, and in so doing he saves him from the rage of the crowd.

Yet there is no charitable Muslim in *The God of Small Things*—not many left in post-Partition India—and no one to speak for

Velutha among his party comrades (though he is a card-carrying member of the Communist party); there is no Good Samaritan among his fellow Christians (after all, Velutha is a Christian if only a third generation convert), nor anyone mindful of Gandhi's campaign in favour of the Harijans (the outcastes), or for that matter of the law that formally abolished untouchability many years ago. Not even his father Vellya Paapen intends to help him in his disgrace—in fact, like a pariah of the old school, one of those who used to "crawl backwards with a broom sweeping away their footprints so that Brahmins or Syrian Christians would not defile themselves by accidentally stepping into a Paravan's footprint,""" not only does he not plead for his son's innocence but is the first to report his supposed crime to Mammachi (Ammu's mother).

As in certain stories set in the Deep South of the United States, where harmless blacks are accused of raping white women and are lynched by the mob—thus Velutha is beaten to death at the Police Station for having raped—in their view of things—a high caste woman; this is really how Ammu is rated, although she is a Syrian Christian, and not so fair-skinned either.

An enigma around which the novel is centered, at least for a Western reader, is how can a community of Christians in a state run by Communist government let such a thing happen as if it were obvious and natural, though unfortunate? Nothing but the author's indignation makes one think that what happens to Velutha is unfair in the eyes of the community—indeed they all seem to leave him to his doom and to blame only him for breaking the rules. And then what rules? Certainly neither those of Communism nor those of Christianity, but rather the unspoken ancient conventions and of a caste society, a thing of the past but still a living reality.

Through a sort of cultural osmosis the Christian communities in India have absorbed the customs of the Hindus and their mentality and have produced a sort of Hindu-Christianity in a long process of contiguity and homogenization. Arundhati Roy describes the infiltration of Christianity into the sub-continent as a slow, gradual process "like tea [seeping out] from a teabag,"[12] but one might claim, that Hinduism itself, even more successfully, has seeped into Kerala's Christianity like tea from a teabag. While carving for themselves a role of respectability and power within the local community, the Christians acquired the new ideology very close to that of the Hindu; or, if they were converts, they never relinquished their old one. More likely still, proximity must have reinforced in the "foreign" community of the Christians certain traits that were to begin with very close to a caste attitude; G. Lemercinier maintains that while they had no formal part in the caste structure, still the Syrians "adopted very widely the social practices of the Hindu groups especially those of the caste Hindus ... they also practised internal discrimination closely resembling that of caste-relations; the Syrian indeed possessed slaves."[13]

Another statement, by a historian of religions seems an appropriate commentary to the events described in the novel: "The religion of the traditional Kerala Christians has always been more a Hindu way of life and worship than a dogmatic system of theological abstractions"[14]; it explains the jarring incongruence between the fierce caste discrimination and the proclaimed ancestral faith of Reverend Ipe's family, Ammu's grandfather, a bishop of the Syrian Orthodox Church.

The family's horror of race pollution leads Ammu and her children to a cruel punishment, and indeed the whole family to a catastrophic end: Ammu is rejected, forced to give up her twins and to escape to another city, where she becomes ill and dies desperately alone, still young; the children's mental balance is shattered; Chaco, Ammu's brother, flees to Canada to hide his shame, Mammachi, her mother dies heartbroken. Falling in love, indeed, is only the last of Ammu's many crimes; there have been previous ones: a divorce, and before that an exogamic "love marriage," probably with a Hindu; "as a *divorced* daughter" ... she had no position anywhere at all. Worse than that, she is "a *divorced* daughter" by "a *love marriage*" and worse still "from an *intercommunity* love marriage." "Well," concludes the author, "words could not describe Baby Kochamma's outrage."[15]

The only survivor of the family, after the catastrophe is, precisely, Baby Kochamma, the spinster aunt who turned Catholic in her youth for love of an Irish priest, a grotesque symbol of aristocratic prejudice and narrow mindedness, a bloated, venomous, bejewelled old woman, who spends her last years watching television in the company of the cook, Kochu Maria, a life-long servant, in the deserted, darkened house.

The Syrian Christians came to absorb a caste mentality very early in the days of their settlement in Malabar, as we learn from the perplexed letters written home by pastoral visitors; one of the reasons is that in pre-Portuguese days (that is, before the Portuguese with their superior power came to protect them from local pressure) they had to lean on to the Hindus to shield themselves from Moslem intolerance. Physical nearness and the need to survive led them to a sort of mimetic process necessary for a minority amidst an alien majority.

Apart from questions of ritual ("the Syrian Christian priests were married")[16] their Christianity appeared on the whole a little strange to an external observer: a letter written after the arrival of the Portuguese reveals that they appeared quite similar to the local people, the Nair, and the Hindus of Kerala. The writer of a letter reports that the Christians had not abandoned Hindu customs such as washing corpses before burial, taking ritual baths, avoiding untouchables"; They have nothing Christian but the name, they believe in witches and fortune tellers, they propitiate evil spirits, sacrifice animals, use charms and amulets, make circles with rice, use Hindu death and wedding ceremonies, use sacred thread, wash dead corpses like the Hindus; they practice untouchability like the Nair who wash themselves after touching a Parayan for fear of becoming themselves Parayan, they confine women 40 days after childbirth, cover the church floor with watered dung, have a suicide squad cutting their bodies, shedding their blood in detestation of injuries done to them, kill whomsoever they meet [...] until they fall victim of someone else."[17]

The Christians who had been latinized (that is brought into the Catholic Churchy by the Portuguese, were nevertheless, according to the same source, totally unwilling to abandon native customs, beliefs and worship system: when Latinisation was imposed, they reacted violently, aware as they were of the need of liberating themselves from foreign missionaries and making the Syrian church independent, with its own priests and bishops.[18]

Another side of the question or rather the question as seen from another angle, a missionary's angle, points to very much the same conclusions. Since the Syrian Christians were similar to the Hindus, a missionary could not do much to change them—in fact he had to turn a little Hindu himself in order to make converts in the Malabar land. The curious story of the Italian Jesuit Roberto de Nobili reaffirms the same problem, while pointing to a solution of high compromise. In the 17th century, De Nobili, a young missionary from a noble family of Montepulciano, in Tuscany, went to Malabar to spread Christian faith; and he made quite a reasonable number of converts—four thousand to be precise—mostly from the low castes and the untouchables, but not enough, in his view, from the social groups he would have liked to conquer. He yearned to convert the spiritual elite of the Indian continent, but the Brahmins were a hard lot to convince, being perfectly happy with their own cults. Thus padre de Nobili resorted to a doctrine worked out in China by his predecessor Matteo Ricci: it was called "doctrine de l'accomodation" and it derived from the observation that Christianizing should not be to Europeanize, that a conversion should not isolate a neo-Christian in his very environment, nor should it severe his many ties with the native culture. Besides, he thought, since the Brahmin has access to all other castes, it would be more practical to convert him, hard as he was to accede to. For that purpose "il faut que le missionaire se fasse passer pour brahme" a missionary must pass for a Brahmin, and de Nobili did so, by conforming in every detail of his behaviour and appearance to the custom of that caste and particularly to the image of a voluntary penitent. Thus he called himself Saniassy and claimed to be a Roman rajah come to do penance in India. He dressed like a sanyasi, took a Brahmin servant who spread around the news of his sanctity and learned perfectly the ancient literature of the Hindus. Theologically, he emphasized the similarities between Hinduism and Christianity by maintaining that their different rituals were nothing but the corruption of one primitive cult—he even identified the Brahmins with the children of Noah, the Biblical patriarch.[19]

To a certain extent he succeeded—he made 26 converts among the Brahmins as the *Dictionnaire de Theologie Catholique* reports; the outstanding feature in this story being, however, not so much his success, but rather his metamorphosis, the extent to which he adapted his religion to that of the Brahmins—who, on their part, do not seem to have swerved too much from their religion in order to become Christians.

It seems to be a story that perpetuates itself through the ages: Henry Dumont reminds us that the Christians in India had separate churches for the low caste or outcaste converts; and *The God of Small Things* might be only an updating of the same question. In Roy's view neither Communism nor Christianity have changed things much for the outcastes. Velutha's sexual crime is only an excuse: in the toes of the inhabitants of Ayemenem, the handsome and brilliant Paravan is guilty of most serious crimes than defiling the purity of a divorced woman. He is guilty, for instance, of being clever and dignified.

It is a matter of no small worry to his father that he walks straight, that he holds his he?'[1] high, that he offers suggestions without being asked, that he disregards suggestions without appearing to rebel. His qualities, that would be perfectly acceptable, perhaps even desirable in Touchables, "in a Paravan ... could be construed as insolence."[20]

As to his cleverness, his ability to construct, create, repair has been a distinctive trait ever since his childhood. At the age of eleven he could work wonders with his hands and a few carpenter's tools:

> He was like a little magician. He could make intricate toys—tiny windmills, rattles, minute jewel boxes out of dried palm reeds; he could carve perfect boats out of tapioca stems and figurines on cashew nuts.[21]

That cleverness becomes a thousand times more evident in his adult years, making him a real asset in the Punnyan Kunju factory; Mammachi promptly hires him when he reappears in Ayemenem after a few years' absence and nominates him factory carpenter, in charge of the general maintenance of her plant.

> Velutha had a way with machines.... He mended radios, clocks, water-pumps. He looked after the plumbing and all the electrical gadgets in the house [...he] knew more about the machines in the factory than anyone else [...] It was Velutha who maintained the new canning machine and the automatic pineapple sheer.

Velutha who oiled the water-pump and the small diesel generator. Velutha who built the aluminium sheet-lined, easy-to-clean cutting surfaces, and the ground level furnaces for boiling fruit."[22]

Although he is paid less than a regular worker, he is still paid more than a Paravan; his fellow-workers resent the fact that an Untouchable should be allowed to be a carpenter—evidently carpentry is a caste job. Besides there are rumours about the clandestine terrorist activities in which he has been involved in the years he spent in Trivandrum; according to these rumours he has become a dangerous political agitator, an extreme leftist, a Naxalite.

Another one of Velutha's disadvantages, in the eyes of the community, is a political one, and it becomes evident to everyone, including Velutha himself, in the scene in which he is seen and recognized by Rahel, one of Ammu's twins, as a participant in the political demonstration staged by the Marxist Labour Union against the Government. On its way to Cochin to see *The Sound of Music* at the local theatre, the Ipe family, on its blue Plymouth, while waiting at a level crossing, is trapped in the middle of a riotous march. Among the marchers, Rahel recognizes Velutha, a great friend of hers,

> in a white shirt and mundu with angry veins in his neck [...] 'Velutha! Velutha!' she called to him.
>
> He froze for a moment and listened with his flag [...] stepped sideways and disappeared deftly into the angriness around him."[23]

The march is not exactly what the Party organizers might have wanted; there are revolutionary shouts, threatening characters surround the car and scare to death aunt Baby Kochamma. "The marchers that day were party workers, students and the labourers themselves," specifies Roy, "on their shoulders they carried a keg of ancient anger,"[24] their acts of vindication are those of a starved, exploited, overworked population, and as she makes it very clear, the keg representing their anger "is lit with a recent fuse"; that anger has "a new edge" to it, and the new edge is Naxalite.

Although there is no certain evidence, Velutha himself is most likely one of the Naxalites; this may very well be the reason why he does not wish to be recognized. For one thing, the Ipe's are his employers; and then he would rather avoid letting know to the party leaders in Aye Menem that he was in the march, since they are certainly loyal to the ruling party, and to pro-Soviet Comrade Namboodiripad, the *'''running dog,* " as Roy calls him, and a *"Soviet stooge."*[25] In the end Velutha's fears prove more than justified: it is indeed Comrade Pillai, the Communist boss, the one who in the end ditches him, after long waiting for a proper reason—he has already a number of improper reasons, such as the other workers' resentment for Velutha's diversity, his privileges, his Untouchability.

Pillai is probably the only person in the whole village who has the power to rescue Velutha from the awful end, which is approaching, but then Velutha is protected by his employers, Chacko and Mammachi and he is, after all, a card-holding member of the Communist Party. But now his political extremism presents itself like a powerful motivation, though an unmentionable one. It also has a secondary advantage of damaging Chacko, the bourgeois, the class enemy (who absurdly enough is himself a sort of intellectual Marxist): Chacko's reputation, after the scandal is destroyed, his factory closes down.

We might ask why should Naxalites have been so dangerous for the public order? Who were they, anyway? From Rabindra Ray's *The Naxalites and their Ideology* we learn that their movement, taking its name from an uprising of workers in the tea-gardens of a North Bengal countryside near Naxalbari, was not a disorganised outburst of peasant anger, but resulted from the political agitation by a group of communist organisers. K.S. Subramanian writes that it "was a development of the latter half of the sixties, [it] started with [...]the peasants struggle but later developed into a political movement with a mass character.... Out of the struggle waged during 1967-69" and adds further on that "the Communist Party of India (Marxist- Leninist)" that is the Naxalites themselves, "came to be formed [...] outside the framework of the established Communist parties." This should be a sufficient explanation for the official Party's hostility to the Naxalites; "it also needs to be noted" concludes the same historian, "that the Naxalite movement as a whole was a complex socio-political phenomenon drawing its inspiration from a variety of sources."[26]

Rabindra Ray in his essay on the ideological nature of the movement describes the difference between the new left and the traditional communists: "During election week all newspapers published in the name of Kerala guards appeared in Kerala, denouncing the CPI(M) leader E.M.S. Namboodiripad as a bourgeois agent and a number one revisionist, in league with the revisionists of the CPI, who fondly believed that Communism could be achieved by the ballot box and democratic means"[27] and describes contemporary episodes of violence caused from food shortages, resembling, incidentally, the march we read about in Roy's novel. Apparently demonstrations in Kerala followed a period of famine, and reduced food rationing during which "police parties were attacked, telegraph wires were cut, railway tracks disrupted, trains and buses stoned [...] in February 1969 the CPI(M) of Kerala called for a general strike and picketing of government offices [...] the *hartal* turned violent."[28]

The butt of these demonstrations was the government of course, but any show of hostility towards the Chief Minister E.M.S. Namboodiripad was also an offence to his glorious party and its local representatives, that is, in Roy's novel, Comrade Pillai, the local printer and pro-Soviet leader. To be sure the marchers' demands in *The God of Small Things* are rather reasonable:

> Their demands were that paddy workers, who were made to work in the fields for eleven and half hours a day—from seven in the morning to six-thirty in the evening—be permitted to take a one-hour lunch break. That women's wages be increased from one rupee twenty-five paisa a day, to three rupees, and men's from two rupees fifty paisa to four rupees fifty paisa a day. They were also demanding that Untouchables no longer be addressed by their caste names. They demanded *not* to be addressed as Achoo *Par ay an*, or Kelan *Paravan*, or Kuttan *Pulayan*, but just as Achoo, or Kelan, or Kuttan.[29]

And yet the people will have to fight hard to obtain them, and perhaps die for them, like Velutha. Because it becomes clear enough in the end, that among the motives to get rid of him, the political one is perhaps the most important. If the levelling of a sexual crime by the caste-conscious Syrian Christians is only a front for another crime, that of having infringed the ancient pollution rules, in a similar way it is also evident that this very last reason (claimed by the police, and by Comrade Pillai, to be the motivation for his "execution"), is, in turn a front for another and more serious reason, which, to paraphrase an American saying, would read: "a good Naxalite is a dead Naxalite." Velutha's death in the end amounts to a political murder. Thus for many intricate historical complications Velutha becomes the scapegoat. His death is only a climax for different tensions and social complications; after the murder things calm down, solutions are postponed for another twenty years, young lives are interrupted, memories are suspended or more likely, with the changing generations, erased.

NOTES AND REFERENCES

1. Francois Houtard and Genevieve Lemercinier, *Genesis and Institutionalization of the Indian Catholicism* (Louvain Lc Neuve: University Catholiquc de Louvain, 1981) 8.
2. Houtard 16.
3. Houtard 18.
4. Houtard.
5. K. J. John, *Christian Heritage in Kerala* (Cochin: F.G. Veliparampil) 12.
6. John.
7. Houtard 66.
8. Genevieve Lemercinier, *Religion and Ideology in Kerala* (University Catholique de Louvain, 1983) 280.
9. George lype, *The Rediff Special, Redijf on the net,* Redif.com/news/sep/18arun.htm
10. Lemercinier 280.
11. Arundati Roy, *The God of Small Things* (London: Flamingo, 1997) 74.
12. Roy 33.
13. Lemercinier 278.
14. John 12.
15. Roy 45.
16. Houtard 79.
17. John 84.
18. George Koilparampil, *Caste in the .Catholic Communities in Kerala* (Cochi: St. Teresa's College, 1982) 95.
19. *Dictionnaire de Theologie Catholique*, Paris 1927.

20. Roy 76.
21. Roy 74.
22. Roy 76.
23. Roy 71.
24. Roy 69.
25. Roy 69.
26. K.S. Subramanian, *Parliamentary Communism; Crisis in Indian Communist Movement* (Delhi: Ajanta Publications, 1989) 96.
27. Rabindra Ray, *The Naxalites and their Ideology* (Delhi: Oxford UP, 1988) 93.
28. Ray 103.
29. Roy 69.

12

Contemporary Short Stories in English by Indian Women Writers

MARY CONDE*

The first short story collections in English by Indian writers, as M.K. Naik has pointed out, appeared well over a hundred years ago (Naik 13): *Realities of Indian Life: Stories Collected from the Criminal Reports of India* by Shoshee Chunder Dutt and *The Times of Yore: Tales from Indian History* by Shoshee Chunder Dutt and Sourindra Mohan Tagore were both published in 1885. Their titles and their publication in London strongly suggest that they targeted an exclusively English audience which regarded India as 'other' and exotic. Short stories in English by Indian writers have been relatively critically neglected; however, even Rudyard Kipling, the master of the short story, is treated solely through an examination of his novel *Kim* by Richard Cronin in *Imagining India* and Ralph J. Crane in *Inventing India*. So this should be interpreted as a symptom of the pervasive critical neglect of the short story as genre. Indian women writers of the short story in the nineteen-nineties, except for Anita Desai and Bharati Mukherjee, have been victims of this. One of the most striking aspects of this overlooked body of fiction is its predisposition to examine itself consciously as fiction, and one of the most striking aspects of this examination is its insistence on the complexities of the influence of English literature. Some writers, it is true, do simply use quotations from and allusions to English literature without any overt commentary.

*School of English & Drama, Queen Mary, University of London, Mile End Road, London E1 4NS England.

One of Lata Jagtiani's protagonists, in "The Lost Pigeon" (39-54) from *Temple Bells and Other Stories* (1996), for example assents to a proposition with the words, "Barkis is willing" (53). Ruby Gupta, in *The Fulfilment: a Collection of Short Stories* (1996) quotes Keats (36, 69), Wordsworth (71) and T.S. Eliot (17) and refers to Gray (60) and Hardy (58). Neelum Saran Gour, more adroit and sophisticated in her use of allusions than Jagtiani or Gupta, refers during the course of her collection *Grey Pigeon and Other Stories* (1993) to Shakespeare (104, 116), Herrick (10), Blake (138-49), Dr. Johnson (118), Ruskin and Carlyle (84), Tennyson (88, 115-24, 123, 124) and Dickens (1). Sathya Saran's whimsical and supernatural collection *Night Train and Other Stories* (1996) not only contains references to Keats and Shelley (101), but seems shaped by a reading of them. In Anjana Appachana's "My Only Gods" (1-9) from *Incantations and Other Stories* (1991) the narrator, in a sentimental reminiscence of her childhood, recalls the way her mother would alternate the reading of the *Ramayana* with *Peter Rabbit*, a childish misinterpretation of which ends the story (9). Children's literature plays a major role in this very characteristic passage tracing the influence of English reading, and therefore of England, on the Indian protagonist. It is from a short story (21-44) from a collection by Nisha Da Cunha, *Set My Heart in Aspic* (1997), the very title of which quotes an English song: "Go Down to Kew in Lilac-time (it isn't far from London)." Aneek is staying at his aunt's cottage in the English countryside with Kim, the Englishman with whom she has fallen in love. Kim's name is presumably meant to recall Kipling's boy hero. At all events, the Bombay-born Aneek looks around her with pleasure, and

> In the bookcase she found old editions of Milly Molly Mandy and the "William" books and Laurie Lee and Flora Thompson. All Aneek's favourite books over the years. How odd my life has been, and is? There must be so many people like me who are odd and all because the English colonized us and gave us their language. We are accidents of history and so many of us are comfortable with that accident. I love these books, I love this countryside, I love Meg and Kim and the mother and baby in Kew. I'm Indian but I love this place more than India. India was only Ma and Papa and now they are gone there's nothing

> there to draw me back. So what does it make me? I won't think of that now, only this peaceful house and the bright squares of this cotton quilt (36).

The ironies here are many. Not only is Aneek looking back over children's books, now very much period pieces, but in Lee and Thompson she is remembering past idylls of rural England. The baby in Kew is now dead. Kim himself is a lecturer in bereavement, and, as we might expect, he dies suddenly before he can marry Aneek, leaving her only with his old aunt Meg as an emotional resource. Aneek cannot live happily within her accident of history for long.

Many collections of Indian women's short stories in the nineteen-nineties confront a collision of cultures, and this is a preoccupation, increasingly, with the collision between the cultures of India and the United States. Jhumpa Lahiri's prize-winning collection *Interpreter of Maladies* (1999) is titled on the cover "stories of Bengal, Boston and beyond," and the lead story (43-69) describes the encounter of Mr Kapasi, the interpreter of the title, with Mr and Mrs Das, both born in the United States, and visiting India as tourists: "The family looked Indian but dressed as foreigners did, the children in stiff, brightly colored clothing and caps with translucent visors" (43-44). Mr Kapasi, who is wistfully attracted to Mrs Das, gives her his address so that she can send him copies of the photographs they have been taking, and, in a rush of self-indulgent daydreaming, begins to hope that they may be able to make some permanent connection. Mrs Das, for her part, endows Mr Kapasi with almost magical qualities, and confides to him that one of her sons is the result of a casual adultery because she hopes that Mr Kapasi may be able to suggest some kind of remedy for her pain, as the "interpreter of maladies" she has styled him on hearing that he works as a translator for a doctor besides working as a guide. He fails her, the family fails to respond to the Indian scenery, and any future contact with them fails as he watches the address, he has given her blowing away. The story ends:

> He watched as it rose, carried higher and higher by the breeze, into the trees where the monkeys now sat, solemnly observing the scene below. Mr Kapasi observed it too, knowing that this

was the picture of the Das family he would preserve forever in his mind (69).

The monkeys, previously predatory and aggressive, regarding tourists as their rightful prey, are now tranquil, and Mr Kapasi will use his memory to replace modern technology, but the tone of this ending is elegiac. The two cultures remain irrevocably disconnected from each other. Modern technology is the expression of American culture in the lead story (1-67) of Manjula Padmanabhan's *Hot Death, Cold Soup* (1996), in which the narrator, an experienced journalist from Delhi, goes into "the wilds of northern U.P." to encounter Sally. Sally, who met her Indian husband at Harvard, now determines to commit sati (which she pronounces "Satty") with the latest modern gadgetry. This turns out to be a farcical failure, but the story is a dark one, not least because it forces the narrator to examine her own cultural reflexes. As she observes, "Even fifty years after Independence, I had found it impossible to resist a direct appeal from a Westerner and an elderly woman at that" (9). Sally is revealed as not only absurd but hateful, effectively the murderer of her husband's lover, but she provokes a milder irritation in the narrator as well, in her "cultural arrogance" (11) in experimenting with the tried and tested combinations of Indian food. The hot death which Sally has hoped to stage-manage is tellingly juxtaposed with the cold soup over which she presides. Many collections reflect on the curious phenomenon of the American "hippie," drawn to India and Indians through what is initially at least an idealistic impulse. The lead story (9-20) of Ritu Bhatia's *Guru & Other Stories* (1996) is a fairly straightforward account of naive, blonde, blue-eyed, American Sherry and her sexual exploitation by the guru she has come to seek in India, her suspicions not even aroused by her own cultural references: "Sherry looked at her Guru's serene face and was instantly filled with joy: it's like the Beatles all over again, she thought" (15). Jai Nimbkar's "The Phantom Bird" (9-60) and "The Lotus Leaves" (200-11) from *The Phantom Bird and Other Stories* (1993) are more subtle examinations of the American infatuation with India. In the first story the young protagonist is caught between two negatives as she turns from the loveless materialist world of her Indian parents to the loveless narcissistic world of the hippies she meets on holiday, and in the second Sarojini is angered by the intrusive interest of an American visitor into the Indian life which she finds dull and stupid. The story ends as she tentatively embraces him but is repelled by the odour of his unwashed body. Like Mr Kapasi and Mrs Das, these two cannot make a connection between the cultures which they represent. Nisha in "Destiny" (173-61) from Shona Ramaya's *Beloved Mother, Queen of the Night* (1993), although, as we might expect, she cannot remain the manipulator she aspires to be, has a very particular cachet in the United States:

> She had always sold the east back there, eastern, oriental, together with its mythical mystique. She had sold the east better than anybody she knew. Exploit what they exploit, and exploit them as part of the game, she had told an Indian friend. That's the way to get on here, if you want to make it. Post-colonial—that's the name of the game now. Academia has discovered the third world (208).

Ramaya is here clearly thinking of herself as fiction-writer as well as of Nisha as anthropologist, and Gauri Deshpande is even more candid in her story "Rose Jam" (141-62) from *The Lackadaisical Sweeper* (1997), in which the narrator introduces the topic of rose jam like this:

> The reason I thought I would begin this account with it is, it's the only really exotic thing about my childhood I can put my finger on: I was brought up eating a jam of roses. You see, over the last few years I have come across a lot of books written by talented writers who left their countries of origin around puberty to settle down in America or Canada or Australia or wherever, and who, before leaving the mother countries, seem to have had enchantingly strange childhoods quite unlike mine, humdrum in retrospect and in comparison. In these books the authors, their parents, grandparents, siblings, schoolmates and surroundings appear so exotic and magical as to be unrecognizable, in spite of the fact that I am quite sure I have ridden the bus and trodden the streets in a few of the spots described; and very probably, though unknowingly, in the company of those same exotic characters (141-42).

The narrator ends by mocking herself because her "golden California boy" (to her truly exotic) does not believe she was brought up on rose jam, and we see that in a sense she was not, precisely because she did not perceive it as exotic.

Many Indian women short-story writers' dwell in detail on the craft of writing. In Githa Hariharan's *The Art of Dying* (1993) the pain and disillusionment of dying and of writing almost become one; Kalpana Swaminathan's Aunt Lalli detective stories are more light-hearted, despite their often morbid content, but here it is still important that the narrator is not Aunt Lalli herself but a would-be writer, whose writing is constantly interrupted by the "real life" of the action and the superior mental powers of an old lady. Chitra Banerjee Divakaruni's *Arranged Marriage* (1997), a collection tracking the "arranged marriage" between the United States and India, although none of the stories has this title, like Shauna Singh Baldwin's *English Lessons* (1999), is much more pessimistic than any of the stories discussed so far. But, as in, for example, the much gentler stories of Nisha Da Cunha, literature is used to signal an outcome. In "Silver Pavements, Golden Roofs" (35-56) the young Indian narrator has a fantasy of arguing with her handsome university professor about the character of Sister Carrie, and Dreiser's philosophy, not seeing how her own life with her uncle and aunt in Chicago is echoing Carrie's in Chicago, and how their existence confirms Dreiser's brutal theories.

Finally, the lead story (7-18) of Nina Sibal's collection *The Secret Life of Gujjar Mal* (1991) early in the decade had offered a witty speculation about the origins of fiction itself. The publisher-narrator observes rather sadly of his business that "... the real income comes from guides. They are the mainstay of university education in Uttar Pradesh: students would be lost; they would not pass exams without them" (8) but adds that he will continue to publish fiction to give himself an interest in life. The writer whom he publishes, Gujjar Mal, visits every evening a prostitute, Rewati Bai, who is equated with his source of inspiration; eventually he leaves, on a kind of intellectual pilgrimage, for the mountains of Nepal which are her own source, in order to solve the mystery pondered by both author and publisher: "What happens when a character in a story speaks? Where does the voice come from?" (9) Meanwhile Rewati Bai bears his child, which is taken over by the publisher and Gujjar Mal's wife Manimala. When Rewati Bai's pimp accuses the couple of having stolen the baby, Manimala replies, "No ... this is my baby, don't you see, it looks just like my husband Gujjar Mal" (18). In other words, the completed work is claimed as a legitimate product wherever it came from, and however dubious its origins.

Contemporary Indian women's short stories richly confront and consider the legacies of language and literature, the collisions of cultures, and the (entirely pragmatic or mysteriously spiritual) origins of fiction itself.

WORKS CITED

Appachana, Anjana. *Incantations and Other Stories*. London: Virago, 1991.

Baldwin, Shauna Singh. *English Lessons and Other Stories*. Fredericton, NB: Goose Lane, 1999.

Bhatia, Ritu. *Guru & Other Stories*. New Delhi: Har-Anand, 1996.

Crane, Ralph J. *Inventing India: a History of India in English-Language Fiction*. Basingstoke and London: Macmillan, 1992.

Cronin, Richard. *Imagining India*. New York: St Martin's Press, 1989.

Da Cunha, Nisha. *Set My Heart in Aspic*. New Delhi: Harper Collins, 1997.

Deshpande, Gauri. *The Lackadaisical Sweeper: Short Stories*. Madras: Manas, 1997.

Divakaruni, Chitra Banerjee. *Arranged Marriage*. London: Black Swan, 1997.

Gour, Neelum Saran. *Grey Pigeon and Other Stories*. New Delhi: Penguin Books India, 1993.

Gupta, Ruby. *The Fulfilment: a Collection of Short Stories*. New Delhi: Har-Anand, 1996.

Hariharan, Githa. *The Art of Dying and Other Stories*. New Delhi: Penguin Books India, 1993.

Jagtiani, Lata. *Temple Bells and Other Stories*. Bombay: India Book Distributors, 1996.

Lahiri, Jhumpa. *Interpreter of Maladies: Stories*. New Delhi: Harper Collins India, 1999.

Naik, M.K., ed. *The Indian Short Story: a Representative Anthology*. New Delhi: Arnold, 1984.

Nimbkar, Jai. *The Phantom Bird and Other Stories*. New Delhi: Indus, 1993.

Padmanabhan, Manjula. *Hot Death, Cold Soup: Twelve Short Stories*. New Delhi: Kali for Women, 1996.

Ramaya, Shona. *Beloved Mother, Queen of the Night*. London: Martin Secker & Warburg, 1993.

Saran, Sathya. *Night Train and Other Stories*. New Delhi: Har-Anand, 1996.

Sibal, Nina. *The Secret Life of Gujjar Mal and Other Stories*. London: Women's Press, 1991.

13

"Why I do not call myself a feminist": Problematic Identity of Feminism in Indian Context

JOEL KUORTTI*

Mahatma Gandhi, on arrival for a visit to London, was once asked a tricky question. The question was: "What do you think of Western civilisation?" Gandhiji's quick answer was: "It would be a good idea."

For me today, the question is: "What do you think of Indian feminism?" I don't have any quick answers but in the following I hope certain relevant issues pertaining to this question will become more familiar to you or that you are reminded of some things.

It was last year when Madhu Kishwar, the editor of *Manushi: a journal about women and society*, published a collection of essays from *Manushi,* titled *Off the Beaten Track: rethinking gender justice for Indian women* (1999). In the book Kishwar declares emphatically her horror of isms and explains for example why she is not a feminist. The most relevant article in this regard, "A Horror of 'Isms': Why I Do Not Call Myself a Feminist," was originally published in 1990 but in the version included in the book it is revised and updated.

The work for women's justice, equality and freedom that Kishwar has done for more than two decades in *Manushi* since 1978 has brought about, as one critic has commented, that "her popular

*Professor of English, FIN-33014 University of Tampere, Finland.

image has always been that of a firebrand feminist."[1] Kishwar herself is very adamant on this issue. From the beginning, she wanted *Manushi not* to be called a feminist journal and she says that she hasn't hardly ever even used the word.[2]

There is, thus, a tug-of-war between her being seen as a feminist and her own refusal to be called one. One result of this has been that not infrequently has she been reproached by feminists for betraying important issues. But what are in fact Kishwar's reservations concerning feminism? How does someone who was once called the high priestess of Indian feminism and the Germaine Greer or the Kate Millet of India justify her criticism of feminism?

To begin with, in her article Kishwar criticises established ideologies or 'isms' in general for not being able to maintain their idealistic agendas. What is done in the name of a given 'ism' is repeatedly an adulteration of the original ideal. In her opinion, such ideologies as Marxism, Leninism and Maoism are time and culture-specific and they do tend to get ossified. Movements with less personified make-up such as feminism, humanism and anarchism share the aspect of culture-specificity and they are also prone to institutionalisation. With feminism, Kishwar decries "the intellectual regimentation demanded in the name of solidarity with the women's movement."[3]

Linked to this general distrust in ideologies is Kishwar's stress on individual choice. She criticises the individualistic foundation of feminism because it has resulted, in the West, in atomisation of society. However, she readily grants individual women a right to determine how they live their life. In an interview she has said: "My business is not to tell women what is good for them."[4] Furthermore, Kishwar in her "inherent mistrust of authoritarian structures"[5] denounces all forms of statist approaches to social reform. The way in which the feminists have tried to get laws passed and implemented for example on pornography is for her not acceptable as it arms, as she says, the "very corrupt and criminalized state machinery with even more repressive powers."[6] One recent issue in which Kishwar and *Manushi* have been vocal against legislative methods and for moral responsibility concerns the constitutional amendment, the Women Reservation Bill that has been debated in the parliament, Lok Sabha since it was introduced in December 1999. In the January-February issue of *Manushi* there was an alternative to the Bill to this effect.[7]

Kishwar's reservations are not, however, only on the level of institutional criticism. Her even more stringent critique concerns Western feminism but the critique Kishwar offers is not against it as such: "in the western context," she says, "the word 'feminism' evokes many positive associations."[8] Neither is she vocal in accusing the "First World" feminists of intervening in Indian affairs. Her criticism is aimed at the way in which Western feminism has been adopted in India. So for example Debashish Mukerji comments that "[i]nstead of the usual targets of feminists, the "patriarchal society," Kishwar's ire seems to be directed at the West, and Indian feminists who have been overly influenced by it."[9] This is true indeed. Kishwar understands feminism first of all as a very culture-specific phenomenon which emerged in the West and benefitted the societies there in making them more equal and democratic. But she does not think that the objectives of feminism are universal. In her opinion, Indian traditions such as the goddess worship and feminine *shakti* provide Indian society with a far more suitable blueprint for voicing women's issues.[10]

In Kishwar's perception, Indian feminism is metropolitan, elitist, statist, patronising and dependent on funding from international agencies. The missionary zeal of such feminists to engage in development projects has not improved the status of women. So for example in her critique of capitalism within development Maria Mies comments that "[i]ntegrating women into development [has] only increased women's workload."[11] Similarly Kishwar sees that not only has feminism been ineffective in accomplishing changes but it has in fact witnessed a decline in the status of women, as the statistics on rape, domestic violence and so on clearly showed for example in Indian media reports around last International Women's Day. Kishwar's conclusion is that one should not, therefore, force foreign concepts into practice where they are not applicable.

Together with her general mistrust in feminism's potential in effecting change, Kishwar thinks Indian "feminist establishment" uses "their pro-poor rhetoric" to advance their own ends.[12] The popularity of the so-called Third World feminism is for her a sign of this. She laments bitterly:

> These days, to declare oneself a third world feminist is to open the gates of many career opportunities which otherwise would not come your way—research grants, fellowships, teaching assignments, invitations to international conferences, project funds, and so on. You are at once admitted as a member of the intellectual elite of the world. In the last decade, with the various international funding agencies promoting feminism in third world countries, to be identified as a third world feminist has become a very lucrative proposition indeed.[13]

In the academic environment we are today, these issues cannot be passed by lightly. This problematic is in fact something which is embedded in my research project which concerns Indian English women's writing and has been funded by, indeed, the Development Studies Subdivision of the Finnish Academy. In the following I will draw attention to some aspects which I encountered when interviewing writers for my research last winter in India.

All the seven writers, five novelists and two poets, expressed reservations as either to the use of the word feminism in the context of their writings or, in more general terms, to feminist discourse. There are a couple of issues which could be considered here. First relevant issue to the topic came up in discussion with Shashi Deshpande. While artistically differentiating from feminism, Deshpande understands feminism in India as activism rather than theory. As she says: "it's not theory. It's not Simone de Beauvoir; it's not Germaine Greer, or anything. Some people will read these, but what changes is activism."[14] Where Kishwar criticises Indian feminism of both relying on (Western) theories and adopting statist strategies, Deshpande acknowledges the achievements in legislation. Although she does not view the changes in society too optimistically in general, there seems to be some hope. As she says: "what has really changed is the awareness that these things have to be taken into account."[15] Through this awareness the changes become possibilities rather than ideals.

She talks also about the second issue: the difficulties in getting published abroad. Extremely small portion of Indian women writers are known outside their language communities. This is true even of Indian English writers. Although she would like to eschew the title of a feminist writer, Deshpande still knew that be it Finland, the

United Kingdom or the USA, "only a feminist publisher would publish" her.[16] Her writing began from the realisation of "what it was to be a woman in this country," but she does not want to be labelled a feminist.[17] In many of her novels, although they are to Deshpande's dismay almost invariably in academic analyses viewed from a feminist perspective, the themes are multilayered, even more so in her later novels. For example in *A Matter of Time* the narrator is a man named Gopal.

Similar regrets are expressed by the novelist Shama Futehally, whose novel *Tara Lane* was understood by one critic as a feminist novel. Futehally says she "wouldn't call it feminist at all."[18] While the novel attests to an awareness of certain limitations within a woman's life, it is an observer's awareness. Futehally concludes her comment by clearing her story of all feminist leanings: "I would say it's a story, a human story. The minute you say feminist or socialist or anything, you get into trouble."[19]

Deshpande on her part laments that the needs for change are not equally understood between men and women. She says: "Women are moving, there's much more awareness among women.... But I think men are not moving fast enough."[20] In contrast, the poet Lakshmi Kannan who thinks it is vital to write also about men, whatever the feminist agenda might say, comments that

> men are changing, and they have to be registered. Recorded. Created artistically in our work. That is my belief. There are a few of us doing that. Despite what feminists, some of these strident feminists who have this one way of understanding, [say].[21]

With the importance of writing about men, here, Kannan refers to that kind of regimentation among feminists which also Kishwar took up above. This third kind of issue is a common objection that the writers I interviewed felt, reluctance to yield to established feminist representations.

In a similar vein, Githa Hariharan talks about her novel *The Thousand Faces of the Night* (1992). At the end of the novel, the story of rebellious Devi and her mother Sita does not come to a neat conclusion. Hariharan comments on this: "Some feminist readers asked me for instance, "Where is the feminist revolution?" And my answer of course was that I was not trying to make any sort of a blueprint for action."[22] Shama Futehally affirms this sentiment on her part: "if that's what you want well why have literature, write a pamphlet."[23]

It is not only in their writing the writers sense an alienation from certain feminist ideas. For example, the novelist Anuradha Marwah-Roy talks about having come up with other kinds of problems. With regard to the divorce process she is going through she has found it difficult to argue why she does not want to give up her right to motherhood. When her novels *The Higher Education of Geetika Mehendiratta* (1993) and *Idol Love* (1999) could be seen as statements on the rights of women, her stance, then, on the custody of her children bears witness to a clash between Indian tradition and feminism. She says: "Some activists feel that insistence on custody only hinders divorcing women. It's so exhausting to convey to them that for me motherhood is a privilege, not a responsibility."[24]

Also Shama Futehally passes a comment on this breach between tradition and feminism on the one hand and between oneself and feminism on the other:

> sometimes one kind, a wrong kind of feminism makes you a little nervous about admitting ... [t]hat the birth of a child, or ... marriage [is] extremely important.... There is a certain tendency within feminist thinking that makes you nervous about admitting that. You think it might be misunderstood. That somehow you are putting yourself in a subordinate position but I'm not doing anything of the sort, I'm just acknowledging something which is humanly very, very important—to me.[25]

What these examples show perhaps most clearly is that the writers are both conscious of the call to be politically correct and reluctant to forego their personal views either in their writing or in their views.

This reluctance applies to poetry as well as to fiction. The poet Sujatha Mathai asserts that in writing a poem, the text is primary. A political programme, she says,

> can never be poetry. Because if it comes so consciously, it can never become a poem.... I mean, if I was consciously thinking

of a text it obviously wouldn't become a poem. It would become an essay.[26]

One last aspect to be drawn from the interviews is expressed by Kannan who argues, in much the same way as Kishwar, that feminism has not succeeded in India. There has even been deterioration and backlash in the status of women. Kannan describes Indian feminism to be "strident, shrew feminism that in *my* view is very stereotypical. Feminism that's just counterproductive—it's a whole lot of noise."[27] The hope for change for her is mixed with huge obstacles. She understands that reality "*is* changing. For the better. Though there are the peripheries, the pockets. Rural India has not changed."[28] Shashi Deshpande, too, senses a stagnation within the process of change: "For most of the women, especially the women in the villages, life has not changed at all."[29]

I have here talked about reservations some Indian authors have expressed about the applicability of feminism in the Indian context. It is not necessary to accept these at a face-value but it is however essential to be aware of these debates. I experienced this when in the course of the interviews, when, while I was referring to the Indian feminist critique of the Indian society and women's issues, one of the interviewees said to me: "But you wouldn't know, Joel. You wouldn't know."[30]

Criticism of development, feminism, postcolonial studies and so on is a worthwhile effort when we are shuttling between unequally equipped cultural spaces. It is in my opinion as important as is the shuttling itself in the first place.

The discussion here does by no means cover the whole field. Instead of a conclusion, I would like to refer briefly to a couple of other approaches. To begin with, there is a booklet by an important Indian women's press, Kali for Women. The booklet, *Some Questions on Feminism and Its Relevance in South Asia*, was originally published in 1986 and reissued last year. In this booklet, Kamla Bhasin and Nighat Said Khan approach the issue in a question-answer format, covering a variety of themes. From my point of view it is a fairly convincing book, too. Bhasin and Kali have also just published another study booklet, *Understanding Gender* (2000). Together with the earlier one, it provides a challenging contrast with Kishwar's position, both of which are deeply rooted in the everyday life of Indian women. The Kali booklets give straightforward arguments as to why feminism is relevant in India and in South Asia in general.

In her recent article on post coloniality and Third World feminists, Ulla Vuorela recognises the discourse on the problematic connection between the issues of development, feminism and cultural criticism. She refers to for example such well known critics as Trinh T. Minh-ha, Gayatri Spivak and Chandra Talpade-Mohanty who already in the 1980s began the discourse on postcolonial feminism. There are quite a few of these critics now and here I would like to draw attention to two more recent, very topical publications. First, there is Chilla Bulbeck's *Re-Orienting Western Feminisms: Women's Diversity in a Postcolonial World* (1998). She challenges the hegemony of Western, meaning Anglophone, feminism and tries to provide a more comprehensive and diverse understanding of feminism. Another book, Irene Gedalof's *Against Purity: Rethinking Identity with Indian and Western Feminisms*, (1999), then, is parallel in its aim at delineating the variety within feminist discourse.

What do you think of Indian feminism? As far as the actual changes in women's issues in Indian society are concerned, the question is not of importance. Only when we begin to consider issues like solidarity and identification do we need to think what feminism actually means, and what it means in India. There are no easy solutions between the universalist and the localist, the individualist and the communalist, or the constructivist and the essentialist approaches. Indian feminism could be any one of these. We could even try to do without it altogether, or replace it with some other term, like the one introduced by some African scholars: "womanism." Whatever our answer might be in the end, I applaud all the approaches as they show how differently things can be thought.[31]

NOTES AND REFERENCES

1. Debashish Mukerji, "Volte-face, what? Books: Madhu Kishwar, *Off the Beaten Track," The Week* 6th Feb. 2000 at http://www.the-week.com/20feb06/life1.htm#1 [visited 29.08.2000].
2. Madhu Kishwar, "A Horror of 'Isms': Why I Do Not Call Myself a Feminist,"

Manushi 61 (Nov. - Dec. 1990) in *Off the Beaten Track: rethinking gender justice for Indian women* (New Delhi: Oxford UP, 1999) 273.

3. Kishwar 268.
4. Jennifer Severn, "Words with Madhu Kishwar, Indian activist, writer and publisher," 1995 available at http://www.freespeech.org/manushi/mk-intvu/mk-intvu.html [visited 29.08.2000].
5. Kishwar 282.
6. Kishwar 274.
7. Jayaprakash Narayan, Dhirubhai Sheth, Yogendra Yadav, Madhu Kishwar, "Enhancing Women's Representation in Legislatures: an Alternative to the Government Bill for Women's Reservation," *Manushi* 116 (Jan.-Feb. 2000) 5-13.
8. Kishwar 276.
9. Mukerji 2000.
10. Kishwar 276.
11. Maria Mies, "'Gender' and Global Capitalism," *Capitalism and Development*, ed. Leslie Sklair (London & New York: Routledge, 1994) 107-22.
12. Kishwar 268, 287.
13. Madhu Kishwar, "When India 'Missed' the Universe," *Manushi* 88 (May-June 1995), *Off the Beaten track: rethinking gender justice for Indian women* (New Delhi: Oxford UP, 1999) 182; available at http://www.umiacs.umd.edu/users/sawweb/sawnet/beauty.html [visited 29.08.2000] and http://www.freespeech.org/manushi/beauty/beauty.html [visited 29.08.2000].
14. Shashi Deshpande "Women are moving: years of silence came to an end": Interview with Shashi Deshpande, Bangalore, 6th Jan. 2000. This and the following references to the interviews are from my yet unpublished book of interviews: *Tense Past, Tense Present: Interviews with Seven Indian English Women Writers.*
15. Deshpande.
16. Deshpande.
17. Deshpande.
18. Shama Futehally, "Women will find ways of breaking out": Interview with Shama Futehally, New Delhi, 1st February 2000.
19. Futehally.
20. Deshpande.
21. Kannan.
22. Githa Hariharan, "The double burden: continual contesting of tradition and modernity": Interview with Githa Hariharan, New Delhi, 3rd February 2000.
23. Hariharan.
24. Anuradha Marwah-Roy, "Stories can never be told to the end completely": Interview with Anuradha Marwah-Roy, New Delhi, 10th February 2000.

25. Futehally.
26. Sujatha Mathai, "Because of the Unbearable Pain," Interview with Sujatha Mathai, New Delhi, 11th March 2000.
27. Lakshmi Kannan, "I could never stop writing poems": Interview with Lakshmi Kannan, New Delhi, 11th March 2000.
28. Kannan.
29. Deshpande.
30. Singh.
31. This article is based on papers presented at two seminars, "Cultural Identity and its Global Manifestations" at the University of Joensuu on 14-16 September 2000 and "Gender, Development and Post-Colonial Theory" seminar at the University of Helsinki, 25-29 September 2000. Thanks to Erkki Sevänen, Jopi Nyman and John Stotesbury in Joensuu and to Ulla Vuorela, Mari Korpela and Anu Hirsiaho in Helsinki. I would like to extend special thanks to Durre Ahmed, Fawzia Mustafa, Mahmuda Islam and Raisa Simola for discussing the papers and for their valuable comments.